D1713561

# Slaughter and Stalemate in 1917

# WAR AND SOCIETY

## Series Editors

MICHAEL B. BARRETT and KYLE SINISI

The study of military history has evolved greatly over the past fifty years, and the "War and Society" series captures these changes with the publication of books on all aspects of war. The series examines not only traditional military history with its attention to battles and leaders, but it explores the broader impact of war upon the military and society. Affecting culture, politics, economies, and state power, wars have transformed societies since the ancient world. With books that cut across all time periods and geographical areas, this series reveals the history of both the conduct of war and its societal consequences.

# Slaughter and Stalemate in 1917

## British Offensives from Messines Ridge to Cambrai

Alan Warren

ROWMAN & LITTLEFIELD
*Lanham • Boulder • New York • London*

Published by Rowman & Littlefield
An imprint of The Rowman & Littlefield Publishing Group, Inc.
4501 Forbes Boulevard, Suite 200, Lanham, Maryland 20706
www.rowman.com

6 Tinworth Street, London SE11 5AL, United Kingdom

British Library Cataloguing in Publication Information Available

**Library of Congress Cataloging-in-Publication Data**

Names: Warren, Alan, 1967– author.
Title: Slaughter and stalemate in 1917 : British offensives from Messines Ridge to Cambrai
    / Alan Warren.
Other titles: British offensives from Messines Ridge to Cambrai
Description: Lanham, Maryland : Rowman & Littlefield, [2020] | Series: War and society |
    Includes bibliographical references and index.
Identifiers: LCCN 2020026790 (print) | LCCN 2020026791 (ebook) | ISBN
    9781538143100 (cloth) alk. paper | ISBN 9781538143117 (epub)
Subjects: LCSH: World War, 1914–1918—Campaigns—Belgium. | Messines, Battle of,
    Belgium, 1917. | Cambrai, Battle of, Cambrai, France, 1917 | Great Britain. Army.
    British Expeditionary Force—History—World War, 1914–1918. | World War, 1914–
    1918—Campaigns—Western Front.
Classification: LCC D541 .D37 2020  (print) | LCC D541  (ebook) | DDC 940.4/31—
    dc23
LC record available at https://lccn.loc.gov/2020026790
LC ebook record available at https://lccn.loc.gov/2020026791

# Contents

# Photos

# Maps

# Preface

In the early morning of June 7, 1917, an electrifying drama erupted beneath Messines Ridge, a vital sector of World War I's principal theater: the western front of France and Flanders. Messines Ridge was crowned by a succession of defense lines built by the army of the German kaiser. From these stout positions, German troops faced west to look out over the trenches of the British Expeditionary Force (BEF).

To the north of Messines Ridge was the British-held town of Ypres. To improve the Allied grip on the Ypres sector, a plan was devised to capture Messines Ridge. In a bid to prise open the oyster at Messines with economy, months earlier British commanders had authorized a mining operation of an unprecedented scale. A set of tunnels was pushed into the ridge, beneath the German front line, and packed with high explosives. When the mines were detonated, an infantry assault on a nine-mile front would storm the ridge.

General Sir Herbert Plumer of the Second Army presided over British troops in Flanders. Plumer and his staff made careful and elaborate preparations to attack Messines Ridge. Success would depend on the harmonious cooperation of infantry, artillery, and engineers. The scheme was meticulously rehearsed on the training ground; huge models of the prospective battlefield were built and studied by large numbers of troops.

Leading up to zero hour—the time at which the mines were to be detonated—a weeklong artillery bombardment was fired at the ridge to cut barbed-wire entanglements and demolish identified strongpoints. In bright weather a cataract of shelling stripped the greenery from the sun-soaked ridge; the villages of Messines and Wytschaete were reduced to crumpled piles of brick. The bombardment strained the nerves of the defenders to the breaking point.

The night before the assault, a radiant and mysterious moon floated brightly in a clearing sky. The night was cool, and flares rose sporadically to cast a lurid, flickering glare upon the western slope of the ridge. At 3:05 A.M. on June 7, the first streaks of dawn filtered across the landscape. As zero hour approached, anxious men, pulses pounding, prepared themselves for a reckless burst of primitive action. Bayonets were fixed; ladders were placed at intervals along trenches; troops crawled over parapets to lie behind white tapes in the scattered grasses of no-man's-land. A relative hush fell upon the front, so much so that nightingales could be heard singing in the shredded foliage of a nearby wood.

At 3:10 A.M. the mines were detonated as simultaneously as was practical. The mine blasts were an awesome spectacle. Right across the front a terrific set of roaring explosions sent great towering jets of crimson flame gushing out of the earth; these pillars of fire, cast skywards with inhuman precision, were followed by cascading columns of soil, stone, and timber. The newspaper correspondent Philip Gibbs wrote of the mine explosions:

> [They were] the most diabolical splendour I have seen in war. Out of the dark ridges of Messines and Wytschaete and that ill-famed Hill 60, for which many of our best have died, there gushed out and up enormous volumes of scarlet flame from the exploding mines and of earth and smoke, all lighted by the flame, spilling over into fountains of fierce colour, so that all the countryside was illumined by red light.[1]

A German observer on the ridge recorded: "Nineteen gigantic roses with carmine-red leaves, or enormous mushrooms, were seen to rise up slowly and majestically out of the ground, and then split into pieces with a mighty roar, sending up many-coloured columns of flame and smoke mixed with a mass of earth and splinters, high into the sky."[2] After the thunderous series of explosions, portions of the German front line vanished beneath dense black smoke clouds; whole companies were entombed in their dugouts.

Once the showers of debris hurled into the air by the explosions had fallen back to earth, British troops poured across no-man's-land. Eighty thousand infantrymen from various parts of the British Isles and Empire set out behind an immense barrage of shellfire nearly half a mile deep. This was to be a "bite and hold" operation; that is, the infantry's advance would halt at the limit of the zone protected by the artillery's creeping barrage.

Enveloped by the churning dust haze of the barrage, the waves of attackers pushed aggressively uphill behind the moving screen of bursting shells. The torn, spread-eagled bodies of the dead and injured lay scattered about the upheaval. Tanks lumbered and nosed a way forward, the drivers picking out a route up a slope honeycombed with shell craters and debris; brightly colored signal flares rose up through the inky smoke hanging in the air. The crest of Messines Ridge was rapidly seized by British troops across the length of the assault frontage. In the afternoon, reserve divisions leapfrogged into the lead in blazing sunshine to seize most of the final objective on the rear slopes of the ridge. In a celebratory mood, Field Marshal Sir Douglas Haig, the BEF's commander in chief, visited Plumer's headquarters soon after 4 P.M. to offer his congratulation.

The long-drawn-out middle period of the war on the western front featured a series of Anglo-French offensives that sought to push the army of Imperial Germany out of northern France and Belgium. The offensive battles fought by Anglo-French forces in 1915 had been followed by the grinding Somme offensive of 1916, and a further round of bitter fighting in the spring of 1917. The German campaign against the French at Verdun in 1916 was the principal deviation from that sequence of events.

The Messines engagement of June 7, 1917, however, appeared to be a brilliant opening to a new campaign. The methods utilized were appropriate to the circumstances of a siege-like war; the hard work of engineers and artillerymen was followed by a well-planned infantry assault. The Messines triumph was a much-needed boost to Allied morale; expectations were raised as to what might be achieved in the rest of the year.

Field Marshal Haig intended the seizure of Messines Ridge to be the first stage of a grand British-led offensive in Flanders. If all went well, this thrust would drive back the German army and capture the submarine bases on the Belgian coast at Ostend and Zeebrugge. Haig believed "that Germany was within six months of the total exhaustion of her available manpower, if the fighting continues at its present intensity."[3] Haig pressed this view on Prime Minister David Lloyd George's War Cabinet with all the conviction he possessed. The support of the First Sea Lord, Admiral Sir John Jellicoe, for Haig's Flanders scheme helped to wrench permission for the offensive from the doubtful politicians.

The Flanders offensive, partly for reasons of geography, would not involve much direct cooperation between British and French forces; this ran the risk of the BEF fighting a large part of the German military on the western front almost single-handedly. This risk did not unduly alarm the British commander in chief. Haig was vaingloriously ambitious for British forces to feature prominently in a victorious campaign, with the French relegated to undertaking localized diversionary attacks on their part of the front. Incredulous French generals were in no position to block Haig's Flanders plan. General Philippe Pétain gave the opinion that "Haig's attack towards Ostend was certain to fail." General Ferdinand Foch felt that, given the flooded nature of Flanders, the scheme to advance toward Ostend and Zeebrugge was "futile, fantastic and dangerous."[4]

At the end of July 1917, some weeks after the Messines battle, the main thrust of Haig's offensive got underway in Flanders. This campaign—which would be known as the Third Battle of Ypres—was driven forward for several months. To the east of Ypres, British troops repeatedly attacked the German Fourth Army in a strongly fortified sector. From behind a series of shallow ridges, massed German artillery rained munitions upon a crowded array of British infantry divisions.

The site of an almost leveled Passchendaele village was finally taken by Canadian troops in early November. By that time a large part of the BEF had been pushed to the verge of exhaustion in return for a five-mile advance beyond the old front line near Ypres. The Passchendaele campaign was described by Winston Churchill as "a forlorn expenditure of valour and life without equal in futility."[5]

In mid-November, Haig decided to close down the Flanders offensive for the year. Yet soon after, at the southern end of the BEF's front, the Tank Corps led an attack by the Third Army against the Hindenburg Line near Cambrai. The Tank Corps had played a minor part in the glacial drive for Passchendaele, only to be given a starring role at Cambrai. The surprise attack made on November 20 was a triumphant success and one of the western front's most dramatic days. In contradiction to that, Haig's attempt to use the Cavalry Corps to exploit the initial success failed to make headway and was reminiscent of an earlier war in a bygone century.

After news of the success at Cambrai had reached London, the War Office arranged for the church bells of the metropolis to be rung in celebration. The fighting, however, continued without any dramatic expansion of the bridgehead seized in the initial assault. Then, seemingly against the run of play, a German counterattack at Cambrai on November 30 achieved a high level of surprise and retook some of the ground taken ten days before. In London there was deep dismay at this rapid turnabout. The War Cabinet was appalled that Haig's staff had failed to detect large German troop movements in a sector that was already the focus of attention.

The bloodletting at Passchendaele and Cambrai left the BEF unnecessarily weakened at the close of 1917. Meanwhile, in the aftermath of the collapse of the Russian war effort, a large force of German troops began to transfer from Eastern Europe to the western front. The war between the Allied powers and the German-led Central Powers seemed far from a conclusion during the winter of 1917–1918.

## ACKNOWLEDGMENTS

I would like to express my thanks to all those who have helped me during the preparation of this book. I am grateful for the confidence and support of my publishers and editors, in particular Susan McEachern, Michael Barrett, Kylie Sinisi, Katelyn Turner, Alden Perkins, and Mark Via. For permission to reproduce illustrations I am grateful to the Imperial War Museum and Australian War Memorial.

# 1

## Stalemate on the Western Front

August of 1914 saw the outbreak of war between the wealthiest and most technically advanced nation-states of Europe. In the decade leading up to 1914, a succession of crises had steadily raised tensions in Europe. Sudden calamity struck on June 28, 1914, when Archduke Franz Ferdinand and his wife Sophie were assassinated by a Bosnian Serb at Sarajevo, the Bosnian capital. The archduke was a nephew of Emperor Franz Josef and heir apparent to the throne of Austria-Hungary. This isolated act of terrorism proved to be the spark that ignited war and tore up the illusion of European harmony. The Austrian desire to punish Serbia, and Russian gestures of support for the latter, resulted in a series of declarations of war. The German-Austrian and Franco-Russian coalitions mobilized against each other; reservists across Europe were recalled by poster and telegram to crowd railway stations and depots. Civilian society was thrown into a turmoil of farewells and departures; complex railway movements began in bright August sunshine.

Britain was soon drawn into the conflict engulfing Europe. The situation was uncertain until Germany invaded Belgium at dawn on August 4. Britain was a signatory to a treaty guaranteeing Belgian neutrality; a British ultimatum to Germany in regard to that expired at midnight of August 4. The British government feared that Germany was striking into Western Europe in a bid to establish a hegemonic position over the Continent.

At the outbreak of war, a relatively small German force was set aside to defend East Prussia from Russian invasion while, in accordance with the prewar planning of the Prussian General Staff, the bulk of German strength was dispatched to overrun France. In Western Europe the left wing of the German army was to stand fast on the Franco-German frontier while the right wing wheeled through Belgium and Luxembourg into northern France. The French army might then be crushed in the

1

jaws of a giant pincer, not unlike the way Hannibal had encircled the legions of Rome at Cannae in 216 B.C.[1]

The frontiers of France and Belgium were littered with clusters of fortifications designed to withstand the largest artillery that could be drawn by teams of horses. Yet, to the surprise of Germany's enemies, when war came, the Germans swiftly pounded to rubble the Belgian forts at Liege and Namur—sited to cover crossings of the Meuse River—with 305-millimeter Skoda and 420-millimeter Krupp heavy howitzers. These giant weapons had been dismantled and hauled forward by train and road tractors before reassembly. The Germans had given a great deal of thought to the design and employment of heavy artillery.

After the frontier fortifications were lost, the Belgian field army retreated on Antwerp. The Teutonic phalanx swept south from Brussels. The British government accepted the necessity of sending an army across the Channel to directly support France. At the northern end of the line of French armies, the British Expeditionary Force (BEF) went into action at Mons on August 23.

The group of German armies that marched down into northern France posed a direct threat to Paris. At one stage German troops could see the great metropolis in the hazy distance; the possibility of a repeat of the siege of Paris of 1870 hung in the air. At the critical time, however, German forces wheeled east of Paris, toward the Marne River. In response, the French garrison of the Paris region seized the opportunity to launch a successful counterattack. When it mattered most, the French were able to redeploy men by rail faster than the Germans could advance on foot. German forces began to retreat northwards on September 9, but halted to take up new positions on high ground behind the Aisne River.

The "Miracle of the Marne" was followed by the "Race to the Sea." The opposing armies rushed troops to fill the one-hundred-mile gap that lay between the Aisne and the English Channel. After the fall of Antwerp, Belgian forces marched down the coast to the Yser River and Nieuport. At the end of October, the sluices were opened at the mouth of the Yser to flood the countryside inland. To the south of Nieuport, fierce fighting at Ypres took place in October and November. A desperate Anglo-French defense held off a series of heavy German attacks. A stalemated front was established that ran for 475 miles from the sand dunes of the Belgian coast all the way to the Swiss frontier and the Alps.

In tandem with the clash of arms in France and Belgium, on the other side of Europe, the Russians had taken the offensive at the outset of war in support of France. Eastern Prussia was saved from the catastrophe of Russian invasion by German victory at the Battle of Tannenberg. In a series of battles across Eastern Europe, the Central Powers stalled the Russian "steamroller" to establish an eastern front that, like the western front, involved armies numbering millions.

The German army mobilized on the outbreak of war failed to execute fully an overambitious war plan. Nevertheless, the seizure of Belgium and northeast France gave Berlin a strong hand in a war that was likely to be concluded by treaty at a peace conference. Across the winter of 1914–1915, German troops improved their fortifications on a set of dominating ridges the length of the western front. That the trenches were on French and Belgian soil made credible Anglo-French claims that the war was caused by German aggression.

In London, Prime Minister H.H. Asquith and his Liberal ministry entered the war hoping that France and Russia would carry the bulk of the burden on land. It rapidly became clear, however, that Britain, too, would need to mobilize a large army for warfare on the Continent. The tall and aloof Lord Kitchener, the hero of colonial wars in Sudan and South Africa, was made secretary of state for war; he wasted no time setting plans in motion to expand the army. Kitchener led the recruiting effort by appearing on a poster bearing the slogan "Your Country Needs You."[2]

At sea, the war proceeded along lines more in accordance with London's expectations. Britain's Royal Navy, which had entered the war with roughly 50 percent more dreadnought battleships and battle cruisers than Imperial Germany, blockaded Berlin's access to the world's oceans beyond the North Sea.

A dramatic development far from the western front was the Ottoman Empire's entry to the conflict at the end of October 1914. In Cabinet, Asquith supported the plan of the First Lord of the Admiralty, Winston Churchill, to seize the Dardanelles and directly attack the Ottoman capital of Constantinople (or Istanbul).[2] An expeditionary force was hastily organized for a campaign in the eastern Mediterranean. After a short-lived naval effort to bombard the forts at the entrance to the Dardanelles in March 1915, a landing by troops was made in the vicinity on April 25. The Turks were able to mass sufficient forces to impose a deadlock that lasted throughout the year. The evacuation of the wretched peninsula was completed in early January 1916.

Meanwhile, with a severe war of uncertain length in prospect, Asquith's Liberals and the Conservative opposition announced the formation of a coalition ministry. This gave the reconstituted government an overwhelming majority in both houses of Parliament. In a ministerial reshuffle brought about by the advent of the new government, the controversial Churchill, who was a Liberal member of Parliament, was removed from the Admiralty in favor of a Conservative.

On the western front in 1915, France's General Joseph Joffre launched offensives in Artois and Champagne that were repetitive and costly. By the close of the year, French casualties in the war numbered almost two million killed, wounded, and missing. Slowly but surely the Allied effort on the western front came to rely on a substantial British presence. The BEF comprised 265,000 troops in January 1915, and expanded to more than one million by the end of the year.

In support of the French, the BEF fought a series of battles in 1915. In particular, the BEF attacked with determination at Neuve-Chapelle, Festubert, Aubers Ridge, and Loos. Across 1915 the BEF lost 285,000 casualties.[3] A War Office study later concluded that the BEF traded five casualties for every two German casualties in 1915.[4] Colonial warfare had not prepared the British Army to attack positions stoutly defended by a "first-class" power. British forces lacked effective artillery and all types of munitions. The German heavy field howitzer of 5.9-inch caliber—150-millimeter—established a formidable and tormenting ascendancy on the western front.

Generalship has always fascinated students of warfare; leadership is vital at all levels of military activity. An important change was made to the British High Command toward the end of 1915. In the aftermath of the Loos campaign, Field Marshal Sir John French was relieved, and from December 1915 the commander in chief of the BEF was General Sir Douglas Haig. Government ministers felt that Field Marshal French, a capable soldier in a colonial setting, lacked sufficient expert knowledge to meet the challenges of a full-blown commitment to Continental warfare.

Given the enormous influence that General Haig would have over the BEF, his career is well worth a blow-by-blow examination. Born to the wealthy family of an Edinburgh whisky magnate in 1861, Haig was the youngest of eleven children. Presbyterian by upbringing, after Clifton school Haig spent three years at Brasenose College, Oxford. He played polo for the university, but left without taking a degree to enter Royal Military College Sandhurst. The humorless Haig grew to be a handsome, self-willed, and notoriously aloof man.

After Sandhurst, Haig joined the 7th Hussars, a cavalry regiment that would soon embark for India. Within three years he was adjutant of the unit, which reveals both a capacity for administration and a strong presence; these would be two of the three defining characteristics of Haig's military personality; the third characteristic was an overweening ambition to rise up the ladder of promotion. The next important step in Haig's career was entry to the Camberley Staff College in 1896. Haig had failed the mathematics paper of the Staff College entrance exam, but he was sufficiently well-connected for that not to be held against him.[5] Upon completing the Staff College course, Haig joined the army fighting the campaign underway in Sudan. Haig was a staff officer to the commander of Kitchener's cavalry; he had his baptism of fire in the skirmishing that preceded the April 1898 Atbara battle. Haig was also at the Battle of Omdurman later in the year, the final bloody action of the long war in Sudan, and a definitive demonstration of the firepower of infantry armed with magazine rifles.

Haig's next appointment was on the staff of General French's cavalry brigade at Aldershot. This formation was among the first to sail for southern Africa and the Boer War late in 1899. Haig was present at the Elandslaagte engagement, at which the cavalry successfully harried a retreating Boer force. Haig was on the staff of French's Cavalry Division when it relieved Kimberley early in 1900.

In the second half of the Boer War, Haig commanded the 17th Lancers in a district of the Cape Colony. The principal action fought during Haig's tenure occurred on September 17, 1901, when a Boer commando led by Jan Christian Smuts overran C Squadron of the Lancers at Modderfontein farm, about fourteen miles from Tarkastad. The camp of C Squadron was poorly sited to withstand a determined assault. On a foggy day the engagement began poorly for the Lancers as approaching

Field Marshal Sir Douglas Haig. (Australian War Memorial)

Boers were mistaken for friendly troops. In a grisly hourlong fight, thirty-two British officers and men were killed and fifty-three wounded. The triumphant Boers looted the camp's stores and vanished again before a relief force could intervene. The losses of Smuts's commando were only one killed and five wounded.[6]

After the Boer War's conclusion, Haig's career continued to prosper; he left for India in 1903 to be inspector general of cavalry, which capped a remarkable rise for an officer who was still a captain early in 1898. The wars in Sudan and South Africa deepened Haig's belief in the importance of cavalry. To the dismay of Kitchener, who had become commander in chief in India, Haig opposed with a "missionary zeal" those within the army who believed that the future of the horsed soldier was to be a mounted infantryman. Haig taught that cavalry still had a sweeping role to play as a shock force. He conducted cavalry exercises based on the great campaigns of the long-departed Napoleonic period.[7] The Edwardian high noon of empire in British India was an ideal military setting in which to examine at leisure anachronistic ideas.

Haig's *Cavalry Studies* of 1907 was a military textbook based on a set of staff exercises. The primary focus of the work was the employment of divisional-sized forces of cavalry. The textbook firmly stated:

> The role of Cavalry on the battlefield will always go on increasing because—Firstly: The extended nature of the modern battlefield means that there will be a greater choice of cover to favour the concealed approach of Cavalry. Secondly: The increased range and killing power of modern guns, and the greater length of time during which battles will last, will augment the moral exhaustion, will affect men's nerves more, and produce greater demoralisation amongst the troops. These factors contribute to provoke panic, and to render troops (short-service soldiers nowadays) ripe for attack by Cavalry. Thirdly: The longer the range and killing power of modern arms, the more important will rapidity of movement become, because it lessens the relative time of exposure to danger in favour of the Cavalry. Fourthly: The introduction of the small-bore rifle, the bullet from which has little stopping power against a horse.

It was conceded that cavalry troopers would need to use their rifles more than previously, but "now as formerly, all great successes can only be gained by a force of Cavalry which is trained to harden its heart and charge home."[8] Haig's devotion to the cavalry, both as a venerated social system and in a military sense, cannot be underestimated: He never swerved from that confident viewpoint.

Haig was socially acquainted with King Edward VII. In 1905, while on leave in Britain, Haig was invited to Windsor by the royal couple for the Ascot races. On this sojourn Haig met the Honourable Dorothy Maud Vivian, one of Queen Alexandra's maids of honor. The lady in question was the shrewd daughter of a titled diplomat. Doris was impressed by Haig's "smart appearance" and seemingly "vital" personality; they were married within a month in the private chapel at Buckingham Palace.[9] The marriage was a success: The first two children to be born were daughters named after their godmothers, Queen Alexandra and Princess Victoria.

Haig left India for a War Office appointment in 1906 and spent three years at that institution. R.B. Haldane, the War Office minister, formed a high opinion of Haig's administrative ability. Late in 1909, Haig returned to India to be chief of the Indian Army's General Staff. In India, Haig added Captain John Charteris to his personal staff. Charteris, a Scotsman, Presbyterian, and Royal Engineer, had attended Quetta Staff College. He was an articulate, untidy, clever, and superficial man—the opposite of Haig in many respects. Charteris became a companion of Haig, though he was never a confidant. Detractors of Charteris called him the "principal boy"; they felt he played out the role of a buffoonish court jester—"a hale and hearty back-slapping fellow, as optimistic as Candide."[10] Nevertheless, Charteris was able to read the taciturn facade of his chief better than most. Haig was a man of steady and redeeming courtesy in his dealings with others, yet he shielded the core of his personality with a frigid outer barrier and was prone to outbursts of suppressed anger.

In February 1912, Haig, now promoted lieutenant general, was selected for the Aldershot command, a corps-sized concentration of infantry, cavalry, and artillery. This was a somewhat unlikely posting as Haig had recently completed a series of staff appointments. As much of Haig's service had been abroad, his arrival at Aldershot with his personal staff, which included Charteris as his assistant military secretary, was termed the "Hindoo invasion." Haig performed poorly in the army maneuvers of September 1912, but he was a safe political appointment from the viewpoint of Haldane and this seemed to override any other consideration.

On the outbreak of war, Haig went to France in command of I Corps; he took part in the difficult campaign that culminated in the stout defensive fighting of the First Battle of Ypres. When the Germans called off their offensive in mid-November 1914, Haig believed that to be a bad error given the thinness of the Allied line.

During 1915, as the First Army's commander, Haig presided over a series of disappointing offensive battles, yet when Field Marshal Sir John French was relieved, Haig was made commander in chief, something for which he had consistently intrigued. Once installed at General Headquarters (GHQ), the immaculately presented Haig needed a chief of staff; the officer appointed was Lieutenant General Launcelot Kiggell. Haig demanded absolute loyalty from his senior staff and subordinate commanders. Kiggell fitted that requirement to the utmost degree. Kiggell's most recent appointment had been at the War Office as director of home defense; he arrived at GHQ without previous service in France. Kiggell had been a prewar commandant at Camberley Staff College. A student recalled Kiggell as

> a tall, gloomy and erudite soldier. . . . The only thing I distinctly remember him saying was: "In the next war we must be prepared for very heavy casualties." His theory of war was to mass every available man, horse and gun on a single battlefield, and by the process of slow attrition wear down the enemy until his last reserves were exhausted, and then annihilate him.[11]

Haig and Kiggell worked well together, though the later remains a shadowy figure behind Haig's domineering personality. Charteris, now swiftly promoted to brigadier general, became GHQ's intelligence chief, a role he combined with the supervision of censorship and the issuance of propaganda. The bustling Charteris had entered intelligence work early in the war as he possessed some knowledge of French and German and was in need of employment.[12]

GHQ had been set up at Saint-Omer late in 1914, but at the end of March 1916, it transferred rearwards to a chateau near Montreuil-sur-Mer, which was a small town eleven miles from the sea, surrounded by medieval ramparts. Haig's headquarters acquired an isolated and detached quality that was much frowned upon during the war and afterwards. This was to some extent inevitable given the scale and static nature of the western front, but it was also in accordance with the personal style and attitudes of Haig. At GHQ—that "City of Beautiful Nonsense"—the red hatbands and red tabs of the General Staff was much in evidence. The newspaper correspondent Philip Gibbs wrote: "Often one saw the Commander-in-Chief starting for an afternoon ride, a fine figure, nobly mounted, with two A.D.C.s and an escort of Lancers. A pretty sight, with fluttering pennons on all their lances, and horses groomed to the last hair."[13] A stern critic complained of GHQ: "There was little or no contact with reality—with the circumstances which surrounded the cutting edge of the Army."[14]

Another vital military appointment was made in London shortly after Haig's elevation to GHQ in France. A new chief of the Imperial General Staff (CIGS), General Sir William Robertson, took up his tenure at the War Office on December 23, 1915. "Wully" Robertson had an extraordinary background for an army general. Born in 1860, he was the son of a village postmaster and tailor from Lincolnshire. Robertson left school at age thirteen to enter domestic service as a footman. At age seventeen he enlisted in the 16th Lancers, to the horror of his mother, who wrote to her son that "there are plenty of things Steady Young Men can do when they can write and read as you can. . . . [The Army] is a refuge for all Idle people. . . . I shall name it to no one for I am ashamed to think of it. . . . I would rather Bury you than see you in a red coat."[15]

Robertson was well suited to army life: He was a strongly built, determined young man, with a deep voice. He quickly rose to be a troop sergeant major. Such an all-round talent deserved support, and Robertson was encouraged to seek a commission. This was a marvelous turn of the wheel of fortune. Promotion from the ranks was rare at this time, but in 1888, Robertson became a second lieutenant in the 3rd Dragoon Guards. It was essential that he proceed directly to India, as he lacked the private means needed to get by as a cavalry officer in Britain.

In India, Robertson was often in need of extra cash. The Government of India granted pay bonuses to officers who were willing to study for and pass Indian language examinations. Robertson leapt at the opportunity and accumulated a proficiency in several languages. This proved to be a gateway to career advancement as he joined the Intelligence Branch at army headquarters by virtue of language qualification. In 1895, Robertson was on the staff of the Chitral Relief Force in the mountains of the northwest frontier. He was wounded when attacked by a treacherous local guide and slashed with a sword.[16]

Robertson returned to Britain to attend the Camberley Staff College, after which, during the Boer War, he served on Lord Robert's staff. In the years leading up to the outbreak of war with Germany, Robertson held a series of staff appointments. Robertson had a blunt manner and short temper, but he was a humorous man and widely admired for the extent of his dramatic rise in the army.

In August 1914, Robertson was appointed quartermaster general of the BEF. In January 1915 he became Field Marshal Sir John French's chief of staff. When the latter was relieved, he recommended Robertson to be his successor; the government, however, did not take up that suggestion.[17]

At the time of Robertson's appointment as CIGS, the Cabinet was urgently looking for an alternative source of advice to Lord Kitchener, the secretary of state for war. Kitchener had lost the confidence of a number of ministers given his lack of Whitehall experience and ad hoc methods. Robertson, fresh from GHQ in France, cannily accepted the appointment of CIGS on condition that he was independent of Kitchener. Robertson thus became solely responsible for issuing orders to commanders in foreign theaters. This arrangement was confirmed by an Order in Council.

In respect to strategy, Robertson, as befitted a former GHQ chief of staff, believed that a maximum level of force should be concentrated on the western front. He wrote in his memoirs: "We could not alter the geography of Europe which conferred upon the enemy the advantage of a central position, and thereby enabled him to keep one of his opponents in check with a part of his armies while he threw the bulk of them into a decisive blow against another."[18] In the early months of 1916, the evacuation of Gallipoli, the siege of Kut al-Amara in Mesopotamia, and the Salonika and Suez Canal theaters were all large British commitments. The 120,000 casualties of the Dardanelles campaign was certainly a substantial toll for a secondary theater. Robertson had no desire to repeat that profitless experience, and he willingly supported Haig's plans for the Western front. "There was never," Robertson was to write, "so far as I know, any material difference of opinion between us in regard to the main principles to be observed in order to win the war."[19] Haig and Robertson, however, were not on terms of close friendship. Haig's habitual courtesy was laced with condescension when dealing with Robertson, whom he regarded as a social inferior. In contrast, Robertson, who was outwardly impervious to the slings and arrows of snobbery, displayed tact in his dealings with Haig so as to maintain the unity of the High Command.

Lieutenant Colonel Maurice Hankey, the secretary to the Cabinet's War Committee, wrote of Robertson: "As a strategist he was sound but rather lacking in imagination. . . . In speech he was slow and deliberate. He never uttered an opinion which he had not thought out." Robertson ruled the General Staff at the War Office with an iron fist. He possessed "a dominating personality," recalled Hankey. "He knew what he wanted, and he nearly always got his way. . . . For him there was only one theatre of war that counted, and that was the Western Front. Taking him all in all he was within his limitations a rugged, dogged and likeable man."[20] The chief of Robertson's limitations, in a strictly professional sense, was his lack of experience as a commander of troops, and, given his cavalry and bureaucratic background, a modest understanding of weaponry at a time of rapid technological change. Like Kiggell, Haig's chief staff officer, Robertson believed the best thing to do on the western front, for want of any worthier idea, was to mount a methodical offensive and grind through the German defenses. Robertson provided the government with as little information as possible; indeed, ministers were hardly better informed about military operations than the heavily-censored-newspaper-reading general public.

At the close of 1915, the Central Powers held large tracts of northern France, Belgium, and Poland, but none of the principal Allied nations had been defeated: The war was far from over. On the western front in 1916, the opening German move was General Erich von Falkenhayn's offensive at Verdun, which began on February 21. Falkenhayn's intention was to bleed white the French army in a gruesomely deliberate battle of attrition. The campaign dragged on for months on ground that was reduced by heavy shelling to a desolate wasteland littered with the rotting remains of the slain.

Meanwhile, final preparations for an Anglo-French offensive in the Somme region were being finalized. A steady stream of fresh divisions had flowed across the Channel to reinforce the BEF. The Somme had been chosen as it was near the junction point of the British and French armies, meaning those two forces could fight side by side. There was no major objective behind the Somme front, just a set of villages and small towns of the kind common to many parts of northern France.

The opening day of the long-awaited offensive, July 1, 1916, was a tragic drama. The German defensive front was deeply mined into chalky, rising ground and protected by dense wire entanglements; the crews of machine guns had clear lines of fire across sweeping, treeless downland. The clumsy assault made by British forces cost sixty thousand casualties within a twenty-four-hour period.

The Somme offensive was badly compromised by its calamitous start; nevertheless, the campaign was pushed onwards until November to attain a maximum advance of seven miles. A succession of blunt and expensive attacks consistently failed to do more than push the line forward a short distance. The German heavy artillery proved an effective weapon of attrition. The strategy behind months of weary slogging was based in part on mistaken estimates of German morale and losses. Charteris, GHQ's intelligence chief, conjured up tallies of German casualties using an arbitrarily eccentric system of accounting. From July 1 to November 30, BEF losses in the Somme battles were 419,654 and French casualties were 204,253.[21] Haig's GHQ asserted that German losses were in excess of 600,000. Postwar investigation, however, found that casualties were traded two to one in the Germans' favor in the British sector of the Somme battlefields.[22]

The cost of the Somme touched many families. The devouring flames of the pyres were fed with rich fuel, including that of Prime Minister Asquith's eldest son, Raymond. Nonetheless, neither Asquith's Cabinet nor Robertson's War Office dared to institute a discreet commission of inquiry into the Somme campaign. In contradiction to that, government-appointed commissions eagerly set about an examination of the failure of the Dardanelles expedition and setbacks in Mesopotamia. Haig and his senior staff dismissed unofficial criticism of their Somme strategy; they took pride in the BEF's expanded role on the western front and firmly believed that victory could be attained only by a full commitment to offensive action.

On the German side of the line, a review of command arrangements took place while the Somme campaign was in progress. At the close of August 1916, Falkenhayn was replaced by the team of Field Marshal Paul von Hindenburg and General Erich Ludendorff, fresh from success on the eastern front against the armies of Tsarist Russia. Hindenburg was made chief of the Prussian General Staff; Ludendorff was given the title of first quartermaster general. In practice, Ludendorff was responsible for the operational conduct of the German army, subject to Hindenburg's distant supervision.

On September 5 the "Eastern Warriors"—Hindenburg and Ludendorff—began an inspection tour of the western front in a specially appointed command train. The headquarters of Army Group Crown Prince Rupprecht was located at Cambrai. This was a convenient place at which to hold a conference to review operational policy for the western front. One of the main outcomes of the Cambrai conference was the decision to build new defense lines behind the existing front. Ludendorff ordered a reconnaissance of possible locations, after which it was decided to build the *Siegfriedstellung* on the line Arras–Saint-Quentin–La Fère–Condé. Work on this carefully laid-out defensive system, which would be known to the Allies as the Hindenburg Line, began at the end of September.[23]

By 1916 it was clear that Britain was deeply and expensively committed to the battlefields of northern France and Flanders. The mounting costs of the conflict lay behind the dramatic upheaval in British politics that closed out the year of 1916. On December 1, David Lloyd George, secretary of state for war since Kitchener's untimely death at sea, demanded of Prime Minister Asquith a reconstruction of the government. Lloyd George was tired of Asquith's rudderless and enervated approach to war leadership; he was also alarmed by the extent to which the making of strategy had fallen into the hands of an inefficient army leadership.

Asquith refused to compromise with Lloyd George, who resigned on December 5, 1916, to bring on a full-blown crisis in the government. Conservative ministers withdrew their support and forced Asquith to resign that evening. King George V asked Andrew Bonar Law, the Conservative leader, to form a new government. Bonar Law, a melancholic and self-effacing man, was unable to meet that request and advised the king to send for Lloyd George. Bonar Law knew that the charismatic Lloyd George was the right man with whom to go tiger hunting.[24]

By December 7, Lloyd George had stitched together a ministry with Conservatives holding many senior positions. Asquith was surprised that the Conservative

David Lloyd George, prime minister of Great Britain, 1916–1922. (A.W.M.)

party's leaders had so readily conspired with Lloyd George, who had been a divisive figure in prewar politics. Asquith was joined on the opposition benches by a number of his former ministers. Crucially, Lloyd George's negotiations with the Conservatives had included an assurance there would be no sudden retrenchment of the military leadership.[25] The brawling instability of British politics created a political need for a stable High Command.

The new prime minister was the most prominent Welshman of his generation; born in 1863, he was a Baptist by denomination and a solicitor by training. Lloyd George entered Parliament in 1890 as a Liberal with a reputation as a fiery platform speaker. A lengthy period as chancellor of the exchequer was the shining feature of Lloyd George's prewar ministerial career. He had a wife and family living at their country home in Wales, and a mistress in London, Frances Stevenson, who was his private secretary. Involvement in financial scandal had added to Lloyd George's notoriety. The prime minister was a strongly built, talkative man of middle height; his longish hair was steadily turning from gray to white. Lloyd George's opponents found him egotistical, devious, and alarmingly effective.

The reformed War Cabinet, which met almost daily, had only five members at the outset; this magnified the influence of the prime minister and other members, as was intended. Lord Milner was invited to join the War Cabinet. Milner had been high commissioner in South Africa during the Boer War and was a senior bureaucrat of long experience. Lord Curzon, a former viceroy of India, was also a member of the War Cabinet and the government's leader in the House of Lords.

As prime minister, Lloyd George had no party machine of his own and no wish for a general election; he was dependent on Bonar Law to manage the Conservative Party's involvement in the government. The Labour Party was also part of the government. Lloyd George's ability to retain the support of Labour and about half of Liberal parliamentarians, in addition to the Conservatives, made him the politician of the day most able to form a broad-based coalition government. The prime minister's position, however, was fundamentally fragile. A wave of ministerial resignations, for whatever reason, would have seen Bonar Law or another politician quickly installed as prime minister. The Asquithian Liberals, if they scented the blood of a quarry, might have supported a fresh ministry merely to bring down the "Welsh wizard."

A matter upon which the Conservatives had a firm opinion was the career of Winston Churchill. The Tory leadership insisted that Churchill not receive ministerial office in the new government. Lloyd George tried to persuade Bonar Law to consent to Churchill being given a responsible position, but to no avail. Bonar Law, an "unsociable teetotaller," neither liked nor trusted the showy Churchill, who had deserted the Tories for the Liberals some years before. Earlier in the war Bonar Law had written of Churchill: "I think he has a very unusual intellectual ability but at the same time he seems to have an entirely unbalanced mind which is a real danger at a time like this."[26] The force and sparkle of Churchill's inventive power aroused suspicion in a man of Bonar Law's bleak disposition.

Across the Channel, General Joffre's tenure in command of France's main field army was drawing to a close. Joffre was sidelined by the French government and replaced by General Robert Nivelle. During the Verdun campaign, Nivelle had played a prominent role. General Pétain, the commander of Army Group Centre, was a more obvious replacement for Joffre, but he was passed over on this occasion.

The emergence of a new British prime minister and a new French commander in chief brought about a lively reexamination of Allied plans for 1917. At a conference in London beginning on December 26, 1916, there was broad agreement that further Anglo-French attacks were needed on the western front to purge the Germans from northern France and Belgium. Allied leaders assembled again in Rome early in January 1917. At the Rome conference, among other heads of business, Lloyd George floated the idea of transferring a quantity of Anglo-French heavy artillery to the Italian front. The French and Italians were unsure of the motives behind the British prime minister's interest in Italy and politely deflected the suggestion.

On the return journey from Rome, Lloyd George met General Nivelle in Paris. Lloyd George was impressed by the vibrant Nivelle, who was invited to London to explain his strategic viewpoint to the War Cabinet. Before the assembled ministers the persuasive Nivelle radiated confidence; his mother was English, and he was fluent in that language. Nivelle wanted to employ masses of artillery to "rupture" the German front and achieve a rapid breakthrough; he envisaged the French taking the lead in a new campaign with the BEF in a supporting role. This pleased Lloyd George, who believed that "much of our losses on the Somme was wasted, and that the country would not stand any more of that sort of thing."[27] The War Cabinet decided to support Nivelle's plans for a French-led offensive. On January 17 the War Cabinet instructed Robertson to order the recently promoted Field Marshal Haig to carry out, "both in the letter and in the spirit, the agreement made with General Nivelle."[28]

In the opening months of 1917, events of great consequence were unfolding far from the western front. At sea a strategic stalemate was firmly established in the North Sea, but beneath the waves a stop-start form of restricted submarine warfare had been practiced by the navy of Imperial Germany since the outbreak of war. Fears of alienating the United States and other neutrals had caused bouts of self-imposed restraint. That all changed, however, when Germany adopted a policy of "unrestricted submarine warfare"; this meant that all merchant shipping—whether Allied or neutral—in designated waters around Britain, France, and Italy was liable to be sunk without warning. This policy commenced on February 1, 1917, and soon caused the United States to break off diplomatic relations with Germany.

Given the deadlock on the western front, Hindenburg and Ludendorff were in favor of the revised submarine policy. The kaiser dared not overrule the combined opinion of his admirals and generals. Chancellor Theobald von Bethmann Hollweg was appalled at this latest development; he complained of the domineering influence of the "demigods" of the High Command. Admiral Henning von Holtzendorff, chief of the Naval Staff, insisted that a concerted campaign against merchant shipping had every chance of bringing the war to a speedy conclusion by putting Britain's food supply in jeopardy.

The dramatic escalation in the submarine war had not been anticipated by Britain's Admiralty. The submarine blockade made an immediate impact as the willingness of neutral shipping to sail to Allied ports plummeted. In April a total of 881,027 tons of shipping was lost to hostile action, the bulk of which—545,282 tons—was British. In addition to this, ports and shipyards became clogged with damaged shipping in need of repair. The toll of Allied shipping losses from February to August would be more than half a million tons in each calendar month.[29] During this fraught period, unrestricted submarine warfare seemed to be tilting the course of the conflict to Germany's advantage.

Meanwhile, preparations for Nivelle's great offensive were pushed forward energetically. Haig's BEF was ordered to fall into line with the plans of the French commander in chief; this arrangement was not permanent and would cease at the conclusion of Nivelle's offensive. For the next round of operations, General Sir Henry Wilson was appointed to coordinate liaison between the British and French High Commands. Wilson was a declared Francophile and had long experience of working with French officialdom.

The Central Powers, however, had their own plans for the western front. By the early weeks of 1917, the Germans were ready to retire to the newly built defensive works of the Hindenburg Line. The Germans were banking on a defensive strategy on the western front for 1917 while the U-boat offensive did its work at sea. At this time there were 154 German divisions on the western front faced by 190 Allied divisions.

From the end of February, the Germans began a stealthy evacuation of a large salient between Arras and Soissons. As part of Operation Alberich, the kaiser's army laid systematic waste to the villages and countryside given up: Houses were demolished, wells poisoned, and trees and orchards cut down. The sum of this devastation was a tremendous gift to Allied propagandists, and fueled demands that hefty payment for war damage be part of any peace treaty. There was heavy fighting where German rearguards chose to make a stand. Haig's cavalry played a minor role across this period, notwithstanding the partial return to open warfare. The German retreat was completed by the end of March.

As the armies on the western front prepared for another year of fighting, the war on the eastern front took a dramatic turn. In March 1917 revolution erupted in Petrograd—the renamed St. Petersburg—sparked by a crumbling economy and food shortages. The hapless tsar abdicated on March 15. A newly created provisional government, which was run by bourgeois liberals, proclaimed an intention to continue the war.

In another part of the world, a further convulsive disruption to the international order took place. On April 6 the United States entered the war. American lives and merchant ships had been lost to U-boat attack. President Woodrow Wilson asked

Congress to accept that a war was already underway. Washington no longer felt able to tolerate the possibility that Germany might come to dominate the Western world, especially a Germany willing to strike at American maritime interests whenever that suited Berlin.

It was unclear at first whether the Americans would send a large army across the Atlantic. There were few precedents for an act of that magnitude. The United States Army was not much greater than one hundred thousand in April 1917. Wilson's administration might opt to fight a naval war against the U-boats, with only a modest commitment on land. Ominously, for Germany, Wilson supported a draft: On May 18 conscription was enacted.

In the Middle Eastern theaters of war there had also been fresh developments. In Mesopotamia, Baghdad fell to British-Indian forces on March 11, 1917. This was an overdue success against Ottoman Turkey given the defeats at Gallipoli and Kut al-Amara. Any captured city or province would be a tradable commodity at a peace conference. In parallel to this, another British Imperial army advanced from the Suez Canal across the Sinai desert to the southern fringe of Palestine; two successive failed attacks at Gaza followed. These false notes were a stern reminder of the fighting prowess of the Turk.

The German withdrawal to the Hindenburg Line disrupted Allied offensive preparations on the western front. In Paris a new prime minister, Alexandre Ribot, took office on March 20, with Paul Painlevé as war minister. Painlevé doubted Nivelle's prospects, as did other French generals such as Pétain, but the ministry let Nivelle's offensive go ahead as planned.[30]

As a prelude to the main French attack, on April 9 the opening blow of the spring season was struck by British troops at Arras in a storm of sleet. An assault was made on a fourteen-mile front. A well-organized creeping barrage paved the way for an advance of three and a half miles in two days; Canadian troops captured Vimy Ridge to gain observation across the Douai plain. This initial success was encouraging, but the offensive rapidly bogged down into another sterile, Somme-type campaign of attrition. The German defensive front had been broken into, but there was no breakthrough into the open countryside beyond. A series of British attacks in the second half of April and early May achieved little. In total the Arras campaign cost 150,000 British casualties; GHQ estimates of German losses were grossly inflated.

Meanwhile, Nivelle's offensive was finally launched on April 16. On the morning of the attack, the weather was discouraging; it had poured with cold rain and sleet all night. On the front between Soissons and Reims, the infantry's assault was preceded by a massive bombardment of the German position on Chemin des Dames ridge. When the barrage lifted, French troops in the Aisne valley pushed up the steep, wooded slopes of the ridge. Useful progress was made during the opening few days of the battle, only for the thrust to grind to a halt in heavy fighting that dragged into early May. Nivelle's offensive achieved a maximum advance of four miles on a sixteen-mile front.

The French casualty toll for April 1917 proved to be higher than any month since 1914. Yet another Napoleonic-type grand maneuver of masses of soldiers had resulted in fields of French corpses and hospitals overflowing with the stricken. French losses for all parts of Nivelle's campaign up to May 9 were 187,000.[31]

The Aisne battle damaged Nivelle's reputation beyond repair; he was persuaded to step down. Pétain took up the post of commander in chief from the middle of May; General Ferdinand Foch became chief of the General Staff in Paris. Earlier in the war, Foch had commanded a group of armies on the western front. To finish off this round of musical chairs, Nivelle and his faded star were banished to a headquarters in Algeria.

Philippe Pétain hailed from a farming family of the Artois region of northern France. Born in 1856, he had attended Saint-Cyr military academy, after which he embarked upon a pedestrian army career. As an instructor at the War College, Pétain specialized in the teaching of infantry tactics. Pétain's political viewpoint is sometimes thought to have hindered his career, but promotion was invariably slow in times of peace unless an officer had a powerful patron or was willing to seek opportunities in France's colonial empire.

In April 1914, Pétain had taken charge of a brigade at Saint-Omer in what was likely to have been a last posting before retirement. The sudden onset of war, however, changed Pétain's destiny. A flurry of rapid promotions catapulted him to command of Army Group Centre. In the spring of 1917, in the wake of Nivelle's brief tenure, Pétain finally became the man of the hour at the head of France's field army.

The stoical Pétain possessed a weight of reserved personality that made an immediate impact on those around him. A subordinate recalled: "I had the impression of a marble statue; a Roman senator in a museum. Big, vigorous, an impressive figure, face impassive, of a pallor of a really marble hue."[32] Pétain's cool realism and sober sense matched the mood of the times and would soon be tested. From the end of April, widespread discontent among French troops became unmistakably apparent. In the days and weeks ahead, as bewilderment and despondency deepened, waves of strikes and drunken riots touched more than fifty French divisions. The units concerned were mostly those involved in the recent offensive. The Germans did not detect a crisis in the French military, as disorders took place in back areas away from the front line. Pétain was privately shaken by events and reported to the government that Nivelle had made too many unfulfilled promises prior to the last round of fighting. From 1914 to the spring of 1917, French commanders had too often thrown away men with the bravura of a bygone era, as if France was still the most populous nation in Europe.

From May 25 to June 10, eighty significant cases of "collective indiscipline" were reported; from June 10 to July 10, this figure fell to twenty, and more or less ceased thereafter.[33] The storm had been weathered. Ringleaders were executed or imprisoned. Pétain later said that fifty-five executions were carried out in the aftermath of the disorders; this was a similar figure to the number of executions carried out in Haig's BEF during the Somme campaign.[34]

It was clear to Pétain that for the immediate future the French army was best suited to a defensive strategy on the western front, with only brief bursts of offensive activity. This approach would at least keep France in the war and in possession of most of that nation's territory.

# 2

## The Road to Flanders

The consequences of the April/May battles were deeply felt across the Channel within Britain's government. Lloyd George had been rash to back Nivelle, an unproven foreign commander. Lloyd George and other members of the War Cabinet found the Nivelle affair chastening. The Prime Minister's confidence in his own military judgment was shaken; he was henceforward reluctant to risk his own position when disputes arose with his generals.

Nevertheless, the war had to be fought to a conclusion; new plans were needed. Lloyd George headed for the next conference of Allied leaders bearing instructions from the War Cabinet to encourage the French to continue the offensive. At the Paris conference of May 4–5, the British prime minister declaimed that "the enemy must not be left in peace for one moment . . . we must go on hitting and hitting with all our strength."[1] Anglo-French civil and military leaders agreed that another round of offensive action was needed on the western front; to stand on the defensive was "tantamount to acknowledging defeat"; fresh attacks for "limited" objectives seemed the most effective way to gain ground with a minimum of loss.[2]

After returning from Paris, Lloyd George suggested to the War Cabinet on May 9 that more effort might be devoted to breaking up the Ottoman Empire. Lord Curzon agreed that possession of Palestine would help to secure Egypt and Mesopotamia. The War Cabinet decided to transfer two of the six British divisions at Salonika to Egypt, but there was no support for a transfer of forces from the western front to the eastern theaters.

In light of the decisions taken at the recent Allied conference in Paris, Field Marshal Haig held a meeting of his army commanders at Doullens on May 7. At this meeting, Haig announced that British forces were no longer subject to French strategic direction; instead, the British Expeditionary Force's (BEF) next major campaign would be in Flanders, at the northern end of the western front. For the past year

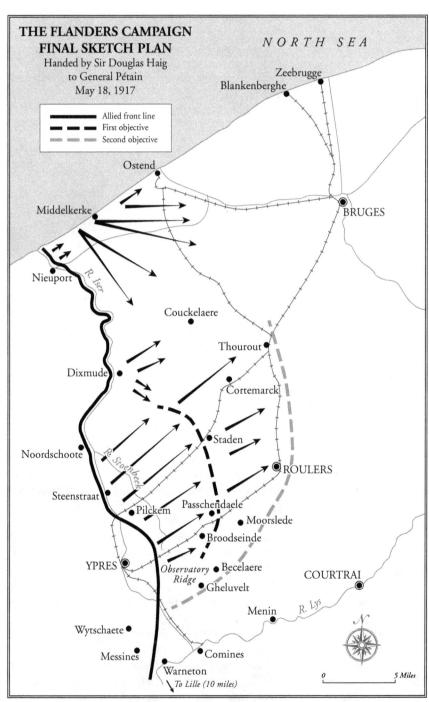

THE FLANDERS CAMPAIGN
FINAL SKETCH PLAN
Handed by Sir Douglas Haig
to General Pétain
May 18, 1917

——— Allied front line
– – – First objective
····· Second objective

*NORTH SEA*

Zeebrugge
Blankenberghe
Ostend
Middelkerke
BRUGES
Nieuport
R. Iser
Couckelaere
Thourout
Dixmude
Cortemarck
Staden
Noordschoote
R. Stoenbeek
ROULERS
Steenstraat
Pilckem
Passchendaele
Moorslede
Broodseinde
YPRES
*Observatory* Becelaere
*Ridge*
Gheluvelt
COURTRAI
Menin
R. Lys
Wytschaete
Messines
Comines
Warneton
*To Lille (10 miles)*

N

0                    5 Miles

**Plan for the Flanders campaign**

Haig had been eyeing the possibility of an offensive in Flanders to clear the Germans from the Belgian coast.

The notion of a campaign in Flanders had also come to the attention of ministers in London. This was because Germany's occupation of the Belgian coast had stirred up a great deal of anxiety at the Admiralty. The German seizure of the Belgian ports of Ostend and Zeebrugge had given the kaiser's navy new bases from which to threaten the sea lanes upon which the Allies depended. Vice Admiral Sir Reginald Bacon's Dover Patrol was the force responsible for covering the eastern entrance to the English Channel. Bacon was a zealous supporter of plans to push the Germans off the Belgian coast, whether by means of an amphibious landing or in conjunction with a land offensive. Whenever Haig and Bacon met, these ideas were avidly discussed. The Belgian ports of Zeebrugge and Ostend were worthy military prizes.

On the other side of the line, German leaders had their own plans for the Flanders coast. When the time came to hammer out a peace settlement to end the war, they intended to claim control of large parts of Belgium, including Bruges and the coastal region of Flanders. If Berlin won the war, the Belgian ports would in all likelihood become permanent bases for Germany's military.

Given the undoubted strategic significance of the Belgian coast, Haig wanted Pétain's French army to support his ambitions in Flanders. In particular, the field marshal earnestly desired that the French launch diversionary attacks to deter the Germans from reinforcing Flanders. On May 18, Haig and Pétain met at Amiens. This was a marvelous opportunity to restart Anglo-French military relations on a harmonious footing. Haig wrote of the encounter: "As regards Petain personally; I found him businesslike, knowledgeable, and brief of speech. The latter is, I find, a rare quality in Frenchmen!"[3] In the course of the discussion Pétain stated that the French First Army of six divisions was ready to directly cooperate with the BEF's plans for Flanders. More importantly, Pétain said he intended to launch a series of local offensive operations in the French sector of the western front. This was exactly what Haig wanted to hear.

Pétain was diplomatic when he met with Haig, but he spoke more freely with General Wilson, the principal British liaison to the French High Command. Wilson noted in his diary for May 20: "In his [Pétain's] opinion, Haig's attack towards Ostend was certain to fail . . . his effort to disengage Ostend and Zeebrugge was a hopeless one." Wilson met General Foch, France's chief of the General Staff, on June 2. "He [Foch] wanted to know who it was who wanted to go on 'a duck's march through the inundations to Ostend and Zeebrugge.' He [Foch] thinks the whole thing futile, fantastic, and dangerous, and I confess, I agree, and always have."[4]

On June 2, General Marie-Eugène Debeney, Petain's chief of staff, visited the BEF's General Headquarters (GHQ) for dinner. Haig wrote: "He [Debeney] brought a letter from General Petain saying that he had commissioned him to put the whole situation of the French Army before me and conceal nothing. The French Army is in a bad state of discipline." As a consequence of that "bad state of discipline," there would be no attacks in the French sector till mid-July at the earliest, though the French First Army remained at Haig's disposal.[5] Wilson wrote in his diary for June 4 that a lack of French support might at least, "I think, and I hope . . . finally dispose of Haig's insane idea of taking Ostend and Zeebrugge."[6] That was not the case: Haig's bewitched eye was firmly fixed upon the Belgian coast.

Haig could face the prospect of another major offensive with grim resolution, as he had ample reserves at his disposal. The BEF's fortunate situation owed much to the French army, which held most of the western front's trench lines that stretched from the North Sea coast to the Swiss frontier. In May 1917 the British held a front of almost 100 miles with 60 infantry and 5 cavalry divisions, whereas the French held 325 miles with 109 divisions, most of which had an infantry strength only two-thirds the usual BEF figure.[7] By this stage of the war, the French had lost almost one million soldiers dead, quite apart from many other casualties from wounds and illness. (The French burden was alleviated by the 130-mile Alsace-Lorraine sector, to the southeast of Verdun, which only needed a light garrison.)

Haig's offensive plans for Flanders would be shaped by the geography of the region. On the coast, the Belgian town of Nieuport lay just within Allied lines. To the south of Nieuport, thirteen miles of inundations along the shallow valley of the River Yser separated the combatants. Not far from the southern end of the flooded

**Haig, his army commanders, and senior staff. Herbert Plumer is to Haig's right and Henry Rawlinson to his left. Julian Byng and W.R. Birdwood are immediately behind Haig. (A.W.M.)**

sector, the town of Ypres sat in a shallow basin only 66 feet above sea level. To the east of Ypres, ridges arranged in a sweeping semicircle rose to 160 feet; to the south of Ypres, the high ground near Messines and Wytschaete peaked at 260 feet.

The front in western Flanders was dominated by the town of Ypres; this gave the region's fighting an isolated quality more typical of an eighteenth- or nineteenth-century battlefield. Ypres provided the sector with a geographic heart the Somme campaign had lacked. As Captain S.J. Wilson was to put it, "If Belgium has been dubbed the Cockpit of Europe, surely the 'Salient' was the cockpit of cockpits."[8]

Ypres had been a prosperous town since the Middle Ages and had featured prominently in the military history of the region. In the late seventeenth century, Marshal Sébastien de Vauban, Louis XIV's master military engineer, directed at Ypres the building of an elaborate system of fortifications. Some of these structures were dismantled in the mid-nineteenth century, but the town center of the early twentieth century still featured brick-faced earthen ramparts and a partial moat. When war came in 1914, the civilian population of Ypres swiftly departed, after which the town was steadily pulverized by bombardment. "Wipers" is thought to have received more shellfire than any other place on the British front. In the center of Ypres, two impressive medieval buildings dominated the town: the large Cloth Hall of the merchant guilds and the Gothic St. Martin's Cathedral. By 1917 war damage had stripped those fine buildings of their roofs. In crumbling interiors weeds grew in the rubble; birds nested in the damaged masonry.

The town wall of Ypres was broken by gates; the Menin Gate issued forth the road that headed toward the town of that name. The intersection of the Ypres-Menin road and Ypres-Roulers railway, about one mile east of Ypres, was known as "Hellfire Corner." Up in the line, working parties ventured out after darkness had fallen to mend wire entanglements and rebuild collapsed trench walls in a landscape polluted and befouled by past battles. The haunting gloom was broken by flares that rose to cast twisted shadows. Dangerous local sectors in the Ypres salient were luridly lit up by streams of flares fired at ceremonial intervals throughout the night.

An officer of the 9th Royal Welsh Fusiliers recalled the condition of Ypres at the close of April 1917:

> So much has been written of Ypres. . . . Everyone who passed through the town formed his own opinion of the place, but all agree that it was an uncanny place. To us, on our move up to the line, though it was a bright moonlit night, it seemed a city of the dead. . . . In the moonlight the city had a peculiar beauty of its own. Shells by the thousand had fallen among its buildings and yet in the dim light little damage appeared on the exterior, but when one looked closely at the houses one saw that only shells remained— the interiors were gutted. By day the City looked gaunt and evil: from a distance the buildings seemed to be undamaged, but as one got closer, windows and doors showed charred and black interiors like the sunken eye-holes of a rotting corpse.[9]

The war-ravaged town's notorious reputation grew more sinister as the military cemeteries behind the lines multiplied.

Part of the ruined Cloth Hall, Ypres, 1917.

The ridgelines to the east of Ypres were low, but high enough to provide the Germans with clear observation over the British trenches that arced around the town's eastern flank. Major C.H. Dudley Ward wrote:

> One speaks of Ypres being overlooked by the enemy, of high ground; but the stranger, visiting the place for a glimpse of the celebrated battlefield, will be disappointed if he expects to see hills in the accepted form; the gentle undulations of an extremely flat country stands before him—a careful study of the map shows him a rise of, say, thirty feet in a mile, or a mile and a half! But, on a winter day, when the foliage does not offer concealment, let him stand on the Menin road. . . . The flatness of the country, the position of Ypres with the enemy's horns on either side, thrust so far forward that their tips were behind the town, gave to the least imaginative the sense of walking into a trap.[10]

Around Ypres an intricate network of small streams and canals had been developed over many generations to drain the farmland, which was prone to flooding due to the flatness of the terrain and frequent rain showers. Small, shell-damaged woods and farmhouses dotted the gentle slopes of the Ypres salient.

A period of relative calm descended across the BEF's front after the collapse of the ill-fated Nivelle-Arras campaign. Major A.T. Paterson recalled:

> May [1917] opened with glorious Spring weather. At daybreak and in the twilight the songs of the birds could be heard all round the shell-torn countryside, and often the call of the cuckoo sounded from the trees. Shrubs and trees were bursting into leaf and bud, and a carpet of wildflowers came to cover the scarred face of No Man's Land and to spread a pall of tiny blossoms over the little mounds with their rough wooden crosses where the dead were sleeping.[11]

There would be little time, however, to contemplate the fragrant scents of spring. After a short interlude the Second Army was scheduled to undertake the opening step of Haig's Flanders campaign at Messines. The aim of this operation was to secure the forbidding Messines-Wytschaete ridge, six to seven miles south of Ypres. The capture of the ridge would open up the constricted Ypres sector for an offensive on a grand scale.

The Second Army's commander was General Sir Herbert Plumer, the "warden" of the Ypres salient. Plumer's hair had turned white during his two years in command there since 1915. The upcoming Messines operation would permit the Second Army to attack rather than ceaselessly defend. The press correspondent Philip Gibbs wrote of Plumer: "In appearance he was almost a caricature of an old-time British General, with his ruddy, pippin-cheeked face, with white hair and a fierce little white moustache, and blue, watery eyes, and a little pot-belly and short legs. He puffed and panted when he walked."[12] Born in 1857, as a young man Plumer had joined what would become the York and Lancaster Regiment; he first experienced active service in the 1884 campaign in eastern Sudan. After attending the Staff College, Plumer was stationed at Jersey before rejoining his regiment in Natal. This was fortuitous, as southern Africa was the scene of much fighting in the years ahead. In the Matabele rebellion and Boer War, Plumer performed his duties with distinction.

Plumer was promoted to major general in November 1902—prior to Haig achieving that rank—and in 1904 became quartermaster general with a seat on the Army Council. Plumer seemed destined for the highest honors the army had to offer, but he was sidelined early in 1906 after a Liberal government took office. Haldane, the incoming secretary of state for war, canceled Plumer's appointment, as the latter seemed too closely associated with the policy of the previous Conservative government.[13] Plumer was put on half pay to await a fresh posting. This caused other rising officers—including Haldane's protégé Haig—to vault ahead of Plumer on the career ladder. Plumer next took command of a division in Ireland; then, after another lengthy period on half pay, he went to Northern Command in 1911 as a lieutenant general.

After the outbreak of war, Plumer was not at first called upon for overseas service, but in January 1915 he went to France to take charge of V Corps, and in May 1915 he moved up a step to the Second Army, which was a station more in keeping with his seniority. By mid-1916 the forty-four-year-old Major General Charles Harington had become Plumer's chief of staff. Like Plumer, Harington hailed from a northern English regiment, the King's Liverpool in Harington's case.

From early in the war, armies on the western front had engaged in tunneling operations to plant mines under the forward trenches of an opposing force. Messines Ridge was a prime opportunity for mining, and tunneling work got underway in that sector in 1915. The following year, the enterprising plan was conceived for a comprehensive mining operation that would involve the sinking of a series of shafts with galleries up to one hundred feet below ground. Beneath a layer of sand on the surface, and a layer of sandy clay beneath, was a deeper seam of blue clay. The heavy clay of Flanders was suitable for deep mining; the sheer depth of the shafts would muffle the sounds of digging.

Tunneling in the Messines sector was pushed forward across 1916. The entrances to the shafts were signed as "deep wells." A large labor force using picks and shovels slowly burrowed and threaded passages into the bowels of the earth by the comforting light of electric lamps; pumping engines kept water at bay. Coal mining was a major industry in Britain, and there was no shortage of mining expertise in the army. The mining work under the ridge took months to complete, and progress per day was measured in feet. The blue clay excavated had to be hidden or transported rearwards to prevent German airmen seeing telltale evidence of mining from high above. A German raiding party returned with a sample of blue clay, but this was assumed to be from an isolated shaft. German miners were also active. At times, especially under Hill 60 on the northern flank of the ridge, it had seemed that rival tunnels were on the verge of intersection, but the chances of two tunnels crossing paths was low, and not unlike the chances of two submarines colliding beneath the ocean.

In the Messines sector, five miles of mine gallery was dug; the longest tunnel was almost half a mile in length. Gigantic mines were planted at the end of the galleries, and in total, nearly one million pounds of high explosives lay packed and ready for detonation. Some of the mines were completed weeks and months ahead of schedule. One particular tunnel was called the "Berlin sap" in mock recognition of the ambition behind the project.

The Germans were aware that preparations were underway for an attack of some sort at Messines. German airmen had spotted expansions to the local light rail network, and the discreet buildup of ammunition dumps and battery positions. German soldiers on the ridge had splendid views in a westward direction; they could see the rising level of activity on the British side of the front. On the other hand, to the relief of British commanders, German prisoners taken in the Messines sector showed little awareness of the great mining operation underway beneath their feet. Indeed, the Germans assessed that British mining activity at Messines had decreased during April and May of 1917; that was true, but only because the work was largely completed.

At this time German forces on the western front were divided into groups of several armies. Royal personalities held key commands. The BEF, at the northern end of the western front, was opposed by the army group of Rupprecht, crown prince of Bavaria. Born in Munich, the forty-eight-year-old Rupprecht had pursued a military career with a praiseworthy seriousness. His wife had died in 1912 and only one of their several children was destined to survive to adulthood. Rupprecht began the war as an army commander; he took control of an army group at the end of August 1916 as a recently promoted field marshal.

German troops in Flanders belonged to the Fourth Army, which was commanded by General Sixt von Armin, a sixty-five-year-old who had been wounded in the Franco-Prussian War at Gravelotte. As a British offensive seemed in prospect, a

**Crown Prince Rupprecht of Bavaria. (A.W.M.)**

conference was held at the Fourth Army's headquarters on April 30 to study the situation. Lieutenant General Hermann von Kuhl, Rupprecht's chief of staff, proposed a retirement of German troops from the most exposed parts of the western face of Messines Ridge. Kuhl was worried by the danger of mines, but his proposal got little support. General von Armin and other senior officers of the Fourth Army opposed the abandonment of any part of the defensive system at Messines.[14] Rupprecht's headquarters later issued specific instructions in respect to the villages of Messines and Wytschaete: "These strongpoints must not fall even temporarily into the enemy's hands. . . . They must be held to the last man even if the enemy has cut them off, on both sides, and threatens them from the rear." In 1917 there was no shortage of German troops on the western front; a number of reinforcing divisions were transferred to the Fourth Army in Flanders, along with a substantial force of artillery.[15]

Plumer's Second Army was to attack Messines Ridge in the early hours of June 7. After the mines were detonated, three corps of infantry would attack on a seventeen-thousand-yard front. The final objective lay two miles distant at the furthest point. The Messines operation was planned in great detail by the Second Army's knowledgeable staff. In preparation for the assault, a large-scale quarter-acre clay model of the ridge was built for curious senior officers to study at their leisure; a high wooden viewing platform surrounded the structure. Some divisions built their own clay models of the local sectors they were to attack; these models were inspected by as many troops as was practical. Units rehearsed for the assault on training grounds upon which topographical features were marked out with tapes. The belts of bursting shells of the creeping barrage were represented by lines of men carrying flags. Drummers, whistles, signal flags, and shouted orders controlled the exercises.

Captain Antony Eden, adjutant of the 21st King's Royal Rifle Corps, wrote of a visit from General Harington, Plumer's chief of staff, in the days prior to the assault. Harington explained to the assembled officers the depth of the creeping barrage and the mines that would be blown. When Harington asked for comments, Eden drew attention to a particular German strongpoint that stood in the path of his unit. "Harington listened and nodded when I had done. . . . He would speak to the Major-General Royal Artillery and recommend that it should be made a particular target for destruction by nine-point-twos. He thought that we could safely count upon it that this would be done."[16] Eden held Harington in high esteem, as did the journalist Philip Gibbs, who gave the general a glowing portrait:

> A thin, nervous, highly-strung man, with extreme simplicity of manner and clarity of intelligence, he impressed me as a brain of the highest temper and quality in Staff work. His memory for detail was like a card-index system, yet his mind was not clogged with detail, but saw the wood as well as the trees, and the whole broad sweep of the problem which confronted him. There was something fascinating as well as terrible in his exposition of a battle that he was planning. For the first time, in his presence and over his maps, I saw that, after all, there was such a thing as the science of war, and that it was not always a fetish of elementary ideas raised to the nth degree of pomposity, as I had been led to believe by contact with other generals and staff officers.[17]

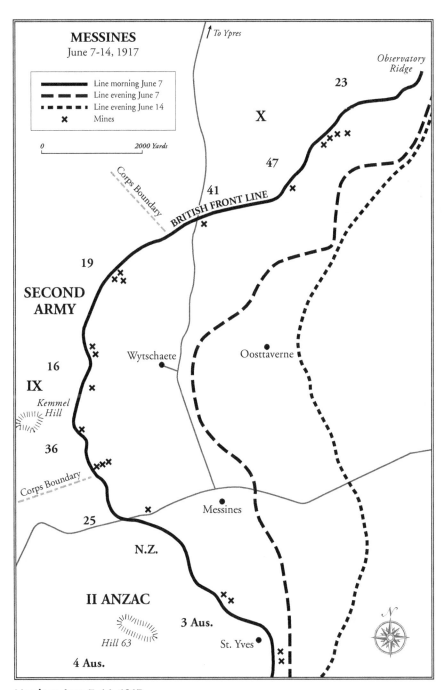

**MESSINES**
June 7-14, 1917

| | |
|---|---|
| Line morning June 7 | |
| Line evening June 7 | |
| Line evening June 14 | |
| ✕ | Mines |

0                    2000 Yards

↑ To Ypres

*Observatory Ridge*

23

X

47

41

*Corps Boundary*

BRITISH FRONT LINE

19

**SECOND ARMY**

Wytschaete

Oosttaverne

16

**IX**

*Kemmel Hill*

36

*Corps Boundary*

25

Messines

**N.Z.**

**II ANZAC**

*Hill 63*

**3 Aus.**

St. Yves

**4 Aus.**

N

Messines, June 7–14, 1917

**Messines Ridge, with the ruins of Messines village on the distant crest line.**

Plumer's and Harington's plans made provision for the seventy-two tanks available to support the Second Army's assault; these tanks were distributed in detachments across the front and allocated specific tasks.

Fresh units assembled in Flanders for the offensive. Private E.N. Gladden of the 11th Northumberland Fusiliers recalled arriving at Ypres about this time: "It was with no little awe that I alighted among the grim ruins of that City of the Dead. As we assembled in the main square, surrounded by spectral shapes, we seemed to be almost encircled by the enemy lights that rose and fell above the low ridges commanding the town." By daylight the bespattered Gladden inspected Ypres from the front line near Zillebeke lake.

> Before my eyes spread the martyred city, whose resistant walls still shaped the remains into the semblance of a dwelling-place of men. A concourse of shattered buildings clustered in the middle distance, with here and there a broken chimney stack or a decapitated church spire jutting a little above the rest. There was no human movement. The place looked as though it had been abandoned half-finished to the elements. But this was only the superficial appearance of the thing, a shell burst among the rubble, demonstrating clearly the cause of the city's dire condition.[18]

The day of destiny for Gladden's battalion was drawing ever nearer.

The Germans held the front at Messines with a garrison of four divisions. The forward trench system ran in a bulging arc around the western base of the ridge. A second system on top of the ridge covered the crest line and the villages of Messines and Wytschaete; behind the crest of the ridge, a reserve line ran through Oosttaverne village.

The German defensive zone had been strengthened by the construction of numerous concrete strongpoints; these were usually called "pillboxes" by British troops. The pillboxes in the forward system were small and might house a few men or a section, but farther to the rear these concrete bastions were larger and had garrisons of twenty-five to fifty men. Steel rods reinforced the concrete; a direct hit from a shell of at least eight-inch caliber was needed to cause serious damage to a well-built structure. Some of the pillboxes were loopholed for machine guns; others were designed primarily as shelters from shellfire and were without loopholes. Earth was heaped up around the low-set pillboxes as camouflage.

The preliminary bombardment for the Messines operation began on May 21 and grew intense from the last day of the month. German positions on the forward slope of the ridge were especially vulnerable to shellfire. Messines and Wytschaete were soon reduced to rubble; at times the villages vanished in drifting clouds of smoke and dust. Bursting shells of the field artillery tore up the barbed-wire entanglements strung out on rows of pickets. The Second Army assembled 1,510 field and 756 heavy guns for the battle. Vast dumps of ammunition fed the massed batteries. Many of the heavy guns merrily firing away were six-inch howitzers.

At a conference on May 30, Haig suggested a premature blowing of the mines, as a rumor had been received that the Germans would soon withdraw from their forwardmost positions. British troops could then dash forward and occupy the craters as a prelude to the main assault planned for a later date. The field marshal's intervention was politely deflected by a skeptical Plumer, who had the seniority to be firm with Haig if he chose to do so.

The screeching bombardment imposed a great strain on the defenders. On the afternoons of June 3 and 5, practice barrages were fired to confuse the Germans. By now the ridge had been stripped of its greenery to create a battered landscape of many shades of brown and gray; patches of concrete shone in the sun on the exposed western face of the ridge. The Australian press correspondent C.E.W. Bean watched proceedings through his telescope during "days of gloriously fine, bright weather— the landmarks on the slope disappeared in a waste of shattered earth crowned by the now formless ruins of Messines village."[19]

British gunners unleashed three and a half million shells from May 26 to June 6. At first the German artillery replied, but this fire soon slackened. A German diarist recorded: "This everlasting murder. They send over shot after shot. The casualties increase terribly. All the trenches are clodded up. The English have also demolished our dug-out. Casualty after casualty. No shelter left. They blow up the earth all round us. To look on such things is utter misery."[20] Erected on watery foundations, concrete pillboxes heaved and swayed from the concussion of nearby shell bursts.

The Royal Flying Corps (RFC) concentrated three hundred aircraft in the Messines sector to support the work of the soldiers on the ground. Aircraft were vital for assisting the artillery to fire effectively at distant targets, especially those beyond the ridge's crest. Squadrons of German aircraft took to the skies as well. The cheerful sunshine of the opening week of June provided excellent flying weather. Reserve *Oberleutnant* Scheele of the 4th Grenadier Regiment recalled:

> The air battles continued to entertain us. The aircraft made a special effort to destroy balloons. If one of the latter was shot down, the observers used to jump and descend to earth by parachute. When the aircraft fired phosphorous [incendiary] bullets, they left long trails of flame and made a most interesting sight. Those of us on the ground were frequently the targets of enemy aircraft; the boldest of these came down to twenty metres to fire at us.[21]

The German observation balloon line lay about ten thousand yards behind the front; it was the intention of RFC commanders to clear German aircraft out of the pale blue sky to the west of that balloon line. The opposing air forces were constantly updating their equipment; the soon-to-be-famous Sopwith Camel made its debut in combat about this time.

General Harington told a press briefing on the eve of the Messines operation: "Gentlemen, I don't know whether we will make history tomorrow, but at any rate we shall change geography."[22] The mined vaults driven under the ridge had taken months to dig and were an unrepeatable freak as a military operation. The mines—if all went to plan—would form the greatest set of man-made simultaneous explosions, three times greater than the previous record during the construction of New York City's subway network.

At dusk on June 6, Plumer's assault troops left their camps and bivouacs behind the front to march for the line under cover of darkness. Eighty thousand infantrymen were preparing to head out across no-man's-land, with a large force of artillerymen, pioneers, engineers, and signalers working in support. Commanding officers were mindful that soldiers should not be overloaded in an assault, but inevitably, heavy loads had to be carried. A steel helmet, rifle, bayonet, ammunition, entrenching tool, haversack contents, water bottle, box respirator, and Mills bombs were all necessary parts of an infantryman's equipment. On top of that, distributed within each platoon were additional items such as picks, shovels, wire cutters, rifle grenades, spare Lewis gun panniers, and flare equipment. Portable light machine guns were a valuable asset, and each platoon had at least one Lewis gun team.

After darkness had fallen, tractors hauled heavy guns to more-exposed positions; horse teams pulled up ammunition wagons to the batteries of eighteen-pound field guns. German gas-shelling—phosgene and chlorine—of Ploegsteert Wood caused five hundred to a thousand casualties, though otherwise final preparations went relatively smoothly. A brief shower fell around midnight amid a burst of lightning and thunder, after which the sky cleared and Messines Ridge loomed up ahead "black and lifeless under the bright moon."[23] A slight mist hung in the air. At one point an aircraft flew low overhead to distract attention from any audible rumbling and clanking sounds made by tanks.

From 2 A.M. on June 7, British artillery fire fell away. A soldier recalled: "The whole countryside seemed wrapped in sleep."[24] A strange stillness prevailed; bayonets were fixed in anticipation; officers tensely studied the luminous dials of their synchronized wristwatches; birdlife was heard singing in readiness for the dawn of a new day. In the last minutes before zero hour, an occasional yellow-and-green flare rose from the German lines. There were bursts of local firing, but nothing more than that. The beaming moon had sunk below the horizon; the first signs of dawn glimmered faintly to the east.

At 3:10 A.M. the guns of the Second Army roared back into life with an ear-splitting din. Out of the gloom to the west, gun flashes were so dense that a line of flickering yellow flame blazed across the horizon. In accordance with long-standing plans, nineteen mines were successfully detonated within about twenty seconds of each other. The sky was lit up by a gigantic flash. An eyewitness recorded: "Suddenly, at 3.10 A.M., great leaping streams of orange flame shot upwards, each a huge volcano in itself, along the front of attack, followed by terrific explosions and dense masses of smoke and dust, which stood like great pillars towering into the sky, all illuminated by the fires below."[25] The violent eruptions threw a reddish glow onto the base of scattered clouds floating in the sky. Civilians in towns and villages up to twenty miles distant thought there was a dangerous earthquake underway. The sound of the detonations reached over the Channel into southeast England. According to a German account: "The ground trembled as in a natural earthquake, heavy concrete shelters rocked, a hurricane of hot air from the explosion swept back for many kilometres, dropping fragments of wood, iron and earth, and gigantic black clouds of smoke and dust spread over the country. The effect on the troops was overpowering and crushing."[26] The explosions were a tremendous surprise for the Germans.

Captain Eden wrote of the mine detonation nearest to his post:

It was an astonishing sight, rising like some giant mushroom to a considerable height in the air before it broke suddenly into fragments of earth, stones and timber falling over a wide area. The whole ground heaved so violently that for a fraction of a second we thought we were over the mine instead of beside it. As the barrage opened simultaneously, the noise of the guns deadened all sound from the mine, except that we could hear, even above this crescendo, the screams of the imprisoned Germans in the crater.[27]

Private Gladden, his senses sharpened by danger, remembered:

The ground began to rock. My body was carried up and down as though by the waves of the sea. In front the earth opened and a large black mass mounted on pillars of fire to the sky, where it seemed to remain suspended for some seconds while the awful red glow lit up the surrounding desolation. . . . Almost simultaneously a line of men rose from the ground a short distance in front and advanced away towards the upheaval, their helmets silhouetted and bayonets glinting in the unearthly redness.[28]

Father William Doyle, a chaplain in the 16th (Irish) Division, wrote of the explosions, "Not only did the ground quiver and shake, but actually rocked backwards and forwards, so that I kept my feet with difficulty."[29]

At an observation post to the rear, the Second Army's staff saw a glare in the sky when the mines were blown. "The Army Commander was not with us," wrote Harington, "he was on his knees in his room, praying for those gallant men who were scaling the ridge." Harington later visited the aftermath of a mine explosion.

> The crater at Spanbroekmolen [in the 36th Division's sector], which had been preserved, was an amazing sight. In a German concrete dugout, close by, I saw four German officers sitting up round a table—all dead—killed by shock. In an officer's pocket was found a copy of a message he had actually sent at 2.50 A.M. saying: "Situation comparatively quiet." He literally was living on a volcano, poor fellow.[30]

The mines that had exploded beneath the German forward system produced craters up to three hundred feet in diameter.

A furious and thrilling infantry assault quickly got underway shortly after the mine explosions had done their work. British troops had assembled as close as possible to the danger zone. In places troops crawled over their parapets to lie behind white jumping-off-tapes on the edge of a darkened no-man's-land. When the order to advance was given, the infantry set out behind an elaborately planned artillery barrage that hurled tons of munitions into the German front. The roaring cloud of the creeping barrage—seven hundred yards in depth—beat up a mist of grit and soil, through which stole the first streaks of dawn. This moving curtain of bursting shells suppressed much of the defensive machine-gun fire that had been so destructive in the battles of 1915–1916.

As shells whined overhead, the waves of attackers bounded swiftly up the slope toward the crest line, rounding up stunned prisoners as they went. Designated "moppers-up" set about clearing captured dugouts after the leading waves had passed onwards. German observers farther up the ridge reported the sight of "masses of infantry advancing in a succession of lines followed by closed columns."[31] The pillbox shelters lay scattered across the ridge like toy bricks. If a pillbox garrison resisted, the attackers were trained to shower the redoubt with light machine-gun fire and rifle grenades while riflemen and bombers worked their way around a flank to rush the emplacement from the rear.

The experience of each British division was particular to its own locality, though much of what happened was common to all sectors. The northern shoulder of the salient was attacked by X Corps with three divisions. Two German divisions—35th and 204th—were posted to defend this vital stretch. The mines blown at Hill 60 wiped out two German companies and opened up a wide gap in the defensive line. Despite the magnitude of the challenge, the attack proved a success across the front of X Corps. Once the summit of the ridge was taken, German infantry and guns could be seen retreating into the distance.

At the center of the Second Army's assault frontage, IX Corps had the most distant objectives and was opposed by the German 2nd Division. In the left-hand sector of IX Corps, the 19th Division advanced toward the wreckage of two small woods. Farther to the right, on the remainder of IX Corps' front, the 16th (Irish) and 36th (Ulster) Divisions attacked side by side. Half a dozen mines had been planted in this sector; the air was thick with pungent smoke and dust after the detonations. The German wire was well cut and troops brandishing rifles surmounted by sharpened bayonets surged forward to occupy the obliterated first objective. The surviving defenders emerged from what remained of their posts, which had been reduced to shattered heaps of earth, concrete, timber, and sheets of twisted corrugated iron. Prisoners were sent rearwards down the slope. Major William Redmond, the Irish home rule parliamentarian, died of his wounds in the advance on Wytschaete village, by now a set of rubble heaps dumped on the hillside. The majority of the tanks that took part in the attack broke down and were ditched. The shell-ravaged forward slope of the ridge was difficult going for a mechanized vehicle.

At the southern end of Plumer's front, II Anzac Corps also attacked with three divisions, and was opposed by the 3rd Bavarian Division and part of the 4th Bavarian Division. In the left-hand sector of II Anzac Corps, the 25th Division, well screened by the shell bursts of the barrage, bounded through a succession of trench lines and pushed deeply into the German front.

The New Zealanders were the central division on the front of II Anzac Corps; their task was to advance two thousand yards to a point beyond Messines village. The New Zealand Division was a de facto national army. Apart from a mounted rifles brigade in Palestine, this infantry division was the small dominion's main field force. After sweeping over the first set of German trenches, the New Zealanders headed

A tank going into action at Messines.

onwards to capture the crest of the ridge. The Auckland Regiment's Second Lieutenant O.E. Burton described the scene:

> The long roll of the heavy guns and the quick, stabbing, bang-snap-bang of the eighteen-pounder blended into one tremendous volume of sound. Up from the enemy positions went the signals of distress and warning, but their urgent appeal met with small response, for the Hun artillery had been overwhelmed by the weight of the British counter-battery work. For hours their field guns were out of action, and the only reply they could make was with long-range guns of heavy calibre.[32]

After the New Zealanders overran Messines village, Germans trapped in the cellars and dugouts beneath the ruins were made prisoner.

At the southern end of the Second Army's assault frontage was the 3rd Australian Division. The principal opposition on this division's front was met by the 33rd Battalion, the commander of which, Lieutenant Colonel L.J. Morshead, would be a divisional commander in North Africa in the next world war. There are obvious comparisons to be made between the Messines infantry assault and the opening night of the Second Battle of El Alamein, a generation into the future. The proper coordination of infantry and artillery has proved an enduring aspect of large-scale modern battle.

By late morning the length of the Messines-Wytschaete ridge was in British hands. The RFC commanded the skies. The reverse slope of the ridge was relatively undamaged; panoramic views along the Lys valley to the southeast revealed villages and small woods basking and shimmering in the bright sunshine.

It was a cloudless day, and the back crest of the ridge was in sight of German artillerymen farther to the east, who knew the range to the yard. A German observer reported that "crowds of British infantry were seen to take off their coats on this warm summer morning and begin to dig in along the skyline of the Ridge; working in their light-coloured shirts they made admirable targets." Artillery fire during the afternoon caused many British casualties on the ridge. The sheer density of the attacking formations had surprised the Germans; officers who had been on the eastern front felt that the British handled massed infantry in a manner that was scarcely different from that of Tsarist Russia.[33]

The attackers now paused behind a protective standing barrage in readiness for the next phase of the operation. The last objective of the day was the German reserve system, which was known as the Oosttaverne Line. The finalized zero hour for this push, following a two-hour postponement, was 3:10 P.M. On the front of X Corps, at the northern end of the assault frontage, the 24th Division came through from reserve to carry the advance onwards to gain most of the final objective. To the immediate south, IX Corps' front had narrowed on the central portion of the ridge so that a brigade-sized force was sufficient to secure Oosttaverne village. At the southern end of the ridge, on the front of II Anzac Corps, two brigades of the 4th Australian Division set out for the final objective with mixed results.

The defensive scheme of Group Wytschaete, the German corps headquarters mainly responsible for the ridge, was sternly tested by the crisis of that morning. Shortly after news of the mine explosions and assault was received, two divisions of the Fourth Army's reserve were made available for a counterattack. The 7th Division and 1st Guards Reserve Division hastily departed their billets. It took some hours, however, for the divisions to assemble and march out for the threatened sector.

The northern of the pair of counterattack divisions—the 7th—was directed toward Wytschaete, but it was 1 P.M. before these troops had crossed the Ypres-Comines canal. As the afternoon progressed, the 7th Division joined up with surviving units of the original ridge garrison and built up a new front wherever that could be managed. Farther south, the leading regiment of the 1st Guards Reserve Division set out for the southern half of the ridge, but shelling and machine-gun fire arrested this movement; the remainder of the division was held to the rear near Warneton.

Over the next three days, troops of the Second Army secured the untaken portion of the Oosttaverne Line in a bout of hard fighting. Additional German reserves arrived to reseal the fractured front. Crown Prince Rupprecht wrote in his diary on June 9:

> The British Army communiqué is celebrating the victory of General Plumer at Wytschaete. It is said that the detonation of the gigantic mines could be heard in London. Some of the mine galleries were completed a year earlier. In the first rush, the British troops succeeded in overrunning the German lines and by midday both Wytschaete and Messines were in their hands. All around Messines the ground was said to have been covered by the bodies of Bavarian soldiers (our poor, brave 3rd Division).[34]

At the southern end of the ridge, the 3rd Bavarian Division suffered losses of ninety-eight officers and thirty-six hundred men.[35]

The all-important ridge was now in British hands. The sweeping view from the summit of the ridge back into the old British front line was revelatory. Philip Gibbs, the press correspondent, wrote:

> From Messines and Wytschaete [the Germans] had absolute observation over a wide tract of country in which our men lived and died—how complete an observation I did not realise until after this battle, when standing in Wytschaete Wood and on the mound by St Eloi, and on the ground rising up to Messines, I looked back, and saw every detail of our old territory laid out like a relief map brightly coloured. "My God," said an officer by my side, "it's a wonder they allowed us to live at all!"[36]

Across the week ahead, the Germans used their heavy artillery to bombard from long range the new British front line on the eastern slope of the ridge, much of which was exposed to direct observation.

The Second Army's casualties from June 1 to 12 proved to be 24,562. Over half the losses were incurred by II Anzac Corps; the dogfight to clear up the Oosttaverne Line in the days after the initial attack was expensive. The New Zealanders lost 150 officers and 4,828 other ranks; the 3rd Australian Division lost 112 officers and 4,010 other ranks.[37] As New Zealand had one fortieth the population of the United Kingdom, the losses of that young nation's division had a far-reaching impact back home.

German casualties for the Messines battle were 23,000, of whom 10,000 were missing. The number of Germans made prisoner was 7,354. There was, however, no large-scale capture of artillery. Typically, Haig's GHQ overestimated German losses as 39,000.[38]

The Messines engagement had been a model "bite and hold" operation; the infantry successfully advanced a predetermined distance behind a well-organized protective artillery barrage. In some respects, the operation was a bigger version of the capture of Vimy Ridge by the Canadians earlier in the year. After the battle Plumer was asked the source of his success, to which he proudly replied: "Perhaps because I am an infantryman, and this is an infantryman's war."[39]

Congratulations poured into the Second Army's headquarters. Press reports in Britain were ecstatic in tone. In a war that seemed to lack brilliant moments, the Messines attack garnered an avalanche of glowing publicity, and raised expectations as to what might be achieved later in the season. The speedy and inexpensive initial seizure of the ridge added fuel to the contentious argument that the offensive done well was a cheaper form of warfare on the western front than sitting on the defensive under heavy shellfire.

# 3

## Interregnum in Flanders

The seizure of Messines Ridge secured the southern flank of Ypres. The scene was now set for the launching of a major offensive in Flanders. Field Marshal Haig believed the time was right to force the issue with Germany on the western front. By mid-1917, however, problems in respect to the British army's supply of manpower were starting to become apparent. The British Expeditionary Force (BEF) had grown to a strength of over two million, and was supported by a large base establishment in Britain. On May 31 the adjutant general, Lieutenant General Sir Nevil Macready, informed the Army Council that there had been a serious shortfall in recruiting over the last six months. The intake was a quarter of a million Category A men below requirements. The BEF was 82,783 below strength in infantry; Macready warned of a "period of exhaustion which will supervene in early autumn."[1]

Another development about this time was an unexpected turn in the air war in the skies over southeast England. Late in the previous year, the zeppelin airship bombing campaign against London had petered out, but in May 1917 a squadron of Gotha heavy bombers began a ruthless series of raids on British targets. From May to July a number of raids struck London and towns in southeast England. These sinister aircraft flew a leisurely course across the sky and were obviously flying from bases in France and Belgium behind the northern end of the western front. The Gothas slipped straight through air defenses that had been built up to combat the night flights of zeppelins.

During the period of the Gotha raids, strenuous discussions took place within the British government in respect to war strategy. Lloyd George had his doubts about a further all-out offensive on the western front in 1917; he was attracted by the argument that the capture of the Adriatic port of Trieste might be followed by the capitulation of the Austro-Hungarian Empire, and the rapid withdrawal of Bulgaria and the Ottoman Empire from the war.

Lloyd George's ministers also wanted their views on war strategy to be given a hearing. On June 7, the day of the Messines attack, Lord Milner observed to the War Cabinet that the "defection" of Russia had derailed Allied plans for victory. Milner went on to say:

> On the other hand, the entrance of America into the war has introduced a new factor, of great ultimate promise but small immediate value. What are we going to do to fill up the time before the weight of America can be thrown into the scale? . . . [It was wrong] to go on without any plan at all. How do we stand about Palestine, about the Balkan campaign, about the continuance of the offensive on the Western Front? I don't know that we have made up our minds about any of them. I feel as if we were just drifting, and as if there was some danger that, in view of the preoccupation of a number of grave but nevertheless minor domestic questions, we might continue to drift.

The following day, at the prompting of Milner, the War Cabinet decreed the establishment of a War Policy Committee "to investigate the facts of the Naval, Military, and Political situations, and present a full report to the War Cabinet."[2]

The newly created War Policy Committee's principal members were Lloyd George, Milner, Curzon, and Jan Christian Smuts; Bonar Law and Robertson often attended meetings; Hankey was the committee's secretary. General Smuts had come to London to join the Imperial War Cabinet as South Africa's representative. The Cambridge-educated lawyer had acquired a spectacular reputation in the Boer War; more recently he had commanded British forces in German East Africa.[3]

The War Policy Committee's first formal meeting was on June 11. At that meeting Robertson argued gamely that further offensive action was needed on the western front. Lloyd George retorted that the Italian front offered better opportunities given the depth of German defenses in northern France and Flanders.

The views of the Royal Navy's leadership were of considerable importance to the formation of British war policy. On June 12 the War Policy Committee heard from Admiral Sir John Jellicoe, the First Sea Lord. As commander of the Grand Fleet from the outbreak of war until late in 1916, Jellicoe had carried a crushing burden of responsibility, as warships could not be quickly replaced in the event of heavy losses. As First Sea Lord, Jellicoe persisted with the careful approach that had been a feature of his tenure at the Grand Fleet. Jellicoe informed the War Policy Committee that it would assist the Admiralty greatly if German submarine bases on the Belgian coast were rendered untenable. Most of the submarines attacking Allied shipping were based at German ports, but some were based on the Belgian coast.

Field Marshal Haig was recalled from France to give his opinion on strategy to the War Policy Committee. The soldiers and civilians met at 11 A.M. on June 19—Haig's fifty-sixth birthday—in Lord Curzon's Privy Council Office at Ten Downing Street. Haig appeared before the committee armed with a raised map to show ministers details of his preferred scheme to clear the Germans from Flanders. Haig believed there was every chance of success; he claimed that German morale was poor and their supply of munitions low. Robertson supported Haig as best he could. The chief of the Imperial General Staff (CIGS) said that the situation was "sufficiently favourable" for a methodical and careful set of offensive operations. In answer to a question from Bonar Law, Haig said that Pétain had promised to make attacks on the French part of the western front to prevent the Germans massing reserves against the BEF.[4]

Haig wrote up his version of events for June 19 in his diary:

> The members of the War Cabinet asked me numerous questions, all tending to show that each of them was more pessimistic than the other. The P.M. seemed to believe the decisive moment of the war would be 1918. Until then we ought to husband our forces and do little or nothing, expect support Italy with guns and gunners. . . . I strongly asserted that Germany was nearer her end than they seemed to think, that now was the favourable moment for pressing her and that everything possible should be done to take advantage of it by concentrating on the Western Front all available resources. I stated that Germany was within six months of the total exhaustion of her available manpower, if the fighting continues at its present intensity. To do this more men and guns are necessary.[5]

At this meeting Lloyd George noticed that Haig "made a dramatic use of both his hands to demonstrate how he proposed to sweep up the enemy—first the right hand brushing along the surface irresistibly, and then came the left, his outer finger ultimately touching the German frontier with nail across." Despite Haig's careful explanations, the prime minister harbored doubts as to whether the plan was practical; the Allies had only a modest advantage in numbers and guns on the western front. Lloyd George asked the soldiers "to realise our own difficulties in regard to manpower. We were now reduced to the point where we had to scrape up men where we could . . . it was very important not to break the country."[6]

At the War Policy Committee meetings of June 20, energetic discussions continued. In the course of these proceedings, Haig made a telling concession to his doubters. "He [Haig] was fully in agreement," recorded the minutes, "with the Committee that we ought not to push in attacks that had not a reasonable chance of success, and that we ought to proceed step by step. He himself [Haig] had no intention of entering into a tremendous offensive involving heavy losses. His plan was aggressive without committing us too far."[7] This reply from Haig soothed some of his audience's anxieties.

On June 20, Admiral Jellicoe again appeared before the War Policy Committee. Curzon asked the First Sea Lord to explain further the implications of Germany's possession of the Belgian ports. Apart from the threat posed by the submarines based on the Belgian coast, Jellicoe was concerned that the Germans had three squadrons of destroyers at Zeebrugge: That figure might be raised to six squadrons when required. If the Germans suddenly attacked with all available forces, they could sweep up the Royal Navy's standing patrol in the English Channel and threaten cross-Channel traffic. The melancholy Jellicoe feared that the war might end in a negotiated peace that left the Belgian coast in German hands, but this could be avoided if the coast was recaptured while hostilities were underway.[8] Haig recorded in his diary that Jellicoe told the committee that

> owing to the great shortage of shipping due to the German submarines, it would be impossible for Great Britain to continue the war in 1918. This was a bombshell for the Cabinet and all present. A full enquiry is to be made as to the real facts on which this opinion of the Naval Authorities is based. No one present shared Jellicoe's view, and all seemed satisfied that the food reserves in Great Britain are adequate. Jellicoe's words were, "There is no good discussing plans, for next Spring—We cannot go on."[9]

Jellicoe's concerns seemed excessive, but the naval viewpoint, by long and illustrious tradition, carried great weight with the civilians inhabiting the corridors of Whitehall.

Despite the series of meetings that had taken place, the War Policy Committee had yet to reach a clear position in regard to the proposed Flanders offensive. Haig and Robertson were firm and united in their opinion that the operation should go ahead; the prime minister, Milner, and Bonar Law were skeptical of the military case, though Smuts, Curzon, and Balfour (foreign secretary) were more inclined to give them the benefit of the doubt.[10] There was no consensus of opinion either for or against the plans of the military.

On June 25 the War Policy Committee met to discuss matters further. In the face of united army and navy opinion, the timid verdict was to let Haig continue with the preparations needed for an offensive in Flanders. The committee wanted assurances that the French would be able to play an active role in support of Haig's proposed campaign. On July 2 the committee was given General Wilson's opinion that the French were capable of the level of aggression needed to hold German reserves on their part of the front. (Wilson's liaison role with the French High Command had recently ended in the wake of Nivelle's dismissal.)

Preparations for the new campaign gathered pace. Haig's chosen commander in Flanders was General Sir Hubert Gough. Born in 1870 to a military family with Irish and Anglo-Indian connections, in the summer of 1917 Gough was just short of his forty-seventh birthday. A man of wiry build, after attending Eton and Sandhurst he had joined the 16th Lancers. Gough was admitted to the Staff College in 1899, but the Boer War intervened and he was posted to Natal and the staff of a cavalry formation. As the war deepened in intensity, a number of irregular mounted regiments were raised: Gough was given command of one of these units.

After the relief of Ladysmith and the capture of the Boer capitals in 1900, Gough's regiment performed a range of tasks as the guerrilla phase of the conflict took shape. In September 1901 the Boer leader Louis Botha stealthily entered Natal with a commando of 2,000 men. Four British columns were sent out to contest Botha's progress, one of which was Gough's regiment of 585 mounted infantry and two fifteen-pound guns.

On September 17, Gough's unit was at De Jaeger's Drift on the Buffalo River when a message was received that Botha's commando was in the vicinity. About noon a patrol reported the sighting of 200 Boers; Gough broke camp and rode with his regiment to join the patrol. The Boers headed for Blood River and dismounted upon arrival. Gough devised a plan to advance with the main body of his force to seize a spur overlooking the riverbed and presumed Boer bivouac. But it turned out that the 200 Boers were only a detachment of a much larger commando. When Gough's troops sallied forth, they were enveloped by Boers approaching from the opposite direction and scuppered in a brisk encounter action. In less than twenty minutes the British force lost 23 dead; Gough and more than 230 officers and men were made prisoner, along with the guns and a lot of valuable ponies, arms, and equipment. Gough subsequently escaped in an evening thunderstorm.[11]

The disastrous action of Blood River Poort might have crippled Gough's military career, but the strength of his social connections enabled him to withstand the embarrassment. After returning to Britain, Gough, undaunted by misfortune, went on to command the 16th Lancers at the age of only thirty-six; this gave him a five- to ten-year advantage in untarnished seniority over a great many officers in the infantry, artillery, and engineers. Gough's entanglement in Irish politics in 1914 at the time of the Curragh mutiny did not seem to imperil his career either.

Hubert Gough went to war in 1914 in command of a cavalry brigade. Haig's chief staff officer at the start of the war was Gough's younger brother, Brigadier General Johnnie Gough VC. Johnnie, however, was fatally wounded by a sniper in February 1915, not long before he was due to take command of a division forming in Britain. According to Charteris, this was "almost the only time in the war" when Haig "allowed a personal incident to interfere with the normal routine of his work." Lady Haig would write: "Douglas was dreadfully upset over the death of General Gough. He told me of his anxiety when Gough was being operated upon in an attempt to save his life, and how his poor wife arrived just in time to get the news of his death."[12]

Henceforward Hubert Gough seemed to take Johnnie Gough's place in Haig's plans. Shortly after the death of Johnnie, Hubert left the cavalry to take command of an infantry division; he moved up a step to command I Corps in July 1915. The following year, Hubert Gough was appointed by Haig to command what would become the Fifth Army.

The controversial performance of Gough's Fifth Army on the Somme, and in the spring campaign of 1917, did not deter Haig from giving his protégé a prize role in Flanders. Gough was chosen because he was thought to be a "thruster," and the right man to push his troops forward rapidly when the campaign transitioned to a more open style of warfare. Gough's chief staff officer was Major General Neill Malcolm, a man with the reputation of a harsh taskmaster. In mid-June 1917, Gough's Fifth Army took over a section of front in Flanders on the left flank of Plumer's Second Army.

In order to cooperate with Haig's plans, Pétain set aside a force of six French divisions—General François Anthoine's First Army. These French troops were slotted into the line on the northern flank of Gough's Fifth Army. To the north of the French First Army, the Belgian army held positions facing the flooded Yser valley.

On the coast at Nieuport, on the northern flank of the Belgian army, the French had maintained a force since early in the war. Pétain agreed to hand over the Nieuport sector to the British, though only for the duration of the proposed offensive in Flanders. The intention of Haig's General Headquarters (GHQ), provided the main Flanders operation made good progress, was for British troops at Nieuport to attack in conjunction with an amphibious landing on the Belgian coast.

Gough's Fifth Army and Plumer's Second Army would play key roles in the upcoming campaign; it was the responsibility of GHQ to coordinate the actions of those armies. Brigadier General J.H. Davidson, the director of operations at GHQ, arranged a conference to finalize plans. Whether the opening phase of the offensive should attempt to "break in" or "break through" the German front was a matter needing resolution. Davidson was inclined to aim for a limited objective on the opening day given the obvious depth to the German defenses, whereas Gough was hoping for an advance of at least three miles. At the conference on June 28, Haig and Plumer supported an ambitious Fifth Army scheme for an "all-out attack" on the offensive's first day. Haig later wrote that the Fifth Army was to "wear out the enemy but at the same time have an objective. I had given two: first the P.S. [Passchendaele-Staden] Ridge; second, the Coast."[13] The Fifth Army was to

> capture the Passchendaele-Staden ridge and the railway Roulers-Thourout. [The Roulers rail junction lay beyond the ridge, about ten miles east of Ypres.] The object of these operations will be to facilitate a landing between the Yser river and Ostend and, in combination with a force so landed, to gain possession of the Belgian coast. . . . The right of your [the Fifth Army's] attack should move on the high ground through Gheluvelt-Becelaere-Broodseinde and Moorslede. As your advance progresses this high ground will be taken over from you by Second Army, which will then be charged with safeguarding your right flank and rear against attack from the south.
> Your left flank should be directed to the south of Houthoulst forest.
> In combination with your advance it is intended to arrange for an offensive along the coast from Nieuport (by Fourth Army under General Rawlinson).[14]

For Haig the Flanders offensive was an ardently held personal goal; if all went well, the Germans would be cleared from the Belgian coast.

German commanders kept a careful eye on Flanders in the aftermath of the Messines operation. On June 8, Ludendorff appointed Colonel F.K. von Lossberg chief of staff of the Fourth Army. Lossberg's predecessor had appeared flustered during the Messines crisis, and that brought about his relief. General von Kuhl, Rupprecht's chief of staff, wrote in his diary for June 12 that General von Armin of the Fourth Army was "rather weak, insufficiently decisive: old, too; not sharp enough." Kuhl believed that Armin should be replaced as well. Lossberg agreed with that point in principle, but he felt he could work through Armin well enough.[15]

Lossberg, an acknowledged expert in defensive warfare, was the product of a Guards regiment, the War Academy, and the Operations Section of the General Staff. Part of the Operations Section's role was to study developments in warfare. Prior to joining the Fourth Army, Lossberg had helped to plan the construction of the Hindenburg Line. Lieutenant Colonel Albrecht von Thaer, the chief of staff of Group Wytschaete, wrote of Lossberg's appointment: "I consider it as a true blessing . . . that Lossberg is in charge. He is a terrifically capable man, a first-class capacity. Everybody trusts him."[16]

From the German viewpoint, the weeks after the Messines engagement was a period of waiting. The reports of airmen indicated that the British were preparing to attack on a wide front. General von Kuhl recalled:

> From the beginning of July the signs began to multiply that the offensive was approaching. The enemy preparations were being driven ahead quite openly. Railways were built, the number of battery positions increased and the number of troops along the British front increased. But still there was no attack. The situation of Army Group Crown Prince Rupprecht was difficult and required the Commander-in-Chief to make serious choices. Concerned, he had to turn his attention to the other fronts; to the Lens area, to Arras and St Quentin where, at any time, there could be an enemy thrust—even if it was designed simply as a diversion or secondary attack.[17]

A staff conference was held at the end of June to review the state of the defenses facing Ypres. "The local commanders," wrote Kuhl, "were . . . unanimous that the current system of positions was eminently suitable for defence from both an infantry and an artillery point of view and that the deployment of reserves had been well prepared."[18] During June additional reinforcements were transferred from the Sixth Army in the Lens-Lille sector to the Fourth Army in Flanders. The task facing German commanders was made more difficult across the summer months as Ludendorff sent a number of divisions from the western front to reinforce the armies in the east fighting the Russians.

Across this period aerial activity over the salient was stepped up as the German air force contested the Allied supremacy achieved during the battle for Messines Ridge. Four squadrons of German fighters, brightly painted single-seaters, were concentrated into a larger wing—*Jagdgeschwader* 1—under Baron Manfred von Richthofen's leadership. On July 6 a large force of German fighters attacked half a dozen FE2ds of the Royal Flying Corps (RFC). In the engagement the Red Baron, flying a distinctive Albatros D.V, was wounded in the head at long range by a British air gunner. Richthofen lost consciousness and the aircraft spun earthwards. Disaster was only moments away when he revived to regain control of the stricken machine five hundred feet from the ground. The Red Baron would resume his command after a brief spell in the hospital.[19]

The RFC's overriding task in Flanders was to aggressively patrol the skies behind the German front in support of the upcoming ground offensive. The RFC maintained No. 2 and No. 5 Brigades near Ypres. Each brigade had a "corps," "army," and "kite balloon" wing. The corps wing comprised squadrons of RE8 two-seater aircraft for artillery spotting and reconnaissance work. The army wing comprised a mix of aircraft types in squadrons of fighters and light bombers: DH4s, DH5s, FE2ds, Nieuport Scouts, Sopwith Camels, and Sopwith Triplanes. By July 1917 the majority of RFC squadrons had relatively new types of aircraft. Competitive technological innovation was a fundamental aspect of the war in the air.

The design of the Flanders campaign included an amphibious landing on the coast of Belgium. The plan was for one division to land from the sea while four divisions of General Sir Henry Rawlinson's Fourth Army pushed along the coast from Nieuport to relieve the bridgehead. The combined force would then march in the direction of Ostend and link up with the Fifth Army. The 1st Division was the formation set aside for the coastal landing. Rawlinson wrote that the division's Major General Peter Strickland was "full of zeal about the landing which he thinks quite a feasible operation and likely to have far reaching results."[20] (Rawlinson had presided over the loss of sixty thousand casualties on the opening day of the Somme campaign.)

On June 20, British troops took over a three-mile coastal stretch from the French at Nieuport that included a bridgehead across the mouth of the Yser. The town of Nieuport—"a roofless shell of a town"—was on the west side of the Yser. The locks at Nieuport were essential for regulating the controlled flooding of the Yser valley. On a clear day the modest splendors of Ostend could be seen in the distance along the coast, with German destroyers entering and leaving the harbor. The bridgehead on the eastern bank of the Yser was only about eight hundred yards deep. The river mouth behind the bridgehead was tidal and varied between one hundred and two hundred yards in width. The main French defense line had been the river; the bridgehead defenses in the sand dunes on the exposed east bank were not well developed.

The Germans were quick to detect that the Nieuport sector had passed into British hands. A patrol returned with British prisoners to verify that state of affairs. Admiral Ludwig von Schroeder's Group North and *Marine Korps Flandern* was responsible for the defense of the Belgian coast. The possibility of an amphibious landing had long occupied the attention of German staffs.

Group North requested and received the permission of Army General Headquarters to launch a preemptive attack on the British-held bridgehead at the mouth of the Yser River. The assault would be made by a reinforced *Marine Korps* division. Exercises to prepare for the operation were held late in June; eleven large torpedo boats were to aid the assault with gunfire from the seaward flank. The force of German artillery opposite Nieuport was strengthened with seventy-three additional batteries and a generous ammunition supply.[21]

In early July, German artillery fire in the Nieuport sector increased. The German attack was due to jump off at 8 P.M. on July 9; a postponement, however, was ordered, as the weather was too poor for the offshore torpedo boats to join the bombardment. The weather was no better the following day, but it was decided to go ahead without further delay.

The morning of July 10 was overcast, with a strong wind blowing from the northeast. German shelling commenced at dawn and grew intense as the day wore onwards. The sector in the sand dunes of the British bridgehead was held by two battalions of the 1st Division. A sustained bombardment got underway from 11 A.M., with occasional pauses to confuse the defenders. Shells from large-caliber guns exploded with devastating impact in the sandhills of the confined perimeter. The reply of the defenders' artillery was sporadic, as many guns allocated to the Fourth Army had yet to arrive. The floating bridges at the mouth of the Yser behind the bridgehead were demolished by the shelling; telephone lines strung out across the river were broken and wireless communications failed.

At 8 P.M. the Germans attacked on a two-thousand-yard front from Lombartzyde to the sea. Troops stormed forward out of the haze in long waves. British positions in the sand dunes had been thoroughly wrecked by the bombardment. Five waves of attackers were supported by teams carrying flamethrowers. The defenders were soon overrun, and the Germans surged onwards to secure the line of the Yser's eastern bank by 8:45 P.M. Once the fighting had petered out, the twilight was spent digging men out of collapsed dugouts.

Only sixty-eight men from the dunes sector escaped back over the river to safety. Farther to the right, the 32nd Division directly defended the ruins of Nieuport. The left-hand brigade of this division became involved in the fighting and, on the whole, held its ground. On the morning of July 11, General Rawlinson ordered a counterattack, but was persuaded against that imprudent course of action. In two days fighting, the 1st and 32nd Divisions lost three thousand casualties.[22]

Haig and Rawlinson were not deterred by the loss of the bridgehead over the Yser. The Germans were obviously alert and holding the Belgian coast in strength, yet there was no drastic adjustment to schemes seemingly set in stone. The plan to mount an attack from the vicinity of Nieuport in support of a coastal landing remained in place. Rawlinson and Admiral Bacon decided that August 8 was the best date for a landing given the expected conditions of moon and tides.

In the third week of July the 1st Division went into camp in the sand dunes near the hamlet of Le Clipon, seven miles to the west of Dunkirk, for specialized training in preparation for the descent on the Belgian coast. The camp of bell tents and Nissen huts was surrounded by a wire fence. The story was spread that a strict quarantine had been imposed on the 1st Division to combat a virulent epidemic that was sweeping all ranks. It was feared a spy might give away the project to the Germans. This so-called hush camp recalled to mind the encampment at nearby Boulogne established by Napoleon's army early in the nineteenth century for an invasion of Britain that never went ahead.

When the time came to launch the amphibious landing, the 1st Division was to embark at Dunkirk in naval monitors and towed pontoons. The flotilla would sail under the cloak of night and approach the Belgian coast before dawn. Destroyers and motor launches were to screen the operation by laying a smoke screen all the way to the Dutch frontier. The plan was to land on open beach between Westende and Middelkerke. In total, 13,750 officers and men were to be landed, along with detachments of tanks and light artillery. Inland from the proposed landing beaches, the Germans had charge of the sluice gates at the junction of the Ostend and Plaaschendaele canals and could inundate much of the coastal area if necessary.[23] That scenario was blithely overlooked by British planners caught up in the bright and breezy atmosphere emanating from GHQ.

The development and use of new types of weaponized poison gas was a distinctive feature of World War I. On the eve of Haig's Flanders offensive, the Germans made an important technical breakthrough in this field. The sudden introduction of mustard gas gave the Germans a dramatic advantage in the sinister realm of chemical warfare.

Suffocating poison gas clouds had been used by the Germans at Ypres in April 1915, after which the British and French quickly set to work on their own gases and countermeasure equipment. An important innovation was the loading of gas in shells, which were then fired by the guns of the artillery or other mortar-like projectors. The use of gas shells avoided the main shortcoming of gas clouds, namely the wind changing direction at the wrong moment. In 1915 and 1916 chlorine and phosgene gases were the most commonly used types of gas.

Mustard gas shells were first used near Ypres on the night of July 12/13, 1917. There had been some light rain in the first week of July, but the weather then became warm, dry, and relatively windless—ideal conditions for gas shelling. The unexpected mustard gas bombardment inflicted many casualties. Among the units shelled was the 6th Cameron Highlanders. The battalion's C Company was billeted in the cellar of a convent. After gas shells fell to earth nearby, the relatively odorless substance was inhaled freely before the troops put on gas masks. After the all clear was given, the masks were removed. The regimental history of the Camerons recorded:

> Actually, the cellar was reeking with the gas, and the whole company of five officers and about 200 other ranks slept in it until about 4 A.M. At that hour the scene in the cellar was dreadful. Everyone was coughing and vomiting. The floor was littered with men writhing and retching in an agony of suffocation, their eyes streaming with water. As quickly as possible, the helpless soldiers were removed to the open air.

The bulk of the company was evacuated in ambulance wagons: thirty-seven officers and men would perish from gas-related injuries incurred in this incident.[24]

In the aftermath of the July 12/13 mustard gas attack, the BEF's medical services received eighteen hundred gas cases at Casualty Clearing Stations.[25] The sectors hit were mainly held by troops of the 15th and 55th Divisions. Many afflicted soldiers suffered from severe conjunctivitis. A medical officer reported: "There were very few who could keep their eyes open, so much so that when some of the milder cases were evacuated each man had to be led like a blind man by an orderly to the ambulance car."[26] The most seriously injured died after a short interval from an agonizing inflammation of the throat and lungs. For the less severely gassed, after a week the condition of their eyes improved; the conjunctivitis passed after a fortnight, though bronchitis and blisters persisted. Debilitating injuries might linger for years to come.

Mustard gas—or dichlorodiethyl sulfide—was not so much a gas as a chemical weapon that took the form of a brownish liquid. The cases of mustard gas shells were marked with a distinctive yellow cross. When mustard gas was first used, the yellow cross shells contained no high explosive; rather, a small burster charge was detonated to spread a mist of fine droplets in all directions. The slight odor of mustard gas was difficult to detect amid the stench of a polluted battlefield. The thud of a gas shell hitting the ground was like a "dud" dropping to earth. The dreadful menace posed by mustard gas was an additional strain on the morale of troops already overburdened by the pitiless hazards of the front line. There was further mustard gas shelling later in the month—especially at Nieuport and Armentières—and whirlwind concentrations were periodically fired at British artillery positions.

On the whole, the Germans led the way in the field of gas warfare, but another dramatic addition to the stock of weaponry available on the western front was the British invention of motorized fighting vehicles. The rise of the Tank Corps within the BEF was a remarkable development. The origins of the Tank Corps can be traced back to the tumultuous opening twelve months of war; officials at the Admiralty, under the dynamic Churchill, and dissident elements at the War Office and Ministry of Munitions, combined to push forward the embryonic tank concept. A steel vehicle that could drive off-road might be of value on the stalemated western front. The Holt tractor caterpillar system from America, or another similar method, held out realistic possibilities. The name "tank" was coined to conceal the function of these mechanical toys; it was a plausible descriptor for a contraption hidden under a tarpaulin on a railway flatcar. The project inspired those possessed of a classical education to daydream of Hannibal's African war elephants and the Punic wars of Carthage and Rome.[27] The British state was heavily invested in the technology of naval warfare; it was high time some of that industrial muscle flowed into the service responsible for the fighting on dry land.

Despite periods when the project seemed to falter for lack of consistent support, the first tank crawled successfully about a workshop in September 1915. On February 8, 1916, King George V took a dignified ride in a tank to give the new invention the royal stamp of approval. A small experimental building program was authorized of 100—later increased to 150—"Land Ships"; these machines would be armed with either six-pound guns or machine guns. This step was a triumph for the small, disparate band of enthusiasts who had possessed the rare combination of vision and relevant technical knowledge. The tank was a contentious intrusion into the Byzantine world of a regular army.

The first tank company landed in France in August 1916. A modestly successful Somme debut was made by a few dozen Mark I tanks on September 15. Haig reported well of this experiment. The tanks were clearly a useful type of engineering equipment. On September 19 a conference on the future of the tanks was held at the War Office; Lloyd George, who was army minister at that time, was present, along with an array of military and civilian officials. Neither Haig nor Kiggell, GHQ's chief of staff, was present; GHQ was represented by Kiggell's deputy. At this conference the decisive step was taken to order the building of a thousand tanks.[28]

The future of the tank now seemed relatively secure, but that was not the case. General Robertson, the CIGS, believed tanks to be "a somewhat desperate innovation." This view was shared by Kiggell at GHQ, who on October 5, 1916, produced a "Note on the Use of Tanks." Kiggell unhelpfully stated that in "the present stage of their development they [tanks] must be regarded as entirely accessory to the ordinary methods of attack, i.e. to the advance of Infantry in close cooperation with Artillery."[29] Major A.G. Stern, the embattled director of the Tank Supply Department at the Ministry of Munitions, had to fight his corner against the mixed feelings of officers far senior to himself. Stern, a former naval officer, recalled:

> Then, on October 10th, I received an official instruction from the Army Council cancelling the order for 1000 Tanks. . . . This sudden cancellation came as a thunderbolt. I immediately went to see Mr Lloyd George, the Secretary of State for War. He said that he had heard nothing of the instruction. . . . Sir William Robertson, the Chief of the Imperial General Staff, then appeared, and Mr Lloyd George said that he could not understand how this order could be cancelled without his knowledge, since he was President of the Army Council. He asked me to tell Sir William Robertson what I had told him. This I did. Excusing myself owing to pressure of work, I then left the room. The order for the production of 1000 Tanks was reinstated next day.[30]

Lloyd George would confirm this account in his memoirs. To the relief of Stern, the cause of the Tanks had enough support in the government to hold at bay hostile elements within the army.

Stern had ambitions for a supply of tanks far in excess of a thousand. "I was continually pressing for still larger orders for Tanks, and in October I wrote to Mr Montagu [Minister of Munitions] to say that we must now decide whether the order for 1000 Tanks for the following year was sufficient."[31] This proposal came to the attention of Robertson, who wrote to Haig on November 1:

> The man Stern, who has something to do with the production of tanks, has been telling Lloyd George that he can put in hand still another 1000 tanks for you. Lloyd George is rather in favour of giving out this further order, but it seems to me that the 1000 you have already asked for is as far as we should think of going at present having regard to the experimental stage of these things and to the large number of personnel they absorb. I therefore told L.G. that I would like to communicate with you first. I should like to know whether you agree with me that we should at present limit our order to 1000. Besides the men they absorb they also take up a great deal of steel, which is now rather scarce, and in general the tanks should not be ordered unless you think they are really necessary.[32]

Robertson got his way. This Luddite act would have serious repercussions later in the war when the demand for tanks grew compellingly urgent. Robertson's intervention left the Tanks organization needlessly disadvantaged in respect to other manufacturing priorities.

Nevertheless, the thousand tanks scheduled for building caused a rapid expansion of the tank force in France from four companies to four battalions, with another five battalions under formation in Britain. Brigadier General Hugh Elles was appointed to command what would become the Tank Corps. A crucial appointment to the Tank Corps was Colonel J.F.C. Fuller, who joined the Tanks' staff in December 1916 and soon became Elles's chief staff officer. Fuller was thirty-eight years old and Elles thirty-six. A fellow officer described Fuller as

> a little man, with a bald head, and a sharp face and a nose of a Napoleonic cast, his general appearance, stature, and feature earning him the title of Boney. He stood out at once as a totally unconventional soldier, prolific in ideas, fluent in expression, at daggers drawn with received opinion, authority and tradition. In the mess his attacks on the red-tabbed hierarchy were viewed in the spirit of a rat hunt; a spirit he responded to with much vivacity, and no little wit.[33]

Elles, on the other hand, was a more conventional officer; he was a Royal Engineer by trade and looked the part of a popular commander. Elles was also a tolerant man well able to bring out the best in his erratic and imaginative chief of staff.

The Tank Corps' three brigade commanders would be Colonels C.D. Baker-Carr, A. Courage, and J. Hardress-Lloyd. Baker-Carr had campaigned in Sudan and South Africa with the Rifle Brigade; he was a recent commandant of the Machine Gun School. Courage and Hardress-Lloyd were both cavalrymen set free from the traditions of that branch. Courage was missing part of his jaw, the other part having been shot away earlier in the war. Hardress-Lloyd had commanded an infantry battalion for a period of months before joining the Tanks.

Meanwhile, new tank designs were examined. During 1917 units were equipped with the Mark IV vehicle. These tanks had a cumbersome maximum speed of under four miles per hour, and carried an eight-man crew that worked in a noisy, hot, fume-filled cabin not unlike a ship's engine room. The large engine dominated the interior of a tank. It took four men to drive the tank and operate the brakes and gears; the other four members of the crew worked the armament. An observer wrote of a tank: "It moved so slowly across country that if you were watching a tank attack you would often find it difficult to tell if the tanks, a few hundred yards away, were moving or not."[34] Tanks were vulnerable to a direct shell hit, but could usually withstand machine-gun fire. Sprays of machine-gun fire, however, might cause flakes of metal and showers of sparks to fly about inside the cabin of a vehicle.

The manufacture of the tanks that had been ordered proved a slow process. This lack of urgency wasted many months. In the spring offensive of 1917, only a single tank brigade was available; this brigade was broken up into small detachments and scattered across the fighting front. The Tank Corps went on to play an unconvincing cameo role at Messines. On the eve of the Flanders offensive, the Tank Corps was still seeking to prove its worth to the army. The leaders of the Tanks felt they had not been given a fair opportunity to show their wares.

# 4

## The Opening Stanza

The Messines battle was followed by a sustained period of near-perfect early summer weather; the gentle slopes of the Ypres salient were soaked by the rays of the northern sun. The Germans took advantage of this and worked feverishly to build up their defenses in western Flanders. Crown Prince Rupprecht's army group, at the northern end of the western front, comprised three armies and sixty-five divisions.[1] The Fourth Army in Flanders mustered five corps-strength formations. Additional reserves lay behind the Fourth Army's immediate front. The disengaged divisions stood ready in the event of a coastal landing, a possibility German staffs had long included in their planning.

The imminent British offensive was likely to be a sustained effort. To meet that likelihood, the Germans built a series of fortified lines on the meadowland slopes east of Ypres. Batteries of heavy artillery took up sheltered positions behind the ridgelines. Rupprecht's headquarters advised that units were to be rotated through the front line more frequently so as to maintain combat effectiveness. "A quicker sequence of reliefs is . . . essential. It must, however, be understood that this necessity . . . is not imposed by heavy losses, but as the result of over-fatigue and the mixing of units, so that the relieved divisions will recuperate comparatively quickly."[2]

A saturating level of bombardment was likely to precede an offensive. The ground east of Ypres was waterlogged and often unsuitable for deep dugouts. The German defensive layout in Flanders came to depend on the kind of small concrete fort already seen at Messines. In preparation for a prolonged battle, German engineers studded the gently undulating countryside with thick-walled concrete blockhouses echeloned in depth. The ruins of farmhouses and outbuildings were useful foundations for oblong strongpoints and all types of field fortification. A pillbox might have a single chamber to house a machine-gun crew; a larger structure might have several rooms and a variety of functions. Captain D. Sutherland of the 5th Seaforth Highlanders recalled that

> the wily Boche had strengthened the crumbling brick walls of these farms with three or four feet of reinforced concrete, and also roofed them in, so that what, to the observer, seemed a harmless farm ruin was really a well-masked concrete redoubt which could generally withstand a direct hit unless of heavy calibre, while the walls had steel shuttered loopholes from which, when required, the deadly machine gun could be turned on to the advancing waves.[3]

Pillboxes could withstand field artillery shelling and heavier shells up to and including six-inch caliber. Nevertheless, troops inside a battered pillbox were liable to shock and concussion injuries. An officer wrote of his experience inside a captured concrete shelter when it was hit by a German 5.9-inch shell: "We didn't get hit with anything, but we were so badly jolted that little drops of blood came out all through our skin. . . . I was deaf for about a week after it."[4] A concrete structure was not difficult to fabricate. On a dark night troops erected a wooden or steel frame that was hurriedly filled with concrete. German engineers in Flanders built more than two thousand concrete shelters.

Rupprecht believed that a British offensive in Flanders was a certainty. With the precedent of Messines in mind, Rupprecht surmised: "I expect the new British offensive to take place on a small front in order to drive us back by snatches with overwhelming concentration of artillery, leaving dents in our lines which can easily be blown up afterwards." Lossberg, the Fourth Army's new chief of staff, faced the future with confidence and declared: "Never has an army been in a better position before a defensive battle."[5]

From the British front line near the low-lying outskirts of battered Ypres, a succession of rises stretched into the distance. On the skyline sat a village with a conspicuous white church spire: This was the quiet, rural backwater of Passchendaele. General Gough's Fifth Army made their final preparations for the push eastwards from Ypres toward Passchendaele ridge and beyond. On June 20, General Headquarters' (GHQ) Intelligence Section reported that the forthcoming offensive would have "a superiority of two to one in infantry, and in guns and ammunition greater still, and support in the air even more assured."[6] Gough was planning for a rapid and deep advance on the battle's opening day. This approach seemed necessary given Haig's ambition to capture the Belgian coast. To support the upcoming offensive, the light rail network was boldly extended behind the Yser canal. Lieutenant Colonel Cuthbert Headlam would write: "The whole, or at any rate by far the larger part of this work on the railway was of course carried out in full view of the enemy, and must have made him amply aware—if, indeed, he required any such additional enlightenment—that an attack on an imposing scale was being rapidly staged."[7]

The Allied air forces massed between the River Lys and the coast added up to more than 750 aircraft. The Germans countered this by concentrating 600 aircraft in Flanders. Across the month airmen fought in the skies over the gathering armies. On July 26 a big dogfight sprawled above Polygon Wood; almost 100 aircraft were engaged at heights from five thousand to seventeen thousand feet. The opposing sets of predators met again the following evening.

The assault was originally scheduled for July 25, but at a GHQ conference on July 7, Gough asked for a delay of five days. The Fifth Army's artillery program had been set back by the late arrival of heavy batteries from other parts of the British front. Haig agreed to a postponement till the 28th. Then on July 21, General Anthoine wrote to GHQ that the work of his artillery was also behind schedule due to cloudy weather and the Flemish haze. He wanted an extra three days. Haig then decided that July 31 would be the new start date. Rawlinson was informed that the coastal operation would also need to be pushed back given the alterations to the schedule.

The Fifth Army's bombardment of the German front relied on an artillery plan similar to that used at Messines. There was, however, a new set of problems in play. In the Messines battle the Germans had been inside a salient, but now it was the British who were jammed inside a salient on the eastern flank of Ypres. The profusion of British batteries was overlooked from a broad sweep of German-held higher ground. Major C.H. Dudley Ward wrote of this period of preparation:

> Every new trench, every trace of new digging, every new track taped out, every building, every hamlet, every wood was bombarded by the enemy with guns and aeroplanes, which became extremely active at this period. As the concentration of troops increased, all attempts at concealment were abandoned, and camps were pitched in the open. The whole area was a "target," and was well described by a gunner who remarked, "Every time a coconut!" Observation, on the other hand, was denied to us.[8]

**A 9.2-inch howitzer of a siege battery.**

For the week of July 6 to 13, casualties in the Fifth Army were 2,275, but for the period of July 13 to 20, the figure rose to 5,930, and for July 20 to 27, to 7,354. Farther south, losses on the Second Army's front mounted to a similar extent.[9] In the last days of July, the German artillery fell quiet by day to hide their locations and then fired steadily by night.

Meanwhile, designated divisions trained vigorously for the new campaign. For instance, the Welsh Guards carried out a practice attack no less than six times on a spacious training ground laid out with a scale representation of their prospective battle sector, complete with assembly trenches and objectives. Lieutenant Colonel J.L. Jack of the 2nd West Yorkshire wrote:

> The day before yesterday a bloodthirsty fellow, Colonel Campbell, the Army bayonet-fighting expert, gave a lurid lecture to a large, thrilled audience on the most economical use of the bayonet, and to arouse the pugnacity of the men. He pointed out that to plunge the blade right through an opponent is a waste of trouble, and that three inches in the heart are quite sufficient. The cold-blooded science of the business seems to me rather horrid, even if necessary.[10]

After training was concluded for the day, the trials of administration dragged on into the night to summon curses from the stoutest of lionhearted warriors. The demands of bureaucracy generated showers of detailed paper work. Lieutenant Colonel F.E. Whitton wrote of the experience of the 2nd Leinsters:

> The preliminary arrangements for the battle [of July 31] were on a comprehensive scale which had come to distinguish major—and even minor—operations in trench warfare. There are the same reams of instructions from both the general and administrative staffs. There was the same preliminary bombardment for days and the same creeping barrage; and a Zero day and Zero hour as before. There is an addition to the memorandum on burials caused by the inclusion of a ghoulish appendix of thirty-nine "authorized cemeteries," sub-divided into "cemeteries now in use," "cemeteries which can be used in case of emergency," "cemeteries which are shelled and should be used only after an advance has taken place," and "cemeteries not to be used."[11]

The mammoth preparations included a vast network of medical facilities, which were expected to play an essential role in the perilous weeks that lay ahead.

During July the Cavalry Corps transferred northwards from the Arras front to camps behind the Ypres sector. The "cavalry-minded" Field Marshal Haig remarked at a July 5 conference that after the capture of the Passchendaele-Staden ridge "opportunities for the employment of cavalry in masses are likely to offer."[12] The cavalry had played a significant role in the fighting of 1914–1915—mostly in a dismounted capacity—but had only been sporadically engaged since that time. After a brief flurry of involvement in the spring fighting of 1917, the cavalry had undertaken a spell of trench-holding duty. At this time the cavalry comprised slightly less than 3 percent of the BEF's combatant strength.[13]

Despite the checkered record of the cavalry on the western front, Haig was as convinced as ever of the all-round versatility of the mounted arm. The Indian cavalry's Colonel W.A. Watson summed up the commander in chief's attitude as follows: "Haig was a cavalry soldier. . . . He had preached the importance of the role of cavalry all his life. He had five Cavalry Divisions behind his line, and he believed that, given a good opening and a convenient terrain, his mounted warriors could still demonstrate the truth of the theories he had inculcated and crown a victory with a paralysing raid."[14] The Cavalry Corps was placed directly under the benevolent oversight of GHQ and ordered to prepare for employment in the new offensive.

Back in London, Hankey, who was secretary of both the War Cabinet and War Policy Committee, wrote in his diary for July 16:

> In the evening Lloyd George gave a dinner at Ten Downing Street to the War Policy Committee (Curzon, Milner, Smuts and self), Balfour [Foreign Secretary] and Carson [Admiralty] being also guests. . . . The final decision was to allow Haig to begin his offensive, but not to allow it to degenerate into a drawn-out, indecisive battle of the "Somme" type. If this happened it was to be stopped and the plan for an attack on the Italian front would be tried.[15]

The committee's members were not enthused by Haig's plans. Hankey added:

> The decision to allow Haig to undertake the Flanders offensive was taken by Lloyd George and by most of his colleagues with reluctance and misgiving. No one believed that a strategic result could be achieved, and all shrank from the terrible losses which they knew it must involve. But the consensus of naval and military opinion was so overwhelming that the War Cabinet could not take the responsibility of rejecting the advice thrust upon them with so much cogency.[16]

After the War Cabinet took the plunge to approve the Flanders plan, the news was conveyed to GHQ, across the Channel. Robertson advised Haig:

> The fact is that the Prime Minister is still very averse from your offensive and talks as though he is hoping to switch off to Italy within a day or two after you begin. I told him that unless there were great miscalculations on your part, and unless the first stage proved to be more or less a disastrous failure—which I certainly did not expect it would be—I did not think it would be possible to pronounce a verdict on the success of your operations for several weeks. . . . He [Lloyd George] is also very keen on capturing Jerusalem and this of course I also had to fight, and I intend continuing to do so.[17]

Robertson passed on to Haig the War Cabinet's desire to know the first objective of the Flanders offensive. The indomitable field marshal answered that the first objective would be "the ridge extending from Stirling Castle by Passchendaele, Staden and Clercken to near Dixmude." In all likelihood, wrote Haig, several weeks of hard fighting would be needed to clear the whole ridge, but after that, progress should be more rapid.[18]

The soldiers and politicians were not the only people focusing their thoughts on Flanders. Robertson wrote to Kiggell, Haig's chief of staff, on July 27: "Everybody seems to know the zero date, down to the lift-man, and many enquiries had been made. The Belgian Minister asked me on what day we should get to Ostend!"[19]

The opening assault of the Flanders offensive was due for July 31, after a preliminary bombardment lasting two weeks. As was the case in previous offensives, the bombardment gave away the possibility of surprise in an overall sense, but did not necessarily reveal the exact moment or precise frontage of an attack. On the Fifth Army's front were deployed 1,422 field and 752 heavy guns. With the inclusion of the Second Army's guns, the offensive had the support of more than 3,000 guns. These guns would fire 4.3 million rounds in the preliminary bombardment; this compared favorably to the 1.6 million rounds fired by 1,681 guns in the bombardment leading into the Somme campaign.[20] The BEF's stock of guns and shells in July 1917 was much greater than twelve months before. A crucial shortcoming to the British artillery effort, however, was a continued reliance on the light field gun that had performed poorly on the opening day of the Somme campaign. The eighteen-pound gun was the mainstay of the creeping barrage, yet lacked the range needed to penetrate a deep defensive zone.

Gough's Fifth Army was going to make the opening assault with ten divisions on a seven-and-a-half-mile front; Anthoine's French divisions would extend that attack front on the northern flank. The Fifth Army's first day objectives were set at a distance of up to five thousand yards. To the south of Gough's army, the Second Army was to mount a diversionary attack on the German outpost line. All three brigades of the Tank Corps were available for the offensive; 136 tanks would be used in the opening day's attack; these tanks were spread across the front in small detachments. An attack across the entire front of the Fifth Army was deemed necessary to prevent the Germans from concentrating defensive fire against a particular local sector. At zero hour, upwards of one hundred thousand infantry would storm forward across the reclaimed marshland.

The German line on Pilckem Ridge, opposite the left and center of the Fifth Army, was heavily bombarded prior to zero day. Due to the weight of shellfire, wire entanglements were effectively demolished. It was a different matter, however, on the Fifth Army's right flank, where the rising ground of Gheluvelt Plateau and a tangle of damaged woods hid a labyrinth of pillbox strongpoints and patches of barbed wire. On July 30 the Fifth Army's intelligence section noted: "The enemy shelled our battery areas and forward communications on all Corps fronts, from time to time firing heavy concentrations."[21] The German artillery remained active and had not been suppressed.

Brigadier General Charteris, the intelligence chief at GHQ, wrote: "There is no justification for anticipating anything in the nature of a [German] panic on any portion of the battle front."[22] On July 29 and the following day, the weather was ominously indifferent. On July 30, Charteris reported: "My one fear is the weather.

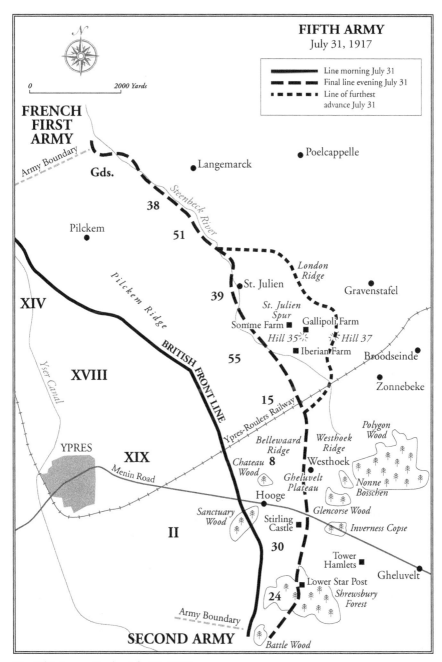

**FIFTH ARMY**
July 31, 1917

Line morning July 31
Final line evening July 31
Line of furthest
advance July 31

*N*

0    2000 Yards

**FRENCH FIRST ARMY**

Army Boundary

Poelcappelle

Langemarck

**Gds.**

*Steenbeck River*

**38**

Pilckem

**51**

*Pilckem Ridge*

London
Ridge

St. Julien

**39**

Gravenstafel

*St. Julien
Spur*

Somme Farm ■  Gallipoli Farm

**XIV**

*Hill 35* ✳  ✳ *Hill 37*

■ Iberian Farm

Broodseinde

**55**

BRITISH FRONT LINE

*Yser Canal*

**XVIII**

Zonnebeke

**15**

*Ypres-Roulers Railway*

*Polygon
Wood*

*Bellewaard
Ridge*

*Westhoek
Ridge*

**YPRES**

**XIX**

*Chateau
Wood*  **8**

Westhoek

*Nonne
Bosschen*

Menin Road

*Gheluvelt
Plateau*

Hooge

*Glencorse Wood*

*Sanctuary
Wood*

Stirling
Castle ■

*Inverness Copse*

**II**

**30**

*Tower
Hamlets* ■

Gheluvelt

*Lower Star Post*

**24**

*Shrewsbury
Forest*

Army Boundary

**SECOND ARMY**

*Battle Wood*

**The Fifth Army attacks, July 31, 1917**

We have had most carefully prepared statistics of previous years—there are records of eighty years to refer to—and I do not think that we can hope for more than a fortnight, or at the best, three weeks of really fine weather."[23] The forecast on the eve of the opening attack was dire. Mist and low, dense cloud would interfere with the plans of the Royal Flying Corps.

Notwithstanding the bleak weather forecast, the British preliminary bombardment was an impressive spectacle. In England, *The Times* military correspondent, Lieutenant Colonel Charles à Court Repington, was in the country for the weekend to play tennis and bridge. "The guns in Flanders were heard very distinctly on the terrace at Glynde. It was a continuous throbbing, the noise of the heaviest guns occasionally rising above the distant din." Closer to events, Haig recorded on July 31: "The heavy firing near here . . . woke me up. The whole ground was shaking with the terrific bombardment."[24]

The rising, frenzied intensity of the gunfire made a vivid impact on the German side of the line. General von Kuhl, Rupprecht's chief of staff, wrote of the thunderous barrage:

> In the early hours of 31st July a hurricane of fire, completely beyond anyone's experience, broke out. The entire earth of Flanders rocked and seemed to be on fire. This was not just drum fire; it was as though Hell itself had slipped its bonds. What were the terrors of Verdun and the Somme compared to this grotesquely huge outpouring of raw power? The violent thunder of battle could be heard in the furthest corner of Belgium. It was as though the enemy was announcing to the world: "Here we come and we are going to prevail!"[25]

British troops in their assembly trenches and shell holes tensely waited for the order to advance. Zero hour was 3:50 A.M. At zero plus six minutes the stationary barrage was to lift and creep forward at a rate of one hundred yards per four minutes; each field gun would fire four shells per minute to churn up the countryside and form a moving curtain of shell bursts. A blue line and black line marked on maps were the Fifth Army's first and second objectives. The green line—or third objective—was the final goal of the day's engagement. A stationary barrage was to be laid down in front of each objective line during the pauses scheduled at those places.

After zero hour, with streaks of dawn visible to the east, the barrage rolled forward in accordance with the prearranged timetable. Projectiles hurtled through the overcast sky toward the German defensive system; exploding shells threw up towers of smoke and debris. At the northern end of the battlefront, two divisions of the French First Army pushed forward twenty-five hundred yards toward Houthulst forest as planned. French troops were supported by 300 heavy guns and 240 field guns, which was the densest concentration of artillery on the Allied front. The two French divisions each lost fewer than one thousand casualties, a modest figure for a major engagement on the western front.

To the south of the French was Lord Cavan's XIV Corps, the left-flank corps of Gough's Fifth Army. After zero hour, the Guards Division, the left-hand formation of XIV Corps, swept across Pilckem Ridge against scattered opposition in a sector littered with ruined farm buildings, but without any villages of significance. The blue and black line objectives were soon taken. By 8 A.M. the third objective had also been captured. The division's reserve brigade came forward to secure the line of Steenbeek stream and establish posts in the shallow valley beyond. A two-and-a-half-mile advance was achieved and more than six hundred prisoners taken. The rest of the day was spent consolidating the captured ground amid sniping and shellfire. There was no counterattack, but rain fell in torrents from late in the afternoon.

Major General C.G. Blackader's 38th Welsh Division attacked on the right flank of the Guards. The blue line was swiftly taken, but pillbox blockhouses studded the ground in front of the black and green lines. Only after hard fighting was the final objective rushed. The 38th Division took seven hundred prisoners, mostly from the 3rd Guards Division and, in particular, the Guards Fusilier Regiment.

To the south of XIV Corps was General Sir Ivor Maxse's XVIII Corps, which had orders to cross the Steenbeek stream, capture St. Julien village, and push onwards in an easterly direction. The 51st Highland Division was the left-hand division of Maxse's corps. To herald the division's assault across a featureless waste, more than two hundred drums of burning oil were hurled from mortars into the German front. This medieval method of war was visually impressive in the dull half-light of dawn. The well-organized barrage screened the advance with a moving wall of fire; troops were able to keep within forty yards of the shell bursts. A Scotsman reported: "Mon, the barrage was that fine ye could have lighted your pipe at it."[26] A number of stoutly manned blockhouses barred the approach to Steenbeek stream, but these local bastions were overwhelmed one by one. After posts were established across the Steenbeek, to the surprise of the infantry, a mounted squadron of King Edward's Horse cantered forward to reconnoiter the ground ahead, picking a way through the shell holes and debris littering the landscape. The 51st Division's history recorded: "On reaching a line 150 yards from the stream, they suddenly came under heavy machine gun fire, and immediately suffered such losses in men and horses that any attempt at a further advance was out of the question."[27] Two tanks later reached the final objective and spent a couple of profitable hours patrolling the vicinity.

On the right flank of the Highlanders was the 39th Division. The opening assault went well, and St. Julien had fallen by 8 A.M.; the cellars and dugouts of the ruined village were cleared of their garrison at bayonet point. The division's reserve formation, the 118th Brigade, then passed into the lead to secure the final objective in a downpour of rain. A maximum advance of four thousand yards was achieved. Patrols fanned out ahead across empty fields seeking contact with any troops nearby.

The German formations under attack had wasted no time appealing for reinforcement. The local German corps headquarters, Group Ypres, set reserve divisions in motion to counterattack the flanks of the break-in. The 50th Reserve Division marched up with horse-drawn field batteries clattering alongside the trudging infantry. From about 2 P.M. German troops worked forward against the posts of the British 118th Brigade, which fell back rearwards as it was too scattered to withstand serious counterattack.

Farther south, on the right flank of Maxse's corps, Lieutenant General H.E. Watts's XIX Corps attacked with two divisions. The 55th (West Lancashire) Division, the corps' left-hand division, used two brigades and one tank company to seize the first two objectives. After that, at about 10 A.M., the division's reserve brigade—the 164th—passed into the lead and, assisted by a second tank company, pushed out across an open slope toward the third objective—the green line. It was a dull, misty morning. The British barrage thinned as the infantry passed beyond the effective range of the field guns. The final objective was reached about noon.

The troops of the 164th Brigade now found themselves in a precarious position, well out in front of the rest of the 55th Division; the brigade had become a sparse advance guard more in keeping with open-field warfare than the trench warfare typical of the western front. Before long German troops were seen gathering in the distance. These soldiers—many of whom hailed from eastern Prussia—belonged to the 221st Division, another reserve formation sent forward by the headquarters of Group Ypres. From midafternoon a determined counterattack was made across the crest of Zonnebeke spur. British troops were short of ammunition and without effective artillery support; the 164th Brigade was pushed back to the second objective—the black line—with losses of seventy officers and thirteen hundred other ranks.

In XIX Corps' right-hand sector, Scottish soldiers of the 15th Division faced blasted, brown slopes devoid of cover. The Ypres-Roulers railway was the southern boundary to the division's sector. The 44th and 46th Brigades attacked with the support of a company of tanks and swiftly captured the blue and black lines; midmorning the 45th Brigade, the divisional reserve, advanced through the other brigades to attack the final objective behind a thinning barrage.

The 45th Brigade set out confidently to burst open the German front. On the left of the brigade line, the 6th Cameron Highlanders battled valiantly to secure their designated objective, but the brigade's right-hand 6th/7th Royal Scots Fusiliers was halted by enfilade machine-gun fire spitting from the tangle of woods beyond their southern flank. Further calamity struck when the left flank of the Camerons was turned by the German counterattack in the neighboring divisional sector. By late afternoon, despite the arrival of reinforcements, the remnants of the 45th Brigade had fallen back to the second objective; rain, which had been a drizzle, fell heavily from 4 P.M.

At the southern end of the Fifth Army's front, II Corps had the most difficult task of the day, namely the scaling of Gheluvelt Plateau. This shallow feature gave German observers commanding views across the flat salient. The road from Ypres to Menin ran up the long slope toward Gheluvelt village, with patches of woodland on either side. These shell-shattered woods lay in front of both the first and second objectives. An ambitious third objective line lay six hundred yards west of Gheluvelt village.

The Germans facing II Corps belonged to four regiments, including all three regiments of the 6th Bavarian Reserve Division. The Bavarians had suffered heavily during the preliminary bombardment. The German outpost line in the Hooge sector was thinly held for fear of mines, a fear that was particularly acute given the recent Messines operation; the defenders were relying on the timely support of the mass of artillery positioned behind the crest lines of Gheluvelt Plateau. The Germans had worked hard to strengthen the fortifications of this vital sector, which was the linchpin to the southern shoulder of the front hemming the Ypres salient.

The commander of II Corps was Lieutenant General Sir Claud Jacob, an Indian Army officer who had come to the western front with an Indian formation earlier in the war. II Corps had been reinforced, as its task was understood to be of particular difficulty. Three divisions of the corps were to attack side by side on a three-mile front.

In the left-hand sector of II Corps, the 8th Division attacked with two brigades. These formations—each accompanied by a section of tanks—were to carry the blue and black lines, after which the division's reserve brigade and a company of tanks was to pass into the lead and take the green line beyond the Hannebeek stream (a tributary of the Steenbeek). Second Lieutenant Hubert Essame of the 2nd Northamptons recalled that at zero hour

> the blast was so deafening that we jammed our fingers in our ears; the ground shook. We could see the flashes of the barrage in the murk ahead. . . . The swish of the eighteen-pounder shells tempted us to crouch down. In fact, although we could not see them, the two leading companies advancing on compass bearings were clinging to the barrage and moving forward each time it jumped a further twenty-five yards.[28]

Bellewaarde Lake and Chateau Wood were the main obstacles to be traversed in this locality; the wood was littered with broken trees and wire.

The first two objectives were taken successfully, after which the 8th Division's reserve brigade—the 25th Brigade—passed into the lead and crossed over Westhoek Ridge "in fine style." The Hannebeek stream lay midway between the second and third objectives, and ran across particularly exposed ground. Before long the brigade came under sustained cross fire from the right flank. Parties of British troops reached the far side of the Hannebeek, but after confused fighting, most finished up back at the second objective. Westhoek hamlet remained in German hands. The 8th Division took six hundred prisoners on July 31, but suffered more than three thousand casualties.[29]

In the central sector of II Corps' front, the 30th Division had the stern task of making a direct attack onto Gheluvelt Plateau. The 30th Division was mostly composed of battalions from Liverpool and Manchester. At zero hour the barrage crashed out a tornado of flame and sound. On the front of the left-hand 90th Brigade, one battalion badly lost direction in the misty gloom, and the rest of the brigade

Disabled tanks in the mud near the Ypres-Menin road.

struggled to keep pace with the creeping barrage; unsubdued pillbox-sited machine guns cut down the khaki figures hastily bobbing and clambering through the scrub. On the division's right flank, the 21st Brigade was heavily and accurately shelled on the start line; the troops fell behind the creeping barrage from the outset, and a day of confusion followed. A brigade of the 18th Division was sent forward from corps reserve to reinforce the 30th Division. These troops were stopped by machine-gun fire in front of Glencorse Wood. Battalions from the 30th Division's reserve brigade were also committed to action and suffered heavy losses. British counterbattery fire in this sector failed to subdue the defenders' artillery.

The ruined woods in the German forward system facing II Corps proved impassable for tanks, which were forced to slowly navigate a passage between patches of tree stumps. A large pillbox equipped with an anti-tank gun commanded the road coming up the slope from Hooge. A series of tanks were suddenly knocked out by shellfire or halted by mechanical breakdown. Tanks bogged in the mud were liable to be hit and further damaged by the shelling that was steadily falling across the sector. Derelict tanks became a feature of the morbid local scenery for a long time to come.

The 24th Division was II Corps' right-flank division; it attacked with all three brigades side by side. The right-hand brigade—the 17th—advanced far enough to maintain touch with the Second Army farther south, but in the center the 73rd Brigade was held up by pillbox machine-gun emplacements in Shrewsbury Forest. The 24th Division's left-hand brigade was also blasted to a halt near the first objective.

It quickly became evident that the attack had failed on the front of II Corps. At 1:30 P.M. a subdued Jacob reported this to the Fifth Army's headquarters. In the Menin road sector, the British thrust had gained only one thousand yards on average. In consequence, the reserve divisions of the local German corps, Group Wytschaete, remained out of action to await further developments. That it proved unnecessary for the Germans to commit any reserves in such a vital sector is a measure of the comprehensive nature of II Corps' defeat at a cost of almost ten thousand casualties.

On the southern flank of II Corps, troops of Plumer's Second Army advanced a short distance against the German outpost line to cover the flank of the Fifth Army and provide a modest diversion. Five divisions played a role in the Second Army's operations and thereby stretched the active front southwards all the way to the River Lys.

Haig and Kiggell visited Gough in the afternoon and received a reasonably clear account of the situation.

> As regards future operations, I [Haig] told Gough to continue to carry out the original plan; to consolidate ground gained, and to improve his position as he may deem necessary, for facilitating the next advance; the next advance will be made as soon as possible, but only after adequate bombardment and after dominating the hostile Artillery.[30]

Haig was doggedly determined to press onwards despite the mixed results of the fighting on July 31.

In the darkness of a black and rain-lashed night, thousands of casualties were evacuated rearwards. The mutilated corpses of the slain dotted the muddy fields. The fighting cost British forces 31,850 casualties from the night of July 30/31 until the night of August 1/2, when units of the assault divisions were finally able to take a roll call. The Fifth Army's losses were 27,001 and the Second Army's 4,849; to these figures can be added the French First Army's losses of almost 2,000. German prisoners amounted to over 6,000, but only twenty-five guns were taken. The heaviest divisional losses in the Fifth Army were incurred by the 8th Division, 3,076; 15th Division, 3,443; 30th Division, 3,365; 39th Division, 3,871; and 55th Division, 3,447.[31]

Despite the lavish preliminary bombardment, the German guns dug in behind the low crests on the eastern flank of Ypres had not been suppressed prior to the assault; the German Fourth Army fired twenty-seven trainloads of ammunition on the opening day of the offensive. Reserve divisions had moved into action where needed to parry the Fifth Army's thrust. Still, German losses were severe, and there was no doubting that further heavy fighting lay ahead. In Group Ypres, the 3rd Guards Division lost 3,000 casualties; 38th Division, 4,000; 50th Reserve Division, 1,500; and 221st Division, 2,150. Lieutenant Colonel von Thaer wrote of the opening day's fighting: "Whole divisions burnt out to slag within a few hours."[32]

Crown Prince Rupprecht's summation of the day's engagement was decidedly levelheaded. The Prince's diary entry for July 31 included:

> This morning the attack, supported by a great many tanks, opened on a front of eighteen kilometres between Steenstraat and the Lys on the Flanders front. I find that I can face this offensive in a calm frame of mind, because never before have we had deployed along a front under attack such strong reserve forces, which have been so well trained in their role. By evening it became clear that the enemy break in to the front . . . has been halted. In view of the massive enemy forces, in conjunction with the fact that experience shows that the initial blow is always the most dangerous, we can take particular comfort from the fact that the battle reserves of Group Wytschaete were barely utilised.[33]

German commanders responded to the British advance in the salient's northern shoulder by rebuilding a defensive front behind Steenbeek stream. The failure of II Corps to make progress up the slope of Gheluvelt Plateau meant that batteries of German heavy artillery behind the ridgelines could remain in many of their original positions. Indeed, the tragic extent of II Corps' bloody repulse was similar to the fate of some formations on the opening day of the Somme offensive the previous year.

The heavy rain that began on the evening of July 31 fell steadily—with intermissions—for four days and nights. A large part of Flanders was reclaimed marshland and vulnerable to flooding. Shell holes brimmed with water; the Steenbeek overflowed; small streams that might have been dry in another year sprang to life to help create a stagnant Stygian mire. A drenched British soldier wryly commented: "Luckily the rain fell with equal persistence on the enemy's side of the line." In practice, however, the water seeped down from the higher ground of the German-held front into the entrenchments of the British.[34]

Divisions of the Fifth Army near the line of the Steenbeek were now in plain view of German observation posts on the main ridge. British field gunners found themselves stranded out on open ground and were regularly battered by shellfire. Camouflage screens were erected in an often vain bid to hide the muzzle flash of a gun when it fired. Captain H. Gordon's 112th Field Brigade was on the front of II Corps. Midafternoon on August 2 the unit's D Battery was hit by an intense box barrage fired by German artillery of 5.9-inch and heavier caliber. D Battery's gun positions became shrouded by shell smoke; jagged splinters hummed spitefully through the air.

> Then suddenly the shelling stopped, and we went out there with stretchers. The place was a shambles, indescribable, a ploughed field of reeking craters with guns pointing in all directions. A few men crawled from their little shelters, bleeding and staggering about, and were led away. A doctor came running from the dressing-station with an orderly, and worked on the badly wounded. Men from adjoining batteries helped with the stretchers. When everyone alive had been taken away, we collected what fragments remained of the dead in blankets and sandbags—a ghastly harvest—and laid them in a dugout to await burial. After a count, the reckoning is that of the forty-six of us at the gun-position, only eleven are left, some badly shaken but game to carry on. Twelve were killed, thirteen wounded, ten shell-shocked.[35]

All of the battery's guns were damaged by the shelling, and one gun was wrecked by a direct hit.

Remarkably, about this time a bar to the Victoria Cross was earned by the medical officer of the 1/10th Liverpool Scottish, Captain Noel Chavasse. (A "bar" to the original award denotes a second award of that decoration.) Chavasse had been wounded on the opening day of the offensive; he was injured again the following day and mortally wounded on the morning of August 2. Major A.M. McGilchrist wrote of Chervasse:

> His bravery was not of the reckless or flamboyant type but the far finer bravery that sprang from his determination that nothing should stand in the way of whatever he considered his duty. More than once he was offered less dangerous work at a Casualty Clearing Station or a Field Hospital to which his long service as a regimental medical officer entitled him, but he preferred to remain with the men he knew and admired.[36]

Chavasse, the son of a bishop of Liverpool, was the only man to win the Victoria Cross and bar in World War I; his first VC had been awarded during the Somme campaign.

On August 1, Field Marshal Haig spoke with a French liaison officer attached to his headquarters.

I saw Colonel de Bellaigue soon after 9 A.M. before he left for French G.H.Q. to see General Petain. I asked him to urge the latter to start his attack as soon as possible in order to prevent reinforcements from being brought against the British by the enemy from the French part of the front. . . . In my opinion, now is the critical moment of the war, and the French must attack as strongly as possible and as soon as possible, so as to co-operate with the British in dealing the enemy as strong a blow as possible.[37]

The effectiveness of further attacks, however, was under threat from the deteriorating weather. At GHQ, Charteris wrote in dismay: "Every brook is swollen and the ground is a quagmire."

August of 1917 would prove to be the wettest August in Flanders for thirty years. In both 1915 and 1916, the month of August had been dry, but in August 1917 rainfall was 127 millimeters. Dull and windless weather meant that the flat, sodden ground was slow to dry; indeed, there were only three rainless days for the whole month.[38] The mournful landscape gleamed with floodwater on days of rainstorm. Winston Churchill wrote of this period:

Soon the rain descended, and the vast crater fields became a sea of choking fetid mud in which men, animals and tanks floundered and perished hopelessly. The few tracks which alone could be preserved across this morass were swept with ceaseless shell fire, through which endless columns of transport marched with fortitude all night long. . . . Ceaselessly the Menin gate of Ypres disgorged its streams of manhood. Fast as the cannons fired, the ammunition behind them flowed in faster.[39]

On August 2, Colonel Fuller, the Tank Corps' chief staff officer, visited the strife-torn front. "The ground was shattered beyond recognition, and in many places slush was two feet deep. On my return, my general, Hugh Elles, asked me: 'How are things going?,' to which I replied, 'Look at me!'—I was plastered with mud from head to foot."[40] How tanks could be used profitably in such a morass was difficult to discern.

Field Marshal Haig submitted to London on August 4 a "Report on the Battle of 31st July, 1917, and Its Results." Haig was not oblivious to the state of the weather during the opening phase of the Flanders offensive; the rain had also fallen on the roof of GHQ. Haig reported: "The space from which the attack had to be launched was very confined and overlooked by the enemy, who had all the advantages of position. . . . The artillery struggle was very severe, owing to the unavoidable exposure of our gun positions." The assault had been launched "over ground which is reported to be now as bad as that with which we had to deal last winter on the Somme and Ancre." Nonetheless, Haig remained confident the campaign was unfolding in a satisfactory fashion.

We have . . . captured over 6000 prisoners and the number of enemy dead on the battle-field is reported to be very large. We know from prisoners that the enemy suffered very heavily in our bombardment and I have no doubt that the total of his casualties exceeds ours very considerably and not improbably by as much as 100 per cent.[41]

The number of prisoners taken, however, did not suggest especially heavy German losses; a more sharply focused analyst might have drawn a different conclusion.

On the other side of the battlefront, Rupprecht wrote on August 5:

> The rainfall of the past few days was so heavy that not only is the crater field occupied by the Fourth Army full of water, so are the trenches in places. Most of the soldiers are taking cover behind their flooded trenches or in shell holes. In the latter case, they are attempting to protect themselves from the wet conditions by huddling under planks or sheets of corrugated iron, daubed with mud. These conditions go a long way to explaining the speed with which the troops are being exhausted and having to be replaced. On average, each division has suffered casualties of 1500 to 2000.

In contradiction to this, Charteris would claim on August 18 that "German losses appear to have been about 3000 per division engaged."[42] Charteris's estimates of German casualties were arrived at by speculative methods that are as lost to translation as the hieroglyphics of a vanished civilization.

Ten days after the start of the offensive, Colonel Baker-Carr of the Tank Corps was asked to give a lecture on tanks to a staff training course at GHQ. After the lecture he went to lunch with Lieutenant Colonel N. Tandy of the Operations Branch. Tandy was an old friend, and he inquired as to Baker-Carr's views on the operations currently underway, to which the heretical reply given was that conditions in the salient were impossible for effective fighting. Baker-Carr's grim news was not well received; after lunch he was given a message from an orderly that General Davidson, GHQ's director of operations, desired an interview. Baker-Carr recalled:

> On entering Davidson's office, I found him seated at his table, his head in his hands.
> "Sit down," he said. "I want to talk to you." I sat down and waited. "I am very upset by what you said at lunch, Baker," he began. "If it had been some junior officer, it wouldn't have mattered so much, but a man of your knowledge and experience has no right to speak like you did."
> "You asked me how things really were and I told you frankly."
> "But what you say is impossible."
> "It isn't. Nobody has any idea of the conditions up there."
> "But they can't be as bad as you make out."
> "Have you been there yourself?"
> "No."
> "Has anybody . . . been there?"
> "No."
> "Well then, if you don't believe me, it would be as well to send someone up to find out. I'm sorry I've upset you, but you asked me what I thought and I told you."
> I took my leave and returned to my headquarters with an uneasy feeling in the back of my mind that I, personally, was responsible for the rain and the mud.[43]

Davidson was reputed to be one of the more enlightened members of Haig's entourage, yet he seems to have been no wiser than the others.

In London, Robertson continued to loyally support Haig's plans despite the dawdling start to the campaign. The Allied armies in Flanders were like stationary sailing boats, treading the wind upon dancing waves, far from a distant shoreline. Haig's commitment to the offensive, however, was unshaken. He wrote to Robertson on August 13:

> In this army we are convinced we can beat the enemy provided units are kept up to strength in men and material. Our opinion is based on actual facts viz: the poor state of German troops, high standard of efficiency of our own, power of our artillery to dominate enemy's guns, etc, etc. An occasional glance at our daily intelligence summaries would convince even the most sceptical of the truth of what I write. Moreover I have been in the field now for three years and know what I am writing about. . . . In my opinion the war can only be won here in Flanders. Even if the Austrians were driven from Trieste, the Germans will still hold the Belgian Coast and Antwerp!

Haig demanded that all available reinforcements be sent to his army without delay. The field marshal added: "Personally I feel we have every reason to be optimistic; and if the war were to end tomorrow, Great Britain would find herself not merely the Greatest Power in Europe, but in the world."[44]

# 5

---

# Stormy Weather

General Gough's Fifth Army headquarters was responsible for the specific planning of the next phase of the offensive. As a first step, the battered and soaked divisions that had taken part in the initial attack were relieved by fresh divisions. The 16th (Irish) Division was among the incoming formations. The historian of the 7th Leinsters wrote of the squalid scene that greeted the new arrivals on the night of August 5/6: "The march out along the Potijze road was a nightmare; the men, shelled as they went along, stumbled at every step through weariness and sore feet. The road was strewn with the debris of battle—destroyed transport wagons, dead horses every few yards, and worse still the numerous dead and dying men, who had collected along that shambles, the one artery of communication to a whole divisional front since the morning of 31st July."[1] Another fatigued Irish officer said of the conditions: "No decent language can express this weather. The country is a marsh: horses up to the breast in mud. Wagons can only move on proper metalled roads. My clothes are a mass of mud; one pair of puttees has simply rotted on my legs." A chaplain stumbled upon a soldier badly burnt by gas, "his hands and face a mass of blue phosphorous flame, smoking horribly in the darkness."[2]

On August 7, General Kiggell, General Headquarters' (GHQ) chief of staff, advised Gough that "Boche killing is the only way to win." This would have to be managed, Kiggell conceded, without incurring more than a "moderate" level of loss. Britain's manpower pool was not without limit. Lord Derby, secretary of state for war, informed Lloyd George on August 9 that "the amount of reinforcements that we send out in this month will barely cover the ordinary wastage."[3] Haig was dimly aware of the impending manpower crisis, but he refused to let that derail or truncate his ambitions.

II Corps, the right wing of Gough's army, had failed to make significant progress on July 31. On August 10 a local operation was undertaken by two divisions of II

Corps to advance the line a short distance. On the left flank, troops of the 25th Division successfully laid claim to some barren acres; the 2nd Royal Irish Rifles overran the leveled ruins of Westhoek hamlet. On the right flank, however, the 18th Division's attack broke down badly; the splintered tree stumps and stoutly defended pillboxes of Glencorse Wood and Inverness Copse again defied capture.

The task of the Fifth Army was made especially difficult as German gunners enjoyed excellent observation from the main ridge overlooking the British front line. Lieutenant Michalk of the 9th Reserve Field Artillery Regiment took part in the engagement of August 10. Michalk wrote of the lively scene visible from his observation post.

> To our front was Ypres laid out like a landscape model and it provided views over all operational activity almost from Langemarck to Wytschaete. That is probably the reason why the division maintained observation there. There was a reasonable selection of telephones available to enable direct communication to be maintained, but inevitably the links were cut whenever the need for them was greatest. In addition radio equipment was available (transmitter only). This worked superbly and, as a result, all important reports were successfully sent to the rear.

Michalk's team was kept busy, as "the British were always up to something, the duty was extremely interesting; I felt like a little general."[4]

Meanwhile, the big German generals reassessed the situation. Crown Prince Rupprecht was visited by the volatile General Ludendorff on August 14. Ludendorff was preoccupied by the situation in Russia. He asked Rupprecht to manage affairs in Flanders "from within our own resources." On August 15:

> I [Rupprecht] spoke to His Majesty the Kaiser who, having toured the fortifications at Heligoland, had travelled to Zedelghem, near Bruges. . . . [He was] in the best of spirits. I did not miss the opportunity to inform him that our losses in Flanders were very significant. At the same time I had the occasion to meet the Chief of the Admiralty Staff, Admiral von Holtzendorff, who assured me that he was of the opinion that our U-boat campaign would defeat England by October. The gentlemen of the navy are dangerous optimists![5]

August of 1917 was the seventh month of the unrestricted submarine campaign; the toll of Allied merchant shipping taken by U-boats remained high.

The restless front line in the salient was close to the Steenbeek and Hannebeek streams, the banks of which were broken by shelling. Nearby abandoned tanks were like "monsters of a prehistoric age." Even on days of relative calm there was abundant tragedy. On the evening of August 14 the 7th Somerset Light Infantry was preparing to play its part in the next phase of the campaign. Captain H.A. Foley commanded B Company. The platoons of the company were strung out in a line, twenty to thirty yards apart from each other. According to Foley:

> I had just left Liddon's platoon and was half-way between it and Goode's in front, when my ear caught the familiar, menacing whine of a heavy shell, which instantly shrieked

to its highest crescendo. There was a shattering roar behind me, the earth trembled and shook under foot; and for a moment I felt stunned as though struck heavily by an immense weight. Then I turned and looked back to see where the shell had fallen. No description of mine can do justification to that scene. Where a few seconds before the thirty men of Liddon's platoon had stood yarning and chaffing together, one's eyes fell now on a pitiable and nauseating scene of carnage and agony. Of many men no trace at all remained; of others torn fragments of their bodies lay scattered about the ground. Desperately wounded men were crying out in their pain; while over the scene the smoke of the shell, and the acrid smell of it slowly floated away.

The projectile that exploded in the middle of the doomed platoon killed seven men and wounded another twenty.[6]

About this time, on a stretch of the British Expeditionary Force's (BEF) front to the south of Flanders, a major operation got underway at Lens. Two Canadian divisions of General Sir Henry Horne's First Army mounted an attack on August 15. In particular the Canadians set out to capture Hill 70 to the immediate north of Lens. On the day of the assault, a swift advance captured most of the designated objective. The Canadians took prisoner 24 German officers and 1,345 other ranks. Hill 70 gave panoramic views eastwards over the Douai plain. It had been a model operation, yet German retaliatory shellfire was heavy; over a ten-day period the losses of the Canadian Corps amounted to 9,198.[7]

In the salient, the Fifth Army had completed preparations for the next attack, which would take place on August 16. At 4:45 A.M., at the northern end of the attack front, French troops advanced methodically to attain their objectives. Cavan's XIV Corps was adjacent to the French sector. In the left-hand sector of XIV Corps, the 29th Division's frontage was a mile wide and the final objective almost a mile distant. Two brigades were launched into this barren square mile of muddy shell holes. Two soldiers of the division's 1st King's Own Scottish Borderers won the Victoria Cross that day, one of whom was Company Sergeant Major John Skinner. Skinner played a decisive part in a brisk fight near Montmirail farm. Captain A.H. Currie, Skinner's company commander, wrote:

> We met with strong opposition during our attack, three blockhouses especially giving a great deal of trouble, and holding us up on the left flank. . . . The three blockhouses were spitting out a terrific fire, and we were obliged to take cover and move gradually forward by squads in quick rushes. At this period Company Sergeant-Major Skinner and I crawled as near to the blockhouses as possible, and succeeded in disabling two of their guns by rifle fire. C.S.M. Skinner, after we had got within seventy yards of the blockhouses, crawled forward on his own initiative, while I covered his advance with my rifle. After ten minutes he succeeded in reaching that on the extreme left, and going round the back of it bombed the team of gunners with Mills bombs and compelled the garrison to surrender. The second blockhouse he put out of action by inserting bombs in the loopholes where the guns were mounted. By this time I had passed orders for the company to advance, and we succeeded in reaching the third blockhouse, though only

after suffering heavy casualties. C.S.M. Skinner's haul was six machine guns, about sixty prisoners, and a few trench mortars. This feat he performed practically single-handed.[8]

By this stage of the war Skinner had already been awarded the Distinguished Conduct Medal and bar and Military Medal, in addition to being wounded several times. He had joined the army aged sixteen and was a veteran of the Boer War, India, Mons, Gallipoli, and the Somme campaign. Skinner would be killed early in 1918 after turning down a home posting. The 29th Division's commander, Major General Sir Beauvoir de Lisle, declared that Skinner was "the bravest man I met in a war won by brave men."[9]

In the right-hand sector of XIV Corps, the 20th Division advanced beyond the Steenbeek stream. An unusually large blockhouse known as Au Bon Gîte was the main German redoubt in the locality. When the assault got underway, British troops, who had spent the night on the start line under intermittent shellfire, went in behind an effective creeping barrage that "fell like a curtain." The unmistakable landmark of Au Bon Gîte was seized by a party of the 11th Rifle Brigade. "Once across the Steenbeek," noted a regimental history, "all movement was very difficult, the ground was nothing but a swampy field of craters right up to the final objective. In order to gain the first objective the only possible formation for the troops was a series of small columns, which wound their way, in single file, between the deep pools of mud and water."[10] The flattened village of Langemarck was overrun; mopping-up parties cleared Germans from the ruins and cellars below ground. After Langemarck was secured, the advance swept onwards to the final objective despite enfilade fire from the right flank.

To the south of Cavan's corps was Maxse's XVIII Corps. Infantry of the 11th and 48th Divisions crossed their start line as planned, but struggled to make any worthwhile progress. The open ground to the east of St. Julien was swept by unsuppressed machine-gun fire.

Farther south, XIX Corps attacked with the 16th (Irish) and 36th (Ulster) Divisions. Ahead lay a slope dotted with fortified farmhouses and pillboxes. The troops were tired and some battalions below half strength. When the assault commenced, the waves of attackers were so thin that "the operation looked more like a raid than a major operation."[11] The heavy going and patches of wire caused the troops to lose touch with their protective creeping barrage. Some gains were made, but at about 9 A.M. German infantry counterattacked over the crest of the Zonnebeke–St. Julien spur behind a hastily improvised barrage. Troops of XIX Corps were driven back to their start line in what proved to be a day of unmitigated disaster.

At the southern end of the attack front, II Corps came to grief again attempting to penetrate the splintered woods and undergrowth leading to Gheluvelt Plateau. In the left-hand sector of II Corps, the 8th Division pushed across the marshy Hannebeek stream. Some units made good initial progress, but raking cross fire thinned the ranks and the survivors fell back toward the start line.

In the right-hand sector of II Corps was the 56th Division. In the days before the attack, the division had moved into the line opposite Glencorse Wood and Inverness

Copse. When the 56th Division attacked, the lightly held German front line was overrun, but the second system of defense proved to be a formidable series of well garrisoned concrete forts and belts of wire. The leading waves were annihilated in a sea of mud; a gallant detachment vanished into Polygon Wood and is thought to have perished there.

The action of August 16 was a catastrophe on most parts of the front for British forces; small groups of tanks sent into action lay stranded in the mud. The desolate, pockmarked plain had become "one vast bog of pestilential slime and filth"; only sixteen hundred German prisoners were taken in exchange for fifteen thousand British casualties.[12] Crown Prince Rupprecht noted in his diary: "British prisoners are saying—and this has never been heard before—that they wished that they had shot their own officers who were leading them into the slaughterhouse. They have had enough of this butchery!" Six days later he wrote: "Of the British prisoners who have been brought in during the past few days, the N.C.Os and men are complaining about the defective leadership of their officers; the officers about the failings of the staff officers. Nobody believes that there is any chance of defeating Germany without American assistance."[13]

Field Marshal Haig's next report to London on August 21 summarized the Fifth Army's most recent attack. "In many places [on August 16] the men could only get forward by assisting each other out of the breast-high mud and water in the shell holes. . . . The gain of ground was therefore comparatively small, but the more important objective of forcing the enemy to expose himself, and causing him heavy loss, was fully attained, and at a modest cost to our troops." Poor weather, added Haig, continued to render "counter-battery work and flying so difficult that our artillery superiority was to a great extent neutralised." The report stated that "the enemy's casualties in Flanders and at Lens [where the Canadians had attacked] since the 31st July inclusive are estimated at approximately 100,000 men." It was claimed that almost all of Germany's 1918 class of recruits had been drawn into service by the extent of their losses and that boys of the 1919 class were starting to appear.[14]

Haig continued to radiate a confident determination: He believed that severe fighting was likely for some weeks to come, but if the weather in autumn proved mild, the prospects for clearing the Belgian coast by winter remained bright. He wrote: "In these circumstances the right course to pursue, in my opinion, is undoubtedly by continuing to press the enemy in Flanders without intermission and to the full extent of our power and, if complete success is not gained before winter sets in, to renew the attack at the earliest possible moment next year." The clearance of the Belgian coast was expected to have "decisive" strategical and political effects. "It will render the enemy's positions in northern France so precarious and so dangerous that it is almost a certainty that he will retire from them."

Meanwhile, on August 17, Gough delivered a broadside to his corps commanders; he told them at a conference that a further attack would be made on the 25th to clear up the objectives not taken on the 16th. Prior to that operation, General Maxse of XVIII Corps supervised an important episode in the development of mechanized

warfare. Maxse willingly backed a plan for a tank-led local attack on a set of fortified farmhouses north of St. Julien that had defied capture in earlier engagements.
Colonel Baker-Carr recalled:

> The plan which I laid before him [Maxse] was briefly as follows: the line of pill-boxes,
> which had held up the infantry, in spite of the most determined and gallant attacks,
> and which were apparently impervious to shell-fire, lay on the far side of the Steenbeek,
> with the St Julien-Poelcappelle road running parallel behind them. If it were possible to
> move tanks along this road, they would be able to attack the pill-boxes from the rear,
> and the solid foundations of the road itself would allow the tanks to approach their
> objectives from a comparatively short distance. I explained that surprise was the essence
> of the attack and that all I required from the artillery was a smoke-barrage to blind the
> enemy's guns. I also pointed out that the only work demanded of the infantry would be
> to take over the pill-boxes, when captured, and that, if the tanks failed in their mission,
> the small number of infantry to be employed would be able to return to their trenches
> without becoming engaged. After some consideration, he [Maxse] agreed to the attempt
> being made.[15]

On the night of August 17/18, Major R.H. Broome's twelve tanks of G Battalion
lumbered into the forward zone and spent the following day in the ruins of St. Julien
decked out with camouflage netting.

In the twilight of dawn on August 19, the tanks moved up the cobbled road
running from St. Julien to Poelcappelle covered by a barrage of smoke shells and
high explosives. A pair of tanks was to attack each identified German strongpoint.
The novel operation was a great success. The defenders were taken by surprise and
surrendered after a brief flurry of gunfire. The small force of infantry advancing in
support of the tanks rounded up the prisoners. The tank crews lost two killed and
twelve wounded; the infantry lost fifteen wounded.[16]

Maxse reported to the puzzled staff at GHQ that the line had been abruptly
advanced five hundred yards on a thousand-yard front for the loss of twenty-nine
casualties. He recorded wryly that the following day "for the first time in the war
Kiggell [Haig's chief of staff] telephoned to ask 'how it was done?', as if one could
explain common sense down a telephone to someone who has never commanded
even a humble company!"[17] The brief engagement was a much-needed triumph for
the tanks, but in general, the Flanders offensive was "a ghastly failure" for the Tank
Corps: The future of the branch was needlessly placed in jeopardy. According to
Baker-Carr: "The tanks failed through being employed in hopelessly unsuitable conditions. If the first submarine had been tested on Salisbury Plain, the results would
not have been encouraging."[18]

On August 22 the Fifth Army conducted a round of local operations to tidy up the
start line for the next big push. XIV Corps, at the northern end of the line, did not
take part, but to the immediate south, XVIII Corps attacked without success. On the
front of XIX Corps, the 15th and 61st Divisions incurred heavy losses at the hands of

the same clusters of pillboxes and strongpoints that had stopped previous attempts to cross the featureless slopes. The two divisions lost three thousand casualties, in return for which the 61st Division advanced six hundred yards and the 15th Division made almost no progress. Farther south, on the front of II Corps, a brigade of the 14th Division attacked Inverness Copse. Some ground was taken, and confused fighting lasted into the following day. On the morning of August 24 a German counterattack reclaimed the corpse-strewn copse.

The plight of the 15th Division by this stage of the campaign provides a cautionary tale. After participation in the attack of July 31, the division had been sent to camps behind the front. The division's history recounted that

> under these adverse conditions reorganisation took place. The recent fighting had reduced battalions to skeleton strength, and to replace casualty drafts amounting to fifty-one officers and 3696 other ranks arrived. Unfortunately they were only partially trained, and there was neither time nor facilities for doing much in that way. The most that could be done was to send parties of 250 from each brigade in turn to the Fifth Army Musketry School, but beyond this nothing was possible. This lack of training was very noticeable, especially during a practice attack.[19]

The 15th Division returned to the line in a poor state of efficiency.

Captain A.F.P. Christison of the 15th Division's 6th Cameron Highlanders took part in the August fighting. He recalled that the attack of August 22 was in many places

> a complete fiasco. Some men flatly refused to go over the top, saying they were not going to fight under officers they'd never seen, and in strange units; that their commanders were deceiving them and that no breakthrough was possible. Some men lay down and refused to move, others arranged with their pals to shoot each other in cushy parts in the first shell hole. The troops had been bluffed and knew it.[20]

The melancholy survivors were paraded in front of Gough, who had been made aware of the extent of the troops' displeasure; Gough gamely asked for expressions of grievance. According to Christison: "He [Gough] said he wanted frank speaking. He got it from the troops all right. It was then he was called a 'bloody butcher.' Afterwards he saw senior regimental officers, and a certain C.O. said 'Why don't you and your staff go and have a look at the ground over which you have been ordering these attacks?' The Army Commander promised to do so."[21] It seems reasonable to assume this was not the only example of dissent in the salient around this time. By the second half of August, morale problems in the Fifth Army had become painfully apparent; the seeds of despair had steadily ripened to full misery; courts-martial and firing squads were resorted to as a bandage solution.

Rain fell with renewed intensity on August 23. Gough canceled the plan for another all-out Fifth Army attack, but a number of failed local attacks were made across the front on August 27. After this latest set of disappointments, the spirits of the Fifth Army sank lower than ever.

Captain E.D. Vaughan of the 1/8th Warwicks took part in the attack of August 27. By evening Vaughan's mud-caked men, faces drawn with exhaustion and eyes cavernous, had taken possession of a German pillbox on the far side of a waterlogged slough. A badly wounded German officer painfully told Vaughan that a shell from a tank had shot through the pillbox doorway and caused numerous casualties within. A soaking, terror-filled night lay ahead for Vaughan's party. "From the darkness on all sides came the groans and wails of wounded men; faint, long, sobbing moans of agony, and despairing shrieks. It was too horribly obvious that dozens of men with serious wounds must have crawled for safety into new shell-holes, and now the water was rising about them and, powerless to move, they were slowly drowning."[22] Pouring rain and gales the following day caused the survivors further hardship. Lieutenant C.E. Carrington of the 1/5th Warwicks remembered:

> August 1917 at St Julien was the worst month the battalion passed through. It had been a series of impossible tasks ordered under hopeless conditions. It had seen continual attacks by weak bodies against strong bodies of troops in concrete fortresses. Communication was always precarious and altogether broke down at critical moments. Runners and signallers had suffered fearsome losses. The tanks on which all operations depended had hardly ever been able to reach the positions of assembly, much less their objectives on the other side. They could never struggle through a sea of mud.[23]

The medical services labored day and night to evacuate and treat the wounded survivors of the fighting.

Not surprisingly, the replacement of the BEF's recent heavy losses was straining resources. The tempo of combat imposed by GHQ took little account of the challenges of constantly rebuilding units shattered in the furnace of combat. Early in the war the army had more recruits than could be equipped, but by 1917 that land of plenty was a distant memory: The supply of recruits was in definite decline. British Army enlistments for the years of World War I were: 1914, 1,186,357; 1915, 1,280,362; 1916, 1,190,075; 1917, 820,646; and 1918, 493,462. When the total for 1917 is broken down into monthly figures, the pattern to the manpower shortage is particularly apparent. The number of recruits fell away significantly in the second half of 1917: January, 85,669; February, 118,841; March, 119,539; April, 87,032; May, 88,494; June, 81,714; July, 60,367; August, 49,359; September, 37,342; October, 36,543; November, 30,823; and December, 24,923.[24] Robertson wrote to Haig on August 17:

> I suggest it is . . . necessary that your Staff should immediately take steps to scrape up all the men they can in France, and if not trained already put them under training so that they may later strengthen your divisions as much as possible. You will remember that I spoke to you about the possibility of combing out some men and collecting those probably and quite naturally hidden away in various places. I attach some figures which are rather instructive. I also spoke to Kiggell, and he rather seemed to regard it as a matter to be attended to after the fight. But I feel very strongly that it ought to be done at

once, and I think you will agree. I repeat that all that we can do at home will be done. In this connection I would like to disabuse you of the idea which seems to prevail in France, namely, that a lot of men who might be sent out are kept at home. I have just been through the classification of the men in Home Service divisions and brigades, and I find there are less than 8,000 "A.1" men.[25]

The comb-out of the BEF's rear services managed to find another 41,000 men for the infantry, but the day of reckoning for Britain's manpower system was drawing ever nearer.

Gough's army was now stranded—cast adrift—in the morass of the salient. At GHQ, far behind the front, Field Marshal Haig was unimpressed by the Fifth Army's sluggish performance. It was time for a change in management. General Plumer and the Second Army's headquarters would lead the next phase of the offensive. On August 25, Plumer was ordered to take over the front of II Corps facing Gheluvelt Plateau. Plumer shrewdly asked for the luxury of three weeks in which to prepare for the next big push.

On August 28, Haig took a high-ranking American official to lunch. At first this was a pleasing encounter, but Henry Morgenthau went on to rashly ask if the British and French could hold out on the western front until the Americans arrived. This was like waving a red rag in front of an angry bull. Haig noted in his diary:

> I replied that every day we seemed to get more of the upper hand over the enemy, and that if the French could only support us in a moderate way there was a chance of ending the war this Autumn. My chief fear was that Germany might offer in October or November terms of peace which the Allied Governments might accept, though not giving all that we ought to receive.[26]

Haig continued to draw strength from the reports of GHQ's intelligence branch. According to this source, forty-one German divisions had been engaged on the Ypres front since July 31, as compared with twenty-three British divisions. This was taken as evidence that the Germans were suffering severely and their resources running low. By the start of September, 10,697 German prisoners and 38 guns had been captured in the offensive. The Fifth Army's casualties from July 31 to August 28 amounted to 68,010.[27]

Given the unsuitability of the terrain, a large part of the Tank Corps was withdrawn from the salient. Haig wrote on August 27 that

> the choice of front on which to make an attack must be made with regard to many considerations, tactical, strategical, political and so forth. In making this choice the tank, at any rate in its present state of development, can only be regarded as a minor factor. It is still in its infancy as regards design. It is of uncertain reliability. Its true powers are more or less a matter of conjecture.[28]

The poor weather and flooded terrain at Ypres dashed any chance the tanks might have had to shine. A pulverized swamp was no place for a tank. For the sake of its institutional future, the leaders of the Tank Corps had already started looking about for profitable work elsewhere on the western front, the more distant from Flanders the better.

The Fifth Army launched a local attack on September 6, when the 42nd Division—veterans of Gallipoli and the defense of the Suez Canal—assaulted a line of fortified farms on St. Julien spur; predictably, little progress was made given the enfilade machine-gun fire the Germans could bring to bear at that place. The Lancashire Fusilier battalions of the 125th Brigade were heavily plundered in the engagement. According to Sir Arthur Conan Doyle, these troops "showed an intrepidity in this attack which in any former war would have been historical, but in this prolonged exhibition of human and military virtue does but take its place among many as good."[29] On September 10 the 61st Division attacked Hill 35 without success. Not much was achieved by these ill-considered, piecemeal ventures, apart from the production of another list of names qualified for inclusion in the newspaper columns set aside for military death notices. The maps of Flanders produced in *The Times* and other British newspapers grew steadily smaller in scale as the stalled campaign dragged onwards.

The infantry was bearing the brunt of the campaign; however, GHQ's artillery adviser, Major General N.F. Birch, was alarmed by the mounting losses of the Royal Artillery. British batteries on low-lying ground were badly exposed to the fire of German artillery sheltering behind the crest lines of Passchendaele ridge and Gheluvelt Plateau. On September 2, Major Francis Graham, commanding officer of C/71st Battery, wrote:

> The weather has again intervened on the side of the enemy. The water-level is never very far removed from the surface in these latitudes, and if we have another couple of days' rain we shall be able to hand over to the Navy, put on our bathing drawers, and swim home. . . . The ground is like one large sponge—the poor old tubes sink farther and farther in. Soon there will be nothing left above ground but the cowls of our dial-sights, and we shall be loading through a periscope.[30]

Field artillery brigades remained in the line for long periods to incur an unprecedented level of loss. For example, A/156th Battery was a six-gun battery, but lost twenty-six guns "disabled" to shellfire; D/162nd Battery lost nineteen guns "put out of action by the enemy."[31] Each artillery unit had its own tale of woe. According to Lieutenant Colonel A.F. Brooke:

> Some batteries remained in the line for three months without a relief, under the most trying conditions, living in a sea of mud, subjected to continual concentrations of fire, and only withdrawn after suffering over 100 per cent of casualties to personnel and equipment. Under such conditions a large proportion of batteries could only be expected to develop a very small percentage of their normal power.[32]

Parts were cannibalized off damaged guns to keep the rest of a unit in action.

Given the Ypres salient's vulnerability to German artillery fire, the casualties of arms other than the infantry were high in the autumn of 1917. Royal Artillery losses during the Somme offensive had been 3.13 percent of total casualties, 4.58 percent at Arras, 4.03 percent at Messines, but were 12.15 percent in the cauldron of Ypres. Royal Army Service Corps and Royal Army Medical Corps losses were also higher than usual.[33] Brooke summed up the Flanders campaign as follows: "We had sacrificed surprise, the enemy was at liberty to employ methods calculated to ensure a lower rate of casualties, whilst the possibility of realising any strategical stroke was denied to us."[34] The German heavy artillery pounded the British front at will from relatively secure positions. German artillery observers surveyed the low-lying salient like gunnery officers in conning towers of a fleet of dreadnought-class battleships.

The Royal Artillery in Flanders had a large number of guns and a plentiful ammunition supply. Part of that largesse, however, was thrown away given the geography of the salient, and crucially, another part of that benefit failed to yield fruit due to the mediocre quality of the equipment in use. The Royal Artillery continued to rely on a stock of light field guns that lacked range and weight of metal. The principal British field gun, the eighteen-pounder, featured a tubular pole trail and spade that prevented sufficient elevation of the barrel. The barrel could only be elevated to a maximum of sixteen degrees because of the pole trail. It is inexplicable that this fault was not corrected speedily once the western front became stalemated. The gun's limited elevation restricted its range to a maximum of sixty-five hundred yards in theory, and less than that in practice.[35] (An updated version of the eighteen-pounder with a maximum range of over nine thousand yards was put in service after the war had ended.)

The BEF had gone to war in 1914 with few heavy guns and this initial handicap had serious consequences after the western front became a deadlocked form of siege warfare. The mainstay of the BEF's heavy artillery was the six-inch howitzer, which was mass-produced in large numbers. The six-inch howitzer was mounted on carriages that allowed a full elevation and an effective range, though it was a cumbersome weapon and difficult to push forward across muddy ground. The main problem with the stock of British heavy artillery in 1917 was that the quantity of guns available was insufficient to prosecute successfully the crude and ambitious style of offensive warfare to which Haig's GHQ was addicted.

To make the task of British gunners more difficult, across the middle period of the war the German artillery underwent an incremental modernization program to improve already efficient ordnance. The standard 77-millimeter field gun was rested on a howitzer carriage to raise the barrel's elevation and increase the range of the weapon. The principal German gunnery advantage, however, lay with ordnance of a heavy caliber. The 10.5- and 15-centimeter howitzers were compact, lightweight weapons and available in quantity from the outbreak of war. A 5.9-inch howitzer could fire a ninety-pound shell up to ten thousand yards. These guns were formidable when firing at long range in a defensive role.[36] The BEF was poorly placed to fight a campaign of attrition given the quality of German equipment.

Away from Flanders, Pétain's long-awaited attack in the Verdun sector finally got underway on August 20, when troops of General Adolphe Guillaumat's Second Army attacked on an eleven-mile front astride the Meuse River. Three thousand guns fired three million rounds in a nine-day preliminary bombardment. During this brief campaign, an advance of three thousand to four thousand yards was achieved; more than ten thousand German prisoners were taken (which was a better haul than at Messines). The west bank heights of Le Mort Homme and Hill 304 fell into French hands. The ability of German commanders to reinforce the front at Verdun had been constrained by the severity of the fighting underway in Flanders. Pétain would close down this battle by mid-September to avoid unnecessary losses.[37]

Elsewhere in August, on the Italian front the Eleventh Battle of the Isonzo commenced on the 17th. Two days before, the persistent Hankey had advised Lloyd George after a War Cabinet meeting "that he ought to investigate" the stalled Flanders offensive. Hankey recorded: "The P.M. is obviously puzzled, as his predecessor was, how far the Government is justified in interfering with a military operation."[38] At the outset of the latest Isonzo campaign, promising reports were received from the British ambassador in Rome. This caused Lloyd George to again prod Robertson about sending forces to Italy. Hankey wrote on August 26:

> About 11 P.M. he [Lloyd George] suddenly decided to write a letter to Robertson about Cadorna's [supposed] victory, urging that Robertson should go to Italy to investigate, with a view to a big transfer of guns and the exploitation of a great victory. He also wrote to Bonar Law on the same tack, pointing out the great opportunity opened up, particularly in view of the failure of the Flanders offensive, consequent on the continuous rain.[39]

Robertson, however, informed the War Cabinet that it was bad strategy to change plans midstream, and that it was impractical to send timely aid to Cadorna as "it was impossible to transfer large numbers of guns to that Front in less than a month."[40]

On August 29, Robertson met with the prime minister for further discussions. Robertson warned that Italy could only be assisted at the expense of abandoning the Flanders offensive. The War Office's director of military operations, Major General F.B. Maurice, told Hankey "that Haig, and still more Kiggell, his Chief of Staff, still believed we could clear the Flanders coast—his reason being that there only remained five German divisions that had not passed through the mill, and that the reserves with which they were filled up were the poorest material." Hankey, however, had little faith in Maurice's speculations. He wrote: "A private letter I received about this time from a valued former member of my staff, now a brigadier-general and a corps Chief of Staff, described the German shelling as heavier than he had ever encountered, and the difficulties of dealing with the myriad of machine guns in wooded country as very great. And he, though a sober judge, has always been an optimist."[41]

On the other side of the lines, the German High Command had also been considering its strategic options. Ludendorff decided to send a number of divisions to Italy, as the situation on the main fronts seemed well in hand. In Russia, German troops were closing on the Baltic port of Riga. On September 1, General Oskar von Hutier's Eighth Army attacked the Russians near the Drina River. The assault was preceded by a sharp five-hour bombardment, fired without prior registration; the overpowered defense quickly collapsed. The Central Powers' war against Russia was on the verge of a successful conclusion. This would have dramatic repercussions for the western front.

# 6

# Menin Road

At the start of September, Field Marshal Haig remained confident that the Flanders offensive was on track. At long last the weather had improved to smother the salient in a blaze of sunshine. Over the next few weeks, the topsoil's crust hardened and the ground slowly turned from a morass into an empty desert-like waste of shimmering gray dust. The proverbial fog of war showed signs of dispersal.

Given the promising weather, the Germans were puzzled that a lull had fallen at Ypres. Crown Prince Rupprecht speculated on September 12: "The Flanders fight seems actually to have ended." Perhaps the British were planning to renew their attack on another part of the western front? The Prince's chief of staff, General von Kuhl, was also perplexed. Lieutenant Colonel von Thaer, Wytschaete Group's chief of staff, joked that the army in Flanders was in danger of getting bored.[1]

The slow progress made at Ypres in August had conspired against the launching of the Fourth Army's operation against the Belgian coast. On August 22, Haig had held a conference at General Headquarters (GHQ) to reexamine the coastal scheme. General Rawlinson gushingly informed his chief: "The chances of success of this attack are distinctly favourable if the wind and weather are good. It would come as a surprise. Preparations are now nearly complete, the troops are very confident of success, and the means at our disposal are adequate to deal with any opposition that may be encountered. . . . I have every confidence that, with reasonable luck, it will succeed."[2] Admiral Bacon told the conference that an advance along the coast to Middelkerke would bring Zeebrugge, Ostend, and Bruges within the range of land-based naval guns. Haig proposed the first week of October as the revised target date for the amphibious landing; the tides and moon would be favorable at that time. The Royal Navy remained firm in its support for the operation. On September 3, Sir Eric Geddes, the recently appointed First Lord of the Admiralty, reminded the War Cabinet of "the importance to the navy of these two harbours [Ostend and Zeebrugge] being rendered useless to the Germans."[3] Pontoons for the coastal landing had been gathered in the Thames estuary.

The troops of the 1st Division awaiting the launch of the amphibious operation remained in camp at Le Clipon, where the steady gunfire at Ypres was audible when the wind blew in the right direction. An obstacle course featuring a replica seawall had been built for training purposes; Haig visited Le Clipon to inspect the preparations. For the soldiers held in camp, the routine among the sandhills and stretches of gleaming beach was monotonous. Apart from tactical training, sport was played and drill practiced to pass the time.

Secrecy at Le Clipon was a priority, but it was decided to permit leave from the camp back across the Channel to Britain. General Strickland saw all officers, warrant officers, and NCOs of the 1st Brigade and announced that their secret operation had been put on hold for an indefinite period. Leave would be made available, and he "trusted to their honour that they would not say anything about where they were or what was going to happen."[4] Lieutenant Colonel A.W. Pagan of the 1st Gloucesters commented: "No one objects to getting leave, but although every man going on leave was personally warned by his commanding officer never to mention where he was or why he was there, yet human nature being what it is, how could he refrain from telling his mother all about it?"[5] Even if mothers were not a security risk, there were plenty of others with whom soldiers on leave could gossip.

Security for the coastal operation had become a matter of some delicacy near the summit of government. Hankey, the War Cabinet's secretary, noted in his diary for August 15:

> In the evening I dined with Lady Cunard. . . . Lady [Eloise] Ancaster, who sat next to me knew far too much about our military affairs, and even knew the secret that at a certain stage in the operations a landing behind the enemy's lines is contemplated—a fact that I have never written down even in the Cabinet Minutes, or in this locked and carefully guarded diary! The real danger of secrets leaking out lies in these high society gatherings. The English ladies learn from their husbands and menfolk—especially young men home from the front who are most indiscreet; they tell their American lady friends, who repeat them to other Americans, who in turn repeat them in neutral countries, where they leak to the enemy. This is how we get much of our information of the enemy, and without doubt it leaks out in the same way.[6]

The navy was less likely than the army to be the source of a leak, as crews involved in the proposed operation remained confined to their ships.

The lull in the salient provided breathing space for decision-makers in London to embark on a renewed bout of politics. Hankey recorded on September 3 that the government had received a telegram from the French proposing the transfer to Italy of one hundred heavy guns from the French First Army in Flanders. General Foch, France's chief of the General Staff, traveled to London to secure Robertson's approval. On September 4, wrote Hankey, "in the afternoon there was a War Cabinet first, followed by a meeting with Foch. The net result was that a conference was arranged between Haig, Robertson, Foch and Petain with a view to scraping up 100 heavy guns for Italy on the basis that Haig should release fifty from the French First Army . . . [and] on the condition that fifty more were got together from other parts of the French front."[7] As it turned out, the latest round of the Isonzo fighting would peter out by mid-September. Nonetheless, given the thousands of Allied guns in France and Flanders, it was remarkable that so much heat was generated by a proposal to transfer a small number to another theater of war. The extremism of Haig's and Robertson's opposition to sending aid to Italy is noteworthy. The British High Command was vehemently determined to concentrate resources in Flanders to drive forward the campaign underway.

Lloyd George's civilian colleagues were reluctant to interfere with the plans of the military. Milner commented to Bonar Law on September 10 that if Haig's forces were weakened to support Italy, the field marshal "would feel that he had not been treated quite fairly and that is a fatal frame of mind for a commander actually engaged in difficult operations."[8] On September 14, Haig noted in his diary that Sir Edward Carson—a former First Lord of the Admiralty and now a member of the War Cabinet—had arrived at GHQ to stay for two nights: "He [Carson] is convinced that the military experts must be given full power, not only to advise, but to carry out their plans. He is all opposed to the meddling now practised by the Prime Minister and other politicians."[9]

On September 5, Lloyd George left London for a sojourn in north Wales; according to Hankey, the prime minister was suffering from "neuralgia and overstrain." Hankey traveled to join Lloyd George on the 14th of the month, where he

> found the Prime Minister had been quite seriously ill with a very high temperature. He was still looking out of sorts and only convalescent. . . . I found him rather despondent at the failure of the year's campaigning, and disgusted at the narrowness of the General Staff, and the inability of his colleagues to see eye to eye with him and their fear of overruling the General Staff.[10]

The war situation was indeed bleak. The possible collapse of Russia had summoned forth the realistic specter of the Central Powers emerging from the war stronger than ever. As a hedge against that contingency, it would be helpful if Britain could wrestle from the Ottoman Turks as much of the Middle East as possible. The newly appointed commander of British forces in the Middle East was General Sir Edmund Allenby. Lloyd George informed Allenby before he departed for Cairo that his objective was "Jerusalem before Christmas." The War Cabinet instructed Allenby "to strike the Turk as hard as possible during the coming autumn and winter" and to "follow up your success as the situation allows."[11] The prime minister had high hopes for success in Palestine; Milner shared this ambition. Allenby estimated that seven infantry and three mounted divisions would be needed to sustain an offensive in Palestine.

Lloyd George had managed, finally, to secure Winston Churchill's return to the ministry after a relatively brief spell in the political wilderness. The prime minister announced the news to the press without consulting Bonar Law, the leader of the Conservatives. On September 12, Churchill, now minister of munitions, sailed across the Channel with his private secretary, Edward Marsh. The two men drove from Calais to Cassel; from there they headed eastwards to visit the fabled trenches, a setting with which the pugnacious Churchill was well familiar given his service in the field of the previous year. Marsh wrote:

> We had been told that Messines was "unhealthy" so we didn't go there, and preferred Wytschaete which was reported "quiet." But no sooner did we begin to walk along the Ridge than six-inch shells began to burst around us. . . . Columns of smoke rose from the ground, sixty to 100 yards from us, and bits of shell fell quite close—five or six yards off—while all the time our own shells were whistling and shrieking over our heads. . . . Winston lent me his excellent field-glasses, through which I could see the emplacement of the Boche lines, about 3000 yards off in the plain—and several towns, including the utter ruin of Ypres. Winston soon began to think it was silly to stay there, and we began picking our way back through the stumps and round the shell-holes of Wytschaete wood. The shells were still falling, all in a radius of about 150 yards—we saw one burst about thirty yards in front of a huge lorry packed with troops which went on as if nothing had happened.[12]

That evening Churchill dined with Field Marshal Haig. Churchill spent several more days in France, during which he joined Haig for an inspection of the New Zealand Division; he also made a flying visit to Paris before returning to Dover.

A steady stream of politicians visited France to sniff the atmosphere of the western front. Haig noted on September 16 that Asquith, the former prime minister, and Asquith's son-in-law had arrived at GHQ for dinner. "Afterwards I had a long talk with Mr Asquith. He said the present Government is very shaky. A. is all in favour of a vigorous offensive on the Western front." Asquith left after breakfast on the 18th: "He [Asquith] said that he had been immensely struck with all he had seen and particularly the grand spirit of confidence existing from top to bottom in the Army. I felt that the old gentleman was head and shoulders above any other politician who had visited my Head Quarters in brains and all-round knowledge."[13] Not long after Asquith's visit, the secretary of state for war, Lord Derby, appeared at GHQ. Derby, a former regular soldier himself, was a resolute supporter of the army's top brass. Haig wrote:

> In the course of a talk after dinner, Derby said that Lloyd George is scheming to get rid of him and Robertson from the War Office. Lloyd George and Painleve (now P.M. in Paris) are desirous of forming an Allied General Staff in Paris to direct operations. This I feel certain cannot possibly work. It seems to be an effort of the French to retain control of operations, notwithstanding that their Army has ceased to be the main factor in the military problem.[14]

The formation of a unified Allied High Command was an obvious counter to the unity of command Germany enjoyed on the western front. Haig and Robertson, however, resented any possible intrusion upon their professional prerogative.

Bonar Law, the Conservative Party's leader, had his own doubts about the situation in Flanders. He wrote to the prime minister on September 18:

> The only thing at all new is that, in speaking to Robertson yesterday, I said to him that I had lost absolutely all hope of anything coming of Haig's offensive and though he did not say so in so many words, I understood that he took the same view. I do not know when the next attack is supposed to take place but I believe it may happen at any time. It is evident, therefore, that the time must soon come when we will have to decide whether or not this offensive is to be allowed to go on.[15]

Earlier in the month Foch had bluntly told Bonar Law that the Flanders offensive would achieve nothing. Robertson later wrote that Haig and his principal subordinates were "better judges of the enemy's condition than I could claim to be, [and] I was not prepared to carry my doubts to the extent of opposing him, and of thereby obstructing the application of that little extra pressure upon the enemy which experience has so often shown may convert an inconclusive battle into a decisive victory."[16]

Robertson wrote to Haig on September 24 that the "whole Cabinet are very anxious to give the Turk as hard a knock as possible this winter; they have heard he is very sick of the whole business." Robertson added: "Of course we shall not win the war merely by holding on to Baghdad. . . . On the whole the situation in the East requires careful watching during the winter months." In a different key, Robertson gleefully told Haig of the ending of Cadorna's offensive. "I do not anticipate that we shall ever hear any more about your sending divisions to the Italian Front."[17] Robertson's anticipation of the likely course of events in Italy was destined to be well wide of the mark.

The fine weather of September caused the war in the air above the salient to rise in intensity. Fighter aces received a great deal of publicity, fame, and popular adulation, but much of the influence wielded by newly invented air power lay with the two-seater reconnaissance biplanes that acted as spotters for the artillery, particularly heavy-caliber batteries endeavoring to fire effectively at long range.

The unglamorous RE8 was the backbone of the Royal Flying Corps' reconnaissance force. One morning early in September, Baron von Richthofen took to the air in a bright red Fokker triplane; he came upon a stray, hovering RE8, soon to be his sixtieth victory. Richthofen recalled: "I approached and fired twenty shots from a distance of fifty yards, whereupon the Englishman fell to the ground and crashed near Zonnebeke. It is most probable that the English pilot mistook me for an English triplane because the observer was standing upright in his plane and watched me approach without making use of his gun."[18] Persistent offensive patrolling over German lines imposed an immense strain on British aircrews. The Royal Flying Corps lost 434 officers in fifty days of aerial combat from July 31 to September 19.[19]

The French air force was also involved over western Flanders. On September 11, Captain Georges Guynemer—a widely lauded national hero—was shot down and killed near Poelcappelle. Guynemer and another French pilot had dived on a German two-seater, only for a flight of escorting German fighters to pounce and send the bullet-riddled Spads plummeting earthwards.

Preparations for the next phase of the Flanders offensive were nearing completion. Plumer's Second Army had a key role to play in the fighting that lay ahead. The Fifth Army would also attack to cover the Second Army's northern flank. Plumer and Harington, the Second Army's chief of staff, were said to know every puddle and contour in the salient. The two men had a clear-cut view as to how a battle should be fought on the deadlocked western front. A "bite and hold" operation seemed the only feasible approach in the circumstances. In light of the experience at Messines, it was believed that an advance of fifteen hundred yards was the limit to what could be hacked from a well-developed defensive system in a single day. This was only a third of the distance Gough had been aiming for on July 31.

The Second Army's immediate objective was to finally clear the devastated woodland area beside the Menin road that had blocked the progress of II Corps for the past month. Beyond that, Plumer's intention was to capture Passchendaele ridge in a four-step-operation, with six days between steps. A meticulously prepared bombardment for the first attack began on September 13 and was scheduled to last seven days. Swans paddled quietly in the moat alongside the ramparts of Ypres as heavy batteries fired at the water's edge. Harington regularly briefed press correspondents to keep them informed of the Second Army's plans. The clamor of the bombardment made it clear to German commanders that something big was in the pipeline.

The attack was due to get underway on September 20 on a front of ten thousand yards; the preceding day was fine and sunny, but drizzle began at nightfall. Rain was falling steadily at 11 P.M., though it ceased not long after midnight. The troops marching up for the assault splashed through a dark night, lit up by the flashes of gunfire and explosions. Field Marshal Haig recalled: "About midnight General Gough proposed that operations should be postponed on account of rain, but General Plumer between 1 and 2 A.M., after consulting his Corps and Divisional Commanders, decided to adhere to plan."[20] During the night whirling rockets soared upwards from the German forward zone. By the light of brilliant showers of flares, anxious watchers on either side of the line scanned the shadowy fields of no-man's-land.

A tinge of light on the eastern horizon marked the breaking of a new day. Finally, at 5:40 A.M. the barrage crashed out in the growing light. The drum fire of field guns saturated the air with shells; batteries of heavy howitzers hurled projectiles high above the tumult to arc down to earth again with a shattering detonation. Through the swelling pall of smoke and fumes rising from the German front, the red flickers of bursting shells throbbed and stabbed briefly in the dust clouds.

The assault battalions heading out across no-man's-land often advanced with platoons and companies in section files—or "worms"; this was an effective way for

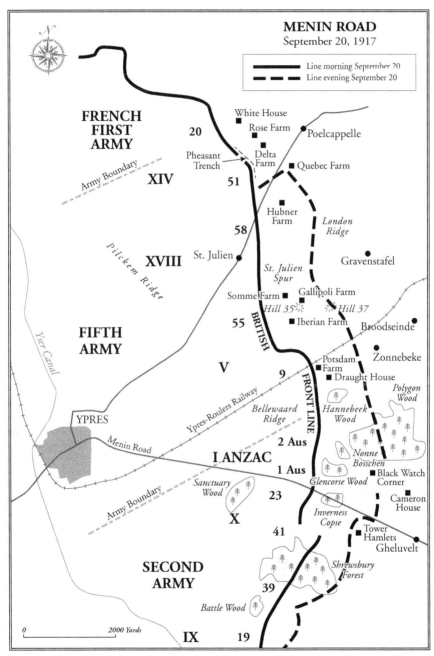

**MENIN ROAD**
September 20, 1917

——— Line morning September 20
- - - Line evening September 20

N

FRENCH
FIRST
ARMY

20

White House

Rose Farm

Poelcappelle

Army Boundary

XIV

Pheasant
Trench

Delta
Farm

51

Quebec Farm

Hubner
Farm

London
Ridge

58

Pilckem Ridge

XVIII

St. Julien

St. Julien
Spur

Gravenstafel

Somme Farm

Gallipoli Farm

Hill 35

Hill 37

55

BRITISH

Iberian Farm

Broodseinde

Yser Canal

FIFTH
ARMY

V

Potsdam
Farm

Zonnebeke

9

FRONT LINE

Draught House

Ypres-Roulers Railway

Bellewaard
Ridge

Hannebeek
Wood

Polygon
Wood

YPRES

Menin Road

2 Aus

Nonne
Bosschen

I ANZAC

1 Aus

Glencorse Wood

Black Watch
Corner

Sanctuary
Wood

23

Inverness
Copse

Cameron
House

Army Boundary

X

41

Tower
Hamlets

Gheluvelt

SECOND
ARMY

Shrewsbury
Forest

39

Battle Wood

0          2000 Yards

IX        19

Menin road, September 20, 1917

junior leaders to maintain control crossing cratered ground. The front was alive with hundreds of these small columns. A thin screen of skirmishers preceded the main force of infantry.

At the northern end of the attack front, the Fifth Army sent five divisions into action in the doleful Steenbeek valley, now a terrible wasteland full of the debris of war. A heavy mist persisted at ground level, and a German diarist wrote that British soldiers appeared like specters out of the fog. On the outer left flank, the 20th Division of XIV Corps advanced a short distance on the south side of the Ypres-Staden railway. To the south of the 20th Division, Maxse's XVIII Corps sallied forth successfully with the 51st and 58th Divisions. The twelve-hundred-yard advance of the 51st Division featured a creeping barrage that included a proportion of smoke shells.

The Fifth Army's right-flank corps was V Corps, which had orders to advance twelve hundred yards on the grim front between St. Julien and Zonnebeke. In the left-hand sector of V Corps, the 55th Division attacked. After a confused day's fighting, the center and left of the division was driven to ground about five hundred yards short of the final objective; the right portion of the division, assisted by reserves, managed to clear the Germans from parts of Zonnebeke spur.

**Stretcher-bearers at work while a shell explodes nearby. (A.W.M.)**

The 9th Division was V Corps' right-hand formation. Major John Ewing of the 6th King's Own Scottish Borderers recalled:

> The ordinary landmarks indicated by the map did not exist; the only one remaining that the eye could pick up without much effort was the Ypres-Roulers railway. All vestiges of roads had been obliterated, and even the Hannebeek brook had ceased to flow. Its banks had been blown in by months of relentless gun-fire and a zigzag trail of shell-holes, rather deeper and more full of water than others, alone gave evidence of its former existence. A bleaker and more repellent battlefield it is impossible to imagine, and even the sun served only to throw into stronger relief the dreadful ghoulishness of the landscape.[21]

Aerial photographs helped officers to pick out the main clusters of concrete shelters dotted on the open slopes, though such places were already notorious to British forces from previous engagements. The 9th Division used a combination of high explosives and smoke shells in its barrage. The division's commander, Major General H.T. Lukin, a veteran of the 1879 Zulu war, had received the permission of higher authority to expend a large stock of smoke shells.

The 9th Division's assault was led by the South African Brigade and 27th Brigade. The right-flank 27th Brigade faced light resistance, but the left-flank South Africans were not so fortunate. In the attack, Lance Corporal W.H. Hewitt of the 2nd (Natal and Orange Free State) Regiment won the Victoria Cross. Hewitt's section attempted to rush the doorway of a pillbox, but the garrison resisted. Hewitt was wounded by a grenade thrown from the doorway, which, in this instance, was on the flank of the pillbox; he hastily took refuge behind the structure.

> I peered round the other side, and there was a jolly loophole with a machine gun firing nineteen to the dozen. I thought, this is where the old bomb comes in. I still had two, so as it looked easy, I lobbed one at the loophole; but it wasn't so easy as it looked and I missed and had to duck back behind the pillbox while it exploded. As I had only one bomb left I decided to make sure, so I crept up right underneath, pulled out the pin, let the lever fly up, counted two and pushed it through the loophole. Some stinker shot me through the hand, but not too badly, and I heard the bomb explode and ran around to the door.[22]

Hewitt, in a smoldering rage, plunged his bayoneted rifle into the first German emerging from the doorway. The remaining survivors of the pillbox garrison took the hint and promptly surrendered.

To the south of Gough's Fifth Army, Plumer's Second Army attacked with six divisions. In the left-hand sector of the Second Army was I Anzac Corps. The commander of I Anzac Corps was Lieutenant General Sir W.R. Birdwood, an India-born Bengal Lancer and protégé of Kitchener. Birdwood, a brave and diplomatic man, had led the Australians since the Gallipoli landings; he had retained the confidence of his troops despite the severity of the bloodletting of the past two and a half years.

After zero hour, the barrage of Birdwood's corps rolled forward at a rate of a hundred yards per four minutes up the long slope leading to Gheluvelt Plateau; the barrage would slow to a hundred yards per eight minutes later in the day. The three weeks of dry weather and gentle sunshine had hardened the ground, though overnight rain made it slippery. The German line of outposts was quickly overrun by shadowy figures looming out of the dust and mist. Lieutenant K.H. McConnel of the Australians' 1st Battalion wrote: "Away along the hillside to the north as far as the eye could see were little groups of men steadily advancing in artillery formation, while further in front small single figures scurried hither and thither, and the little white bursts of bombs showed where some German machine gun nest was being rooted out."[23] The 1st and 2nd Australian Divisions reached the second of three objectives about 7:45 A.M.; prisoners were rounded up and shoved off in the direction of the old front line. The troops then halted for the next two hours behind a protective barrage. There was no German counterattack, though snipers harassed the unwary and unlucky to deliver death and injury when least expected. At 9:53 A.M.—rather like a carefully drawn-up railway timetable—the barrage began to roll forward again. The troops followed the barrage on to the final objective, after which they spent the rest of the day consolidating the new line under steady shellfire.

To the south of the Australians was the 23rd Division of X Corps. The 23rd Division's sector straddled the Menin road, and included patches of marshland. The attack in this sector unfolded successfully. The troops, despite the numerous pillboxes in their path, overran the litter of debris that marked the place where Inverness Copse had once stood; six hundred prisoners were taken, along with three field guns and forty-five machine guns. A large number of German dead would be buried in the vicinity.[24]

**Battle of Menin Road: a front-line trench from which the attack had commenced earlier in the day.**

On the right flank of the 23rd Division, the 41st Division had the difficult task of seizing the Tower Hamlets feature. When troops of the 41st Division attacked, they were caught in a devastating hail of machine-gun and rifle fire on exposed ground; further attacks that evening and next morning also fell short of the final objective.

To the south of the 41st Division, the 39th Division attacked with a single brigade on a narrow front; these troops struggled to make progress given the severity of enfilade fire coming from the Tower Hamlets sector. Finally, to cover the southern flank of the assault front, the 19th Division also advanced a short distance. The division's commander, Major General Tom Bridges, was among the seriously injured. Late in the afternoon he visited the headquarters of his brigade commanders in tunneled dugouts beneath Hill 60. As he was leaving this underground complex, a shell burst nearby and almost severed his right leg, which was later surgically removed.[25]

The weight of the British attack put the German front under great pressure. The relentless assault was a catastrophe for those German units directly in its path. In most places the attackers swiftly plowed into the heart of the local defensive system. *Unteroffizier* Ludwig Schmidt of the 28th Bavarian Ersatz Regiment recalled that

> the British fired smoke bombs and smoked off the entire area. At first we thought that it was gas. There was a wall of smoke twenty metres to our front. We could no longer see to shoot them. Suddenly, emerging out of the smoke, were swarms of British soldiers with fixed bayonets. For us it was all over. The few of us had no chance of resisting an assault at that range against such numbers. It was a matter of hands up, drop equipment and throw away ammunition. My pockets were still full of bullets. In consequence, when a British soldier searched me, he hit me in the groin with his rifle butt. I was relieved that nothing worse happened to me. Our main concern was to escape from the clutches of these drunken British soldiers as soon as possible. I cannot express in words my own thoughts at that time. I stood and watched as a British soldier spun round and shot one of our comrades in the back as he made his way to the rear. As we passed our own front line, we saw that the British positions were crammed with reserves. They lay there shoulder to shoulder, waiting to advance.[26]

Farther to the rear, prisoners were collected together and sent to a holding cage prior to transfer to a camp.

By the afternoon, the new front line was far enough advanced for British observers to see right across Gheluvelt Plateau to the crest lines of Broodseinde and Passchendaele. Several German reserve divisions had been in position immediately behind the front, but the Royal Flying Corps dominated the radiantly clear skies. Airmen aloft in reconnaissance biplanes were able to direct artillery fire onto any German troops spotted in the distance. For example, the 16th Bavarian Division was among those troops waiting in reserve. At 9 A.M. the 11th Bavarian Regiment was ordered to counterattack, but a ferocious artillery barrage halted the troops in their tracks and sent them diving for cover in shell holes. The 21st Bavarian Regiment was also set in motion. Two battalions of the regiment entered Polygon Wood, but a curtain of exploding shells prevented any further progress.

**Battle of Menin Road: a German shell bursts near Glencorse Wood.**

In the Menin road action, British troops advanced a maximum distance of fifteen hundred yards. A great deal of publicity was given to the day's fighting in the press. Plumer's splendid reputation—already high in the wake of Messines—was reinforced in the popular eye. In the afternoon Haig visited the headquarters of the Second and Fifth Armies and, encouraged by promising reports, wasted no time fixing a date for the next big attack. The Germans were to be given no respite.

British losses on September 20 amounted to 22,000; the divisions principally engaged suffered about 2,000 casualties each, though the figure for the 41st Division was 3,123.[27] The German artillery had not been suppressed by the preliminary bombardment and fired steadily throughout the day. The shelling of German heavy guns was usually delivered from long range; these batteries were beyond the effective retaliation of all but the heaviest-caliber British guns. A "continuous rain" of howling five-nines caused many casualties after the troops had carried the final objective. The number of German prisoners taken on September 20 was 3,243.[28]

Back in Britain, Prime Minister Lloyd George and War Cabinet Secretary Hankey returned to London from Wales on September 23. The following day, the War Cabinet received news from Italy that Cadorna's exhausted army would be moving onto the defensive for the winter. On the evening of September 24, the prime minister and Hankey departed London for Dover, and crossed the Channel to Boulogne in a destroyer early the following morning. Lloyd George and Paul Painlevé, the new French prime minister, met in a railway carriage after breakfast; a more solemn conference took place in the afternoon and was attended by Robertson and Foch.

At Boulogne, Lloyd George and Painlevé discussed the desirability of establishing an inter-Allied war council with its own permanent general staff. The Allied powers needed to find a better way to coordinate the actions of their militaries. In French parliamentary circles pressure was also mounting for the British to take over a longer portion of the western front. The two prime ministers agreed in principle that this should happen. Robertson suggested that an adjustment might best take place once the campaign currently underway had ended. After the conference, a party that included Lloyd George, Robertson, and Hankey motored to GHQ to further study the situation.

Meanwhile, Field Marshal Haig's fevered strategic imagination continued to flourish in Flanders, seemingly unchecked. The recent Menin road action had been most encouraging for Haig and his staff. Admiral Bacon was summoned from Dover for discussions regarding the amphibious landing planned for the Belgian coast.

September had been a dry month, and the fine weather was forecast to continue. Preparations for the next attack went ahead rapidly. A fresh set of infantry divisions was assembled; the artillery was pushed forward across the bare sweep of crater field to positions that were more exposed than ever. Pioneers extended plank tracks that radiated and snaked eastwards from Ypres across the flat landscape. The German heavy artillery remained shrouded from direct observation behind the ridgelines. German shelling of the British front across the period from September 21 to 25 was distressingly persistent.

RE8: a Royal Flying Corps aircraft type commonly used for reconnaissance work. (A.W.M.)

In the skies over the salient, the opposing air forces continued to duel. The German ace Lieutenant Werner Voss was shot down and killed by a patrol of SE5s of No. 56 Squadron. Voss had forty-eight victories to his name.

About this time, Bonar Law received tragic news in respect to his eldest son, who was a fighter pilot in the 60th Squadron. On September 21, Captain James Law was shot down and killed; this was the second son lost by Bonar Law to enemy action in less than six months, and he was stunned with grief. Lieutenant Charles Law of the King's Own Scottish Borderers had been reported missing at Gaza, Palestine, in April.

# 7

## Polygon Wood to Broodseinde

The Menin road engagement compelled German commanders to reassess the situation in Flanders. Crown Prince Rupprecht noted on September 23: "We cannot tolerate the idea of the enemy firmly in control of the Zonnebeke heights or the Gheluvelt [Plateau]. They are now so close to achieving this that the fear must be that they will achieve it with their next attack. We must ensure that our counter-strokes during the next enemy assaults are driven right up to their planned objectives." He added the next day: "It appears as though fresh attacks against Groups Ypres and Wytschaete are about to take place."[1]

In a bid to disrupt the timetable of the British campaign, on September 25 a German counterattack took place to the south of Polygon Wood. Two regiments of the 50th Reserve Division moved out at 5:30 A.M. on either side of the Reutelbeek stream, after a brief hurricane bombardment. On a hazy morning German troops advanced seven hundred yards, but were unable to progress farther than that.

Haig's offensive was not derailed by the 50th Reserve Division's counterattack. The next big effort by Plumer's Second Army was planned for September 26. Plumer's intention was to make a short advance across Gheluvelt Plateau to seize Polygon Wood and the southern part of Zonnebeke village. The Second Army's thrust would involve I Anzac Corps and X Corps. Divisions of the Fifth Army would advance as well to cover Plumer's northern flank. In total, seven divisions were to attack on a front of eighty-five hundred yards in a bid to reach objectives only one thousand to twelve hundred yards away.

Zero hour on September 26 was 5:50 A.M., at which time the complex artillery barrage commenced. The ground was dry as powder, and shell bursts threw up clouds of dust. At the northern end of the assault frontage, the Fifth Army's 58th and 59th Divisions advanced out of the morning mist to successfully take most of

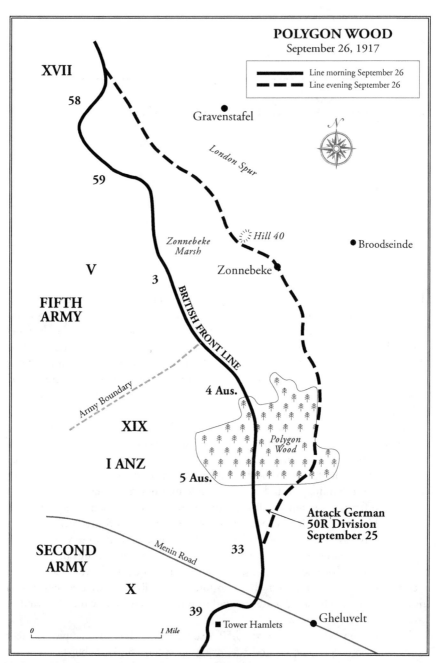

**POLYGON WOOD**
September 26, 1917

| | |
|---|---|
| ——— | Line morning September 26 |
| - - - | Line evening September 26 |

XVII

58

Gravenstafel

*London Spur*

N

59

*Zonnebeke Marsh*

Hill 40

Broodseinde

V

3

Zonnebeke

FIFTH
ARMY

BRITISH FRONT LINE

Army Boundary

4 Aus.

XIX

*Polygon Wood*

I ANZ

5 Aus.

Attack German
50R Division
September 25

SECOND
ARMY

*Menin Road*

33

X

39

0 — 1 Mile

Tower Hamlets

Gheluvelt

Polygon Wood, September 26, 1917

their designated objectives. Farther south, troops of the 3rd Division fought their way into ruined Zonnebeke.

To the south of the Fifth Army, the Second Army's I Anzac Corps advanced behind five belts of barrage fire that formed a moving wall of shells, dust, and smoke a thousand yards deep. In the left-hand sector of Birdwood's I Anzac Corps, the 4th Australian Division's front lay between Zonnebeke and Polygon Wood. The morning was misty, and aircraft droned overhead as the troops set out across ground broken by shell holes. The barrage "was the acme of perfection—a gigantic thunderstorm of bursting steel hurled out of the lips of thousands of guns. . . . So close overhead was it, that the warm air caused by the friction of the shells could be distinctly felt."[2] The final objective was carried by 8 A.M. German troops could be seen in the distance retiring over the crest of Broodseinde Ridge. The Australian infantry spent the rest of the day consolidating the newly won patch of ground under heavy shellfire.

In the right-hand sector of I Anzac Corps, the 5th Australian Division had the task of capturing Polygon Wood, which was defended by a German infantry regiment. The polluted wood was over half a mile wide and a similar distance deep. The wood had once been a training base for Belgian artillerymen. In the center of the wood was an oval riding track; the northeast corner of the splintered wilderness featured a large, thirty-foot-high mound known as "the Butte," which had originally been a stop-butt for the practice firing of cannonballs.

The 5th Australian Division had a pivotal role to play in the day's battle. The division's commander was Major General Talbot Hobbs, an English-born West Australian and an architect by profession. The division was to attack with two brigades on a narrow eleven-hundred-yard front; each brigade was to use a single battalion to reach the first objective—the red line. Once that line had been taken, the barrage would halt for an hour to allow the infantry to regroup; the attack would then resume, each brigade using a further two battalions to capture the final objective—the blue line. For direct artillery support, six field brigades and one hundred heavy guns were available. The creeping barrage was to open 150 yards in front of the assembly line and then roll forward after a brief interval. Many of the division's Vickers machine guns would fire as part of the lavish barrage. A squadron of aircraft was to patrol the skies over the wood; the infantry were given instructions to light vivid flares to keep the airmen informed of their progress.[3]

In the early hours of the morning of September 26, the troops of Hobbs's division assembled behind jumping-off tapes, nerves stretched to the highest pitch. A stupendous barrage broke out at 5:50 A.M. and roared ahead like a bushfire. A line of skirmishers closely followed the barrage into the gray mists of dawn, with section columns close behind. The concussion of the barrage dazed German soldiers sheltering in pillboxes, and killed or wounded many of those in less well-protected earthworks. Where a pillbox fort resisted, machine guns flashing from loopholes or a nearby trench parapet, a local drama unfolded; there was the usual confusion as to when, how, or if the survivors of an overwhelmed garrison might be made prisoner. A sharp-eyed commanding officer reported on the lively scene:

> For but a short space of time beaters and worm section formations held together, but soon the area was covered with little parties of eight or nine men deployed, each looking for its shell-hole or pill-box full of Boche, and they found him too, but the cringing Kamarading Hun was not willing to fight, everywhere surrendering rapidly. Indeed, he did not get much opportunity to show resistance, because our men pounced on him immediately the barrage passed over him. Detachments were left behind to clear each pill-box, and parties of from thirty to forty from two of these strongholds were quickly escorted to the rear.[4]

The final objective was reached by the left-hand 14th Brigade soon after 8 A.M.; losses in the advance were light, but steady shelling for the rest of the day took a rising toll. The right-hand 15th Brigade had a more difficult task, as that formation was vulnerable to enfilade fire from the southern flank. The first objective was taken almost on schedule, but after holdups, the advance to the final objective was only resumed at noon with partial success. About six hundred prisoners were taken at Polygon Wood and many German dead left upon the field.[5] German reserves set in motion behind Polygon Wood were repelled by the weight of the barrage.

On the southern flank of the Australians, the 33rd Division's attack also made good progress, but farther south the 39th Division came to grief against the portion of Tower Hamlets spur still in German hands. The main cause of this setback was the "Quadrilateral," a menacing unsuppressed network of interlocking strongpoints.

On the surface at least, September 26 was another successful day's fighting for the British Expeditionary Force (BEF). German units in the forward zone were over-run and their remnants scattered to the rear. There were no German counterattacks of any great danger. At 5 P.M. Haig, Plumer, Gough, and their senior staff met at General Headquarters (GHQ) in a jaunty mood of self-congratulation. Nevertheless, another 15,375 casualties were lost; the reward for that crop of sorrow was no more than a sliver of shattered ground.[6] The Germans had massed a substantial force of artillery opposite both Gough's and Plumer's armies; these guns, often firing from long range, steadily flayed exposed targets. The number of German prisoners taken on September 26 was only 1,600.[7] A disappointing feature of the day's fighting was the British barrage's obvious inability to penetrate deeply the German defensive zone. The limited range of the standard British field gun was a consistent operational handicap.

Lloyd George had dined at Haig's headquarters the evening before the Polygon Wood engagement. "I found there an atmosphere of unmistakable exaltation. It was not put on. Haig was not an actor. He was radiant. He was quiet, there was no swag-ger. That was never one of his weaknesses, but he had the satisfied and confident de-meanour of a leader who was marching his army step-by-step surely and irresistibly, overcoming all obstacles."[8] On the morning of the Polygon Wood engagement—the

**German *Panzerlafette* (anti-tank gun) captured near Sterling Castle on September 20. Eight tanks were put out of action in the vicinity of this gun, including the vehicle in the background. (A.W.M.)**

26th—the field marshal, prime minister, and Robertson had met in conference. War Cabinet Secretary Hankey was also on hand to leave an account of what transpired.

> There was a big attack that morning. All the time at the conference messages were coming in from the front. Haig had a great map showing the line we wanted to reach, and it was very interesting the way first one bit was filled in on the map, then another. . . . [During the middle part of the day] we drove on to the rear of the Army through the usual paraphernalia of dumps of ammunition, aerodromes, herds of "tanks," like great mastodons, roads made of planks, etc. At the cross-roads outside Poperinghe a big eleven-inch shell whistled over our heads and burst 100 yards away—too close to be pleasant. Our destination was a cage for prisoners brought down from the day's battle containing a number of nerve-shattered, tired, unshaved, and dirty men, who nevertheless sprang to attention as though under review by the Kaiser.[9]

Lloyd George pounced upon this incident in his memoirs with the verve of a prosecuting counsel:

> During this visit [to GHQ], Sir Douglas Haig and his staff dwelt repeatedly on the visible deterioration in the physique and smartness of the German soldiers, judged by the specimens captured in recent victories. I expressed a desire to see them. The proposition

was received without any enthusiasm. Would I not prefer to see Vimy Ridge where I could get a view of the German positions? I preferred to see the last batch of prisoners. I saw the last "cage," and I thought the men were a weedy lot. They were deplorably inferior to the manly samples I had seen in earlier stages of the War. It was some years after the War that I ascertained . . . that on that occasion G.H.Q. rang up Fifth Army and stated that the Prime Minister was coming down and would go to Corps Headquarters to see German prisoners. Instructions were given to inform the Corps—I forget which one it was—of this, and to tell them to see that able-bodied prisoners were removed from the Corps cages.[10]

Lloyd George did not accuse Haig of being directly involved in the deceit, which was arranged by a subordinate. A staff officer at the Fifth Army's headquarters, Major Wilfred Greene, a future judge, would confirm the veracity of the prime minister's version of events.[11]

The Polygon Wood engagement had firmly established the Second Army on Gheluvelt Plateau. Haig was confident that the next round of operations in the salient would bring further noteworthy success. At the War Office, however, Robertson was not as convinced. On September 27 he wrote to GHQ:

My views are known to you. They have always been "defensive" in all theatres but the West. But the difficulty is to prove the wisdom of this now that Russia is out. I confess I stick to it more because I see nothing better, and because my instinct prompts me to stick to it, than because of any good argument by which I can support it. Germany may be much nearer the end of her staying power than available evidence shows, but on the other hand France and Italy are not much to depend upon, and America will require a long time.[12]

Haig was in no mood to pay much attention to Robertson's point of view. Haig wrote in his diary for September 28: "I am of opinion that the enemy is tottering and that a good vigorous blow might lead to decisive results."[13] At an army commanders' conference that day, the field marshal spoke of the Germans' declining morale. On September 29, Haig advised Admiral Jellicoe that "good progress has been made on the Ypres front and there may still be an opportunity for launching the coastal attack about the end of October when the tide and moon are favourable."[14]

Haig's offensive in Flanders would benefit from another French attack on their part of the western front. This might draw German reserves away from the BEF's sector. Haig recorded on September 29 that

Colonel de Bellaigue, head of the French mission, came to see me at 9 A.M. He was most insistent that I should know that he had done all in his power to get the French to attack on the Aisne as soon as possible. As a matter of fact, they cannot attack till the 10th or 15th October because they will not be ready. I limited my remarks to reminding him that Petain had promised to "attack on or about the 15th October."

Commandant E.A. Gemeau, another French liaison officer, assured Haig that "the morale of the French troops is now excellent"; the attack planned for the Aisne sector had lagged behind schedule only for reason of material preparation.[15] As had been the case the previous month, it was Haig who was pressing Pétain to attack and not the other way around.

Haig dearly wanted to involve the cavalry in the next round of operations. On October 1 he met with the Cavalry Corps' Lieutenant General C.T.M. Kavanagh to sketch out the role the cavalry might play. Brigadier General A.F. Home, Kavanagh's chief staff officer, also attended the meeting. Home wrote: "I think there is a chance. We shall lose heavily; on the other hand we ought to make a big bag of guns and men. It is for the Chief [Haig] to decide whether it is worthwhile; if he says, then we go through with it. . . . The fine weather continues—if we have a fine October many things may happen."[16] The Cavalry Corps had spent August and September engaged in regimental and brigade-level training behind the front.

The BEF's next operation was intended to capture Broodseinde Ridge and the eastern fringe of Gheluvelt Plateau. Haig and his army commanders conferred on October 2 to finalize the details.

> I [Haig] pointed out how favourable the situation was and how necessary it was to have all necessary means for exploiting any success gained. . . . Both Gough and Plumer quite acquiesced in my views, and arranged wholeheartedly to give effect to them when the time came. At first they adhered to the idea of continuing our attacks for limited objectives. Charteris emphasised the deterioration of German Divisions in numbers, morale and all-round efficiency.[17]

The date for Plumer's next attack was brought forward by two days, as the most recent round of fighting had fulfilled expectations. Haig went on to tell the conference:

> The time may come shortly when the enemy's troops will not stand up to our repeated attacks, or when he may not have sufficient fresh troops immediately available to throw into the battle. The enemy failed to take advantage of his opponents on 31st October, 1914, and did not push forward when his repeated attacks had exhausted the British forces on the Ypres Front.[18]

That was a mistake Haig did not intend to make.

To maintain the desired level of pressure, fresh divisions were needed in Flanders to relieve those that were exhausted. Among the new arrivals to the salient was the 3rd Australian Division, the commander of which, Major General John Monash, set up his headquarters under the thick ramparts of Ypres' town walls. Monash described his situation in a letter home:

> It is in every respect like the underground workings of mines, narrow tunnels, broadening out here and there into little chambers, the whole lit by electric light. . . . It is cold and dank and overrun by rats and mice . . . but here I shall have to stay for nearly three

weeks. . . . The town of Ypres, once a marvel of medieval architectural beauty, lies all around us a stark, pitiable ruin. . . . For three years it has been dying a lingering death, and now there is nothing left of its fine streets, its great square, its cathedral, the historic Cloth Hall, its avenues, and boulevards of fine mansions, its hospitals, its town hall, or its straggling suburbs, but a charred collection of pitiable ruins—a scene of utter collapse and desolation.

At night Ypres was subject to intermittent long-range shelling; these projectiles fell on the lines of traffic on the roads that converged upon the town. Monash added: "If you could stand for half an hour at what we know as the Asylum Corner, at the southern entrance to Ypres, where the roads from Dickebusch and Poperinghe meet, you would see this never-ending stream [of traffic] ploughing its way slowly and painfully through the mud, man and horse plastered to the eyes in mud, and a reek of petrol and smoke everywhere."[19]

Back in London, the War Policy Committee continued its work. On October 3, Lloyd George pointed out to the committee that progress in Flanders was not fulfilling the predictions of the military leadership. That day Field Marshal Haig was given the news by Robertson—"a great bombshell"—that the government had "approved in principle" French requests that the BEF take over a longer portion of the western front at a time to be decided.[20] A few days later, Haig sent a strongly worded memorandum to Robertson setting out his opposition to an extension of the BEF's front. Haig went so far as to write: "It is necessary, in my opinion, to refuse to take over more line and to adhere resolutely to that refusal, even to the point of answering threats by threats if necessary."[21] In reality, there was little either Robertson or Haig could do, as the British and French governments had already decided the matter.

German commanders in Flanders had been alarmed by the sheer weight of British attacks in the second half of September; units in the forward zone had been smashed and successive lines of elaborate defenses given up. Lieutenant Colonel von Thaer, chief of staff of Wytschaete Group, wrote on September 28: "We are going through a really awful experience. I do not know anymore what to do in the face of the British."[22] Something that could be done, however, was another local counterattack to disrupt British plans.

At dawn on October 1, a sudden torrent of heavy shelling fell on a fifteen-hundred-yard front stretching from the Reutelbeek stream northwards to Polygon Wood; this was soon followed by an assault. Two German regiments attacked in a bid to regain some of the ground that had been lost five days before. Heavy defensive fire drove the German infantry to cover in the craters of no-man's-land; they only reached the British line at one point. Another counterattack to the north of Polygon Wood was planned for October 3; this counterattack, however, was postponed to October 4 to permit more-thorough preparations.

The next attack in the salient by the Second and Fifth Armies was also scheduled for October 4; twelve divisions were to press forward on a fourteen-thousand-yard front. The Second Army's artillery strength on paper was more abundant than ever,

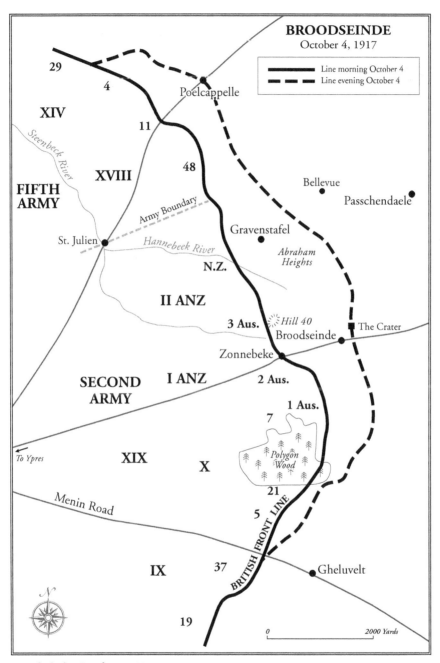

**BROODSEINDE**
October 4, 1917

| | |
|---|---|
| —— | Line morning October 4 |
| - - - | Line evening October 4 |

29

4

Poelcappelle

XIV

11

XVIII

48

Bellevue

FIFTH
ARMY

Steenbeck River

Passchendaele

Army Boundary

St. Julien

Hannebeek River

Gravenstafel

N.Z.

Abraham
Heights

II ANZ

3 Aus.

Hill 40

Broodseinde

The Crater

Zonnebeke

SECOND
ARMY

I ANZ

2 Aus.

1 Aus.

7

To Ypres

XIX

X

Polygon
Wood

21

Menin Road

5

BRITISH FRONT LINE

IX

37

Gheluvelt

19

0

2000 Yards

Broodseinde, October 4, 1917

yet gun strength on the ground had dropped due to losses to shellfire. In August the Second Army had 234 eighteen-pounders destroyed, and another 350 in September—"replacement was only gradual."[23] The German five-point-nines were an ever-present danger for British gunners.

Rain began falling on October 3; the climate had finally broken after a lengthy spell of fine weather. By evening low clouds were rolling across Flanders, blown by a gale from the southwest. Overnight the moon was hidden behind clouds; twilight before dawn was overcast and drizzly.

The Fifth Army's share in the engagement of October 4 can be quickly summarized. The intention was to reach objectives about twelve hundred yards away. After the usual tension-filled, sleepless night preceding an assault, the troops sallied forth with the air above them full of rushing shells. On the Fifth Army's left flank, units of the 4th and 29th Divisions advanced a short distance. On the Fifth Army's right flank was Maxse's XVIII Corps (11th and 48th Divisions). A well-organized bombardment helped this corps seize most of their objectives. The infantry entered the village of Poelcappelle with the support of ten tanks. The tanks were able to crawl along the cratered St. Julien–Poelcappelle road. The northern part of Poelcappelle, however, remained in German hands.

Farther south, in the left-hand sector of the Second Army's front, the New Zealand Division (II Anzac Corps) was given the task of advancing a thousand yards on a two-thousand-yard front to secure Gravenstafel spur. The New Zealanders attacked with two brigades. Among the German soldiers sheltering in the craters of Gravenstafel was Lieutenant Groth of the 77th Regiment. He recalled:

> Far out to the right the red flares were going up; the fire became ever more frenzied. A loud uniquely endless droning racket filled the air and enveloped the positions so it was impossible to distinguish one sound from another. Many men lay silent, apathetic, pressed hard against the walls of the craters. Others crouched down, murmuring prayers; their staring eyes struggling to take in the gruesome scenes of death all around them. Suddenly above the row could be heard . . . "*Herr Leutnant,* here they come!" . . . It was true, the British were on their way approaching from half left in long lines; wave after wave. . . . My telescope was smashed by a bullet as I looked through it. Fortunately I only suffered a few scratches. Meanwhile we were under a hail of enemy hand grenades and the machine gun was knocked out. A little later, the enemy suddenly appeared in strength ten metres behind us. We were completely surrounded! We were under heavy fire from all sides and grenades continued to be thrown. The machine gun crew was shot down, the few remaining men were overwhelmed, bayoneted, bludgeoned with rifle butts and robbed. The four or five who were left were led away bleeding profusely.[24]

After this successful attack, the New Zealanders secured 1,159 prisoners and reported seeing an unusually large number of German dead on the field of battle.[25] The New Zealand Division suffered losses of 330 killed and 1,323 wounded. Sufficient high ground was gained to afford fine views to the southeast over distant Flemish lowlands. On the right flank of the New Zealanders, the 3rd Australian Division also attained their objectives on schedule.

To the south of II Anzac Corps, Birdwood's I Anzac Corps had the main task of the day, namely the capture of Broodseinde Ridge. The Germans, however, had a surprise of their own in store for Birdwood's corps. About 5:20 A.M. the Germans on Broodseinde Ridge started firing yellow-colored flares instead of the previous white flares. German guns in this sector began to fire a heavy barrage at 5:30 A.M. It seemed that the plan for the Second Army's attack had been discovered. German shells hurtled down upon the Australian troops opposite. Soldiers sheltering from the rain in shell holes beneath their waterproof capes were poorly situated to endure intense shelling. The bombardment was laced with trench mortar bombs, which could be seen arcing through the gloom. Losses from shellfire were heavy; roughly one seventh of I Anzac Corps' assault force was killed or wounded drawn up behind the jumping-off tapes.

At 6 A.M. the Second Army's bombardment struck up as scheduled and quickly drowned out the sounds of the German shelling. The British barrage fell 150 yards in front of the jumping-off tapes, remained there for three minutes, and then moved forward at an initial pace of 100 yards per four minutes. The shrouded landscape ahead was dimly lit up by the glow of dawn. The Australian infantry leapt to their feet and set out to get clear of the shelling they had been under for the past half hour. Lieutenant E.R. Shelley of the 3rd Battalion recorded:

> At this point I turned for a few moments and faced the west, being rather far forward, waiting for our men to come up. I was rewarded by one of the finest sights of the war. In the slowly breaking dawn I could see, not tens, not hundreds, but literally thousands and thousands of stabs of orange flame belching from the mouths of our guns to north, south, and west. It looked for all the world like some gigantic field packed full of twinkling lights—a wonderful spectacle.[26]

The troops of I Anzac Corps had to cross a slight dip of open ground before moving onto the gentle upslope of Broodseinde Ridge. The infantry was closing up to the barrage when shadowy figures were seen in the murky twilight thirty yards ahead. Firing broke out once it was realized that the gray-coated men in no-man's-land were the enemy. A confused round of brawling and scuffles caused the Germans to break rearwards; they had been stunned by the barrage that had unexpectedly rolled across them. Seldom did such large bodies of opposing infantry collide in a hand-to-hand melee.

The Germans in no-man's-land belonged to the 212th Reserve Regiment of the 45th Reserve Division; these troops and supporting detachments had been waiting to attack from 6:10 A.M. on a two-thousand-yard front from Polygon Wood to Zonnebeke. Among the Germans opposite was Major Lincke, who commanded the 2nd Battalion of the 212th Reserve Regiment. The day did not turn out as Lincke had hoped:

> Shortly before 6 A.M. and far behind the British lines, a previously unknown light signal, comprising three blue, red and green flares was fired and hung, plainly visible in the sky

for several minutes. This signal was the trigger for the sudden start of a concentration of enemy light and medium calibre shells on our trenches. The fire was of an intensity which even the battle hardened officers and men had never previously experienced. Despite this fire the companies of the centre of the attack got to their feet . . . exactly as ordered and went their final way. What actually happened in that swampy area in the dark and in the fog, no pen of a living author can ever write. No report ever reached the battalion commander, a sure sign of the intensity of the battle.[27]

The attack of the Australians rolled into the 212th Reserve Regiment. Lincke was wounded in the arm by a shell splinter and made prisoner. He wrote of the aftermath:

We finally reached the old German front line, which had been torn from the possession of the Guards [4th Guards Division] during the battle. Dotted around in the swampy landscape were concrete pillboxes, with space for about one section. . . . At one of them I saw what, for me, was the most gruesome sight of the war. Hanging from one of the four metre long vertical steel reinforcing rods by his legs was the corpse of a German soldier, headless and with his chest torn open. He must have been thrown there by a shell. . . . I kneeled next to a runner from 8th Company who was close to death and begging for water. I shall never forget his beaming face when he recognised me, his commander . . . he thought that we must have won the battle. I gave him the last drops in my water bottle then held his hand for the few remaining seconds it took him to die.[28]

After the initial clash with German troops waiting in no-man's-land, the Australian infantry pushed on to secure the first objective on the forward slope of Broodseinde Ridge. Captain E. Gorman of the 22nd Battalion noted: "In one dugout in the vicinity of De Knoet Farm the occupants refused to surrender. Bombs had to be dropped through the ventilator, and next morning twenty-three corpses were removed."[29] At 8:10 A.M. the barrage moved forward again, and by 9:30 A.M. I Anzac Corps had secured the final objective. A shallow valley lay ahead between Broodseinde Ridge and Passchendaele ridge to the northeast.

Late in the afternoon Major Lincke was taken to the rear as a prisoner. Lincke stopped at the headquarters of an Australian formation and conversed with an officer of about thirty years of age who spoke German with a Berlin accent. The Australian officer said he was a lawyer and militia soldier who had studied in Germany. Lincke fainted from his wound and had to be revived with whisky, tea, and biscuits. The Australian officer, wrote Lincke,

asked me how I had been treated by his men. I told him truthfully that apart from being robbed there were many good things to report. At that he stated that though his men were a rough lot when they were fighting, on the other hand they showed good will towards courageous opponents whom they could respect. It was a complete mystery to him how we expected to be able to win the war when we were opposed by the men and material of the whole world. He put it very bluntly: "The cannon fodder of the entire world is at our disposal." What he meant by this was that the manpower reserves of the enemy alliance were inexhaustible, whilst on the other side, as he stated and the events of today's battle had proved, the best soldiers of the Kaiser were being killed, wounded or captured and in any case were no longer available to fight. To his question, "When will your revolution begin?" I parried with pride, "Do not forget, general, that we are Germans not Russians."[30]

The captured crest of Broodseinde Ridge was bare but for a paved road running from Becelaere to Passchendaele. The hamlet of Broodseinde was a heap of rubble. As was often the case in this campaign, the Germans heavily shelled the positions they had recently forfeited; this exacted a heavy toll as the day wore on. The losses of the 1st and 2nd Australian Divisions in the engagement would tally up to 2,448 and 2,174, respectively.[31]

At the southern end of the assault front, another four divisions of the Second Army attacked in a bid to secure the eastern edge of Gheluvelt Plateau. On the immediate right flank of the Australians, the 7th Division advanced on the northern side of Reutel stream. According to the division's history: "The British barrage gave the attacking battalions the greatest possible satisfaction: it was accurate, regular, and most effective, while its slow pace enabled the infantry to keep well up with it."[32] By midmorning the day was already a success. Germans were seen fleeing into the distance; the field was strewn with the dead. The 7th Division's haul of prisoners amounted to six hundred, most of whom belonged to the 4th Guards Division.

To the south of the 7th Division, the 21st Division advanced to the western edge of Reutel village. Farther south again, the 5th Division attacked rising ground to the north of Gheluvelt village and the Ypres-Menin road. This rising ground was dominated by the derelict ruins of Polderhoek Château. The unit historian of the 14th Warwicks, J.E.B. Fairclough, would write:

> In the peaceful days before the war, Polderhoek Chateau was a residence of some importance, situated in large grounds and just north of the Menin Road. A photograph of the chateau before the war, issued just prior to the attack, showed a charming house and a picturesque garden with a large lawn bordered with tall trees and shrubs, with here and there ornamental flower beds. But when we arrived all these had disappeared; in their place was found a ruined shell of a building reinforced with concrete and converted into a strong fortress, standing up conspicuously as an island, surrounded by swampy ground pitted with countless shell holes full of water.[33]

From a pillbox at Polderhoek Château, *Hauptmann* Wolf watched the British attack develop amid a deafening racket of shell bursts and small-arms fire. Three tanks lumbered toward the German lines. Wolf wrote of the drama that followed:

> Protz [Wolf's batman] said, "I do not think that they will be able to get through the swamp." We shall just have to see. Oh yes—one has already bogged down. Good! The crews climbed out. Our machine gun fire deals with them. What about the second? Clang! One of those British shells which gives off a reddish smoke hits it squarely. Very many thanks for the support! As for the third, what is it going to do? It turns away, so that was that dealt with.[34]

British troops entered the grounds of the château, but a fleeting opportunity for success quickly passed and the advance came to a halt in front of the ruined building.

To the south of the Ypres-Menin road, probes by the 37th Division toward Tower Hamlets spur made little progress. By evening, rain was falling heavily upon the salient's bleak landscape.

The Broodseinde engagement cost the BEF another sixteen thousand casualties; almost five thousand German prisoners were taken, which was the best haul since July 31; many German dead and dying littered the battlefield. Ludendorff wrote of the day's onslaught: "The battle on the 4th of October was extraordinarily severe, and again we only came through it with enormous losses."[35] He added: "Opposite the 1st Anzac Corps alone . . . the 45th Reserve Division lost eighty-three officers and 2800 other ranks and the 4th Guards Division eighty-six officers and 2700 other ranks. Foot Guard Regiment No. 5 described it as the worst day yet experienced during the war."[36]

On October 4 the line was advanced a maximum of fifteen hundred to two thousand yards at the spearpoint of the thrust. This was an impressive achievement by the standards of the time. Plumer's "bite and hold" approach pulverized those German regiments caught in the path of the assault and negated any scheme of defense based on reactive counterattack.

Plumer's army now held most—though not all—of Gheluvelt Plateau. Charteris wrote, "We gave the German a great beating. A few more . . . and we shall be in Ostend before [Christmas] and the war will be won."[37] Charteris joked to Harington: "Now we have them on the run—get up the cavalry!" Plumer grandiosely described October 4 as "the greatest victory since the Marne [the French victory of 1914 that saved Paris]."[38]

Nevertheless, the German front remained unbroken. The shallow advance was insufficient to threaten the German artillery that was firing into British lines from a wide arc of positions stretching from northeast of Passchendaele to south of Gheluvelt. Each time British forces edged forward, they occupied a more pronounced and more dangerous salient.

# 8

## Final Steps to Passchendaele

Reports of the Broodseinde action received at General Headquarters (GHQ) were unusually encouraging. The next attack was scheduled to take place on October 9. Field Marshal Haig believed that the time was ripe for his Cavalry Corps to take a more active part in the campaign. The cavalry was ordered to concentrate behind the Yser canal in preparation for action in the pristine countryside beyond Passchendaele ridge. If the German front suddenly crumpled, the massed horsemen were to make a dramatic sweep toward Roulers, Thourout, and onwards to the Belgian coast. Captain L.R. Lumley of the 11th Hussars summed up the situation:

> The plans for the cavalry were that the 1st and 5th Cavalry Divisions were to lead, the 1st on the left with the Fifth Army, and the 5th on the right with the Second Army. . . . If called upon to advance, it [the 1st Cavalry Division] was to move forward north of St Julien to a position of readiness west of the Passchendaele Ridge, and from there was to make its first bound beyond Westroosebeek, clear of the worst part of the shell-broken country. If they went through, the cavalry were to overrun the enemy's gun area and exploit the situation.[1]

As the cavalry prepared for action, the rain began to pour down: The principal dry spell of the autumn of 1917 had ended. General Home at Cavalry Corps headquarters noted that GHQ was "cheerful and determined to carry out the attack—rain or no rain." Haig and his staff continued to think in terms of maps "scored by sweeping pencil strokes to mark the indefinite hope of a cavalry advance."[2]

In Paris, an emotional General Foch told a press interviewer: "Boche is bad, and *Boue* [mud] is bad, but Boche and *Boue* together—ah!" The Frenchman threw his hands in the air to emphasize his point. On the evening of October 7, Lieutenant Colonel Repington, the influential newspaper correspondent, interviewed General Pétain. The unwelcome prospect of the collapse of Russia was much on Pétain's

**Pioneers laying duckboards near Zonnebeke, October 5, 1917.**

mind. "Petain is prepared to admit," wrote Repington, "that anything from thirty to sixty German divisions may come West, and that we shall be duly appraised of their advent." Pétain went on to say that he "had the greatest respect for Haig and admired his tenacity and the great achievements of our Armies, but could not think that our attack in Flanders was good strategy. What did I [Repington] think of it, and was not the strategy imposed upon us by our Admiralty?" Pétain was far from impressed with Haig's senior staff. "He [Pétain] said that Charteris killed off the Germans too quickly, and that he and Davidson egged on Haig to believe that he was winning the war when we were still far from that desirable consummation."[3] Pétain conceded that morale in the French army had been poor in June, but that was no longer the case.

In contrast to Pétain, Haig believed that the bitter campaign in Flanders was on the verge of strategic consequence. He told Robertson on October 8: "It would be better for the future of our race to fall in the next year's offensive than to accept the enemy's terms now when after more than three years of splendid effort we have brought German resistance so near to breaking point."[4] Heavy rain, however, was fast turning the salient back into a landscape of flooded shell craters and ditches. An observer compared the stretches of muddy water to the sight that might greet a sailor from the porthole of an oceangoing vessel. Meteorologists were not expecting the weather to improve in the days ahead; menacing storms were rolling out of the North Atlantic to the west of Ireland.

On the German side of the lines, commanders had also reviewed the past fortnight's cruel fighting. The Fourth Army in Flanders issued a directive that reemphasized the need to fight a "deep" defensive battle. "The foremost shell-crater area," wrote General von Kuhl,

to a depth of 500 to 1000 yards was to be considered merely as an advanced zone and only to be occupied by a thin line of sentries with a few machine guns. In the face of a big offensive these few troops were to retire on the main line of resistance at the back of the advanced zone, while the artillery were at once to lay down and maintain a dense barrage of shells in front of it.[5]

On October 6, Ludendorff spoke with Rupprecht by telephone; the former said that the military situation was favorable for Germany; there was even the chance that the war would be won by the end of the year. The Crown Prince of Bavaria did not share so optimistic a view.

Final preparations for the next push in Flanders were hastily completed. Zero hour on October 9 was at 5:20 A.M., after an inky black night. The attack was to take place on a 13,500-yard front. At the appointed time, in the northern part of the attack front, French troops and neighboring troops of Cavan's XIV Corps—the Fifth Army's left-flank corps—set out across no-man's-land. Over a mile of swampland was taken in a series of short, bitter clashes.

The Fifth Army's right-flank corps—Maxse's XVIII Corps—endeavored to advance along Poelcappelle spur. The 11th and 48th Divisions each attacked with a brigade, but these troops were cut down by raking machine-gun fire. That evening, after darkness had fallen, a tank engineer officer left St. Julien and headed up the road toward devastated Poelcappelle.

**Battle of Broodseinde, October 4. German prisoners working as stretcher-bearers. (A.W.M.)**

As I neared the derelict tanks, the scene became truly appalling; wounded men lay drowned in the mud, others were stumbling and falling through exhaustion, others crawled and rested themselves up against the dead to raise themselves a little above the slush. On reaching the tanks, I found them surrounded by dead and dying; men had crawled to them for what shelter they would afford. The nearest tank was a female. Her sponson doors were open; out of these protruded four pairs of legs.[6]

On the southern flank of the Fifth Army was the Second Army's II Anzac Corps. In the left-hand sector of II Anzac Corps, the Yorkshiremen of the 49th Division attacked along Bellevue spur, an offshoot of the main ridge. Captain P.G. Bales of the 1/4th Duke of Wellington's wrote of the ruined landscape: "Could the prophetic eye of Dante have looked so far forward into the future, he might readily have introduced this desolation as the setting to one of the lowest circles of Hell."[7] The 49th Division attacked with two brigades supported by a feeble creeping barrage. The leading troops made slow progress across the waterlogged landscape, and then faced barbed-wire entanglements and scything machine-gun fire from loopholed pillboxes on Bellevue spur. The attack had failed by midmorning. Many soldiers spent a harrowing day stranded in the mire of no-man's-land waiting for darkness and the chance to crawl to safety.

In the right-hand sector of II Anzac Corps, the 66th Division attacked up the spine of the main ridge leading to Passchendaele village. When the attack commenced, the infantry trudged into the wasteland with bayonets fixed. The torrid slime of the ground, a howling wind, heavy loads, and unburied corpses looming suddenly underfoot were features of the day. The East Lancashire and Manchester units of the left-hand 198th Brigade were held up, short of the first objective, by enfilade machine-gun fire from Bellevue spur. The advance of the right-hand 197th Brigade was more successful, and by 10 A.M. these troops—Lancashire Fusiliers — were near their final objective. About 11 A.M. a British patrol entered Passchendaele village and found it deserted; these soldiers, however, fell back again for lack of support. Despite a promising start, by afternoon the 197th Brigade had given up most of its gains. On the right flank of the 66th Division, troops of the 2nd Australian Division also attacked and failed to make any worthwhile progress.

At the far southern end of the attack front, X Corps sallied forth in another bid to secure the eastern edge of Gheluvelt Plateau. The 7th Division captured the village of Reutel amid a sea of mud. On the right flank of the 7th Division, the 5th Division again attempted to capture Polderhoek Château. After a rainy night the château's muddy grounds were entered, but the lethal fire of machine-gun posts in and around the ruins held up the advance. The troops finished the hopeless day back on their start line.

Total British losses for October 9 were close to 13,000, and included 2,585 and 3,119 for the 49th and 66th Divisions, respectively.[8] The day's engagement would be called the Battle of Poelcappelle for want of a better name. The attack secured 2,100 prisoners.

**A battalion headquarters on Broodseinde Ridge, October 5, 1917. (A.W.M.)**

The day had been an especial disaster for Lieutenant General Sir A.J. Godley's II Anzac Corps, but this was not properly appreciated at headquarters far behind the firing line. An airman reported the sighting of signal flares at the final objective, and this news was gratefully accepted by the "top brass" as evidence of success. Plumer signaled GHQ: "I am of opinion that the operations of the 49th and 66th Divisions, carried out today under great difficulties of assembly, will afford II Anzac Corps a sufficiently good jumping-off line for operations on October 12th, on which date I hope that II Anzac Corps will capture Passchendaele."[9] There is no question that the High Command was woefully ignorant of conditions at the front. Up in the line, however, the full extent of the recent debacle was readily apparent. On October 10 a lieutenant surveyed the macabre sights of Ravebeek valley:

> The slope . . . was littered with dead, both theirs and ours. I got to one pillbox to find it just a mass of dead, and so I passed on carefully to the one ahead. Here I found about fifty men alive, of the [66th Division]. . . . Never have I seen men so broken or demoralised. They were huddled up close behind the box in the last stages of exhaustion and fear. Fritz had been sniping them off all day . . . the dead and dying lay in piles. The wounded were numerous—unattended and weak, they groaned and moaned all over the place.[10]

The speed with which the dead could be buried lagged well behind the pace of their accumulation upon the field of battle. Under a wan, neutral sky, the survivors went about their duties in a state of confusion.

Meanwhile, back in London, the political world continued to slowly turn. Lloyd George remained unconvinced of the High Command's competence, yet he was unable to persuade his ministers that he possessed a strategic vision of superior merit. Lloyd George, however, had not climbed to the political summit of the British state for lack of guile. In a bid to discover other strategic alternatives, the prime minister suggested that fresh military advisers be consulted. Lloyd George told the War Policy Committee on October 9: "If a patient was very ill no one would limit themselves to taking the advice of a family doctor. They would call in a second opinion."[11] When Robertson got wind of what Lloyd George had in mind, he offered his resignation to Lord Derby, the secretary of state for war.

On the evening of October 10, Lord Curzon called on Hankey, the War Cabinet's secretary, and told him the news of Robertson's offer to resign. Hankey recorded in his diary: "Curzon then went on to tell me that, if the Prime Minister drove out Robertson: Robert Cecil, Balfour, Derby, Carson, and he himself, probably, would leave the Government, which would then break up." The following day Hankey recorded:

> Before the War Cabinet I walked round St James's Park with Lloyd George. . . . I repeated Curzon's warning in very straight terms and he—Lloyd George —took the hint very quickly. I told Curzon what I had done and he said I had rendered a very considerable public service. Balfour [the foreign secretary], with whom I walked to the Foreign Office after the meeting, remarked on how admirable the Prime Minister had been. I told him of my warning to Lloyd George which he warmly endorsed.[12]

Lloyd George, a prime minister without a party, could not set aside the strongly held views of key political backers.

Faced by a political impasse, Lloyd George took a different tack and specifically sought the views of Field Marshal French and General Wilson; they were among the few senior soldiers not beholden to the whim and whimsy of Robertson's and Haig's patronage. The prime minister confided to Wilson that Robertson was "afraid of Haig, and . . . both of them are pigheaded, stupid and narrow-visioned."[13]

About this time the War Cabinet turned its attention to the question of losses in the still-unfinished Flanders campaign. Smuts pressed for detailed statistical information; Curzon and Lloyd George agreed that the War Office needed to be more forthcoming in that respect.

The battle of October 9 had not carried the front any appreciable distance toward Passchendaele ridge. Haig and Plumer, however, rashly chose to trust reports that the day had gone well. Orders were given for another attack on October 12 to complete the capture of the ridge. Near Nieuport, the Fourth Army remained poised for a descent on the Belgian coast. General Rawlinson wrote in his diary for October 10: "G.H.Q. sent a letter this morning saying we are to be prepared to carry out the coastal operation in its entirety at the end of the month if necessary."[14]

On October 11, the day before the next engagement, Field Marshal Haig granted an audience to the principal press correspondents. These troubled gentlemen were

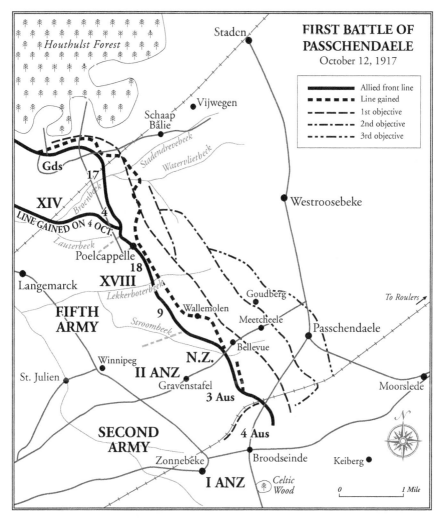

**FIRST BATTLE OF PASSCHENDAELE**
October 12, 1917

Legend:
— Allied front line
■ ■ ■ Line gained
— — — 1st objective
—·—·— 2nd objective
—··—··— 3rd objective

Houthulst Forest

Staden
Vijwegen
Schaap Bālie
Stadendrevebeek
Watervlietbeek
Gds
17
XIV
4
LINE GAINED ON 4 OCT.
Broenbeek
Lauterbeek
Westroosebeke
Poelcappelle
18
Langemarck
XVIII
Lekkerboterbeek
Goudberg
To Roulers
FIFTH ARMY
9
Wallemolen
Meetcheele
Stroombeek
Passchendaele
Winnipeg
N.Z.
Bellevue
St. Julien
II ANZ
Gravenstafel
Moorslede
3 Aus
SECOND ARMY
4 Aus
Zonnebeke
Broodseinde
Keiberg
I ANZ
Celtic Wood
0        1 Mile

**First Battle of Passchendaele, October 12, 1917**

appeased with the revelation that "we are practically through the enemy's defences. . . . It was simply the mud which defeated us on Tuesday. The men did splendidly to get through it as they did. But the Flanders mud, as you know, is not a new invention. It has a name in history—it has defeated other armies before this one." Haig added: "He [the German] has only flesh and blood against us, not blockhouses—they take a month to make."[15] For Haig the campaign had become an obsession; his lust to attain his stated objectives had a vice-like quality. Haig's persistence can be likened to the hopeful conceit of a compulsive gambler. The British Expeditionary Force (BEF) sailed onwards, rather like the ocean liner *Titanic* plowing through an ice field.

Preparations for the next attack took place in poor weather; ruined Ypres loomed drearily out of the mist beneath a slate-gray sky. Hundreds of seriously wounded soldiers from the previous attack still helplessly littered the forward zone awaiting a team of stretcher-bearers to carry them away. On October 11 cold showers fell in the morning and steady rain had set in by evening. Heavy, low-lying clouds packed the sky. Gough would recall: "It poured with rain . . . and in the evening I telephoned to Plumer to say that I thought the attack should be postponed. He said he would consult his corps commanders, and shortly after eight o'clock he called me up to say that they considered it best for the attack to be carried out. The only course for the Fifth Army was to follow suit."[16] During the rainy, pitch-black night of October 11/12, flares rose regularly from the German front, where the garrison was apprehensive and vigilant.

In the twilight dawn of zero hour on October 12, the drizzle turned to rain, which fell, on and off, throughout the day. On the outer left flank of the assault front, the French First Army and troops of the Fifth Army's XIV Corps made another short advance toward the ruined fringe of Houthulst forest. Farther south, XVIII Corps mustered two divisions for a futile attack. The creeping barrage laid down was flimsy and erratic. Shells from worn and unstable guns frequently fell short at random amongst British troops. According to Major Ewart: "Rain and mud constitute the chief explanation for the failure of the [9th] Division in this battle, which should not have been fought; no man could progress at more than a snail's pace, and sheer exhaustion was a factor more potent than the enemy in bringing the advance to a standstill."[17]

To the south of the Fifth Army, Plumer's Second Army attacked again along the spine of the ridge toward Passchendaele village. On the front of II Anzac Corps, the New Zealanders had relieved the 49th Division. When the New Zealanders

**Troops on Broodseinde Ridge, October 5, the day after the capture of the ridge.**

advanced, it was clear that something was amiss with the barrage from the lack of the usual sounds of intense gunfire. From the slopes of Bellevue spur German machine gunners in pillboxes, seemingly afloat in a sea of mud, fired upon heavily laden soldiers waddling through the slough. The rearmost waves of the two-brigade attack force closed up behind the leading waves; all were pinned down by grazing machine-gun cross fire. Astride the Gravenstafel-Bellevue road, and to the south of the road, deep wire entanglements had not been sufficiently breached by the inefficient bombardment. There was only a single lane through the wire at the sunken road; many men were killed by machine-gun fire in that gap, which was "a veritable lane of death."[18]

On the right flank of the New Zealanders, two brigades of the 3rd Australian Division advanced up the same shallow slope that had thwarted the 66th Division three days before. At the outset, sections and platoons moved forward steadily and soon neared the first objective line, which amounted to a gain of a thousand yards. Before long, however, the left-hand brigade was halted by enfilade fire from Bellevue spur on the northern flank. In spite of this setback, a party of twenty men managed to pick their way forward along the shallow Ravebeek valley. A German pillbox garrison was surprised and surrendered at Crest farm, which was a vital position on the final approaches to Passchendaele. The party went on to reach the shell-damaged village church, but, in the absence of support, soon made a hasty retreat; the Germans gratefully reoccupied Crest farm. Meantime, the division's right-hand brigade was forced to ground by heavy firing; these troops ended the day not far from the start line held at dawn, their notional objectives stranded upon the distant horizon.

To the south of the railway running from Ypres to Zonnebeke and Roulers, a brigade of the 4th Australian Division spent a difficult day covering the flank of the active battlefront. The embankment of the railway drew steady artillery fire; mangled heaps of the dead littered the embankment alongside those alive and seeking shelter.

On October 12 another thirteen thousand British casualties were lost in what would officially be called the First Battle of Passchendaele. Only a thousand Germans were made prisoner in the day's fighting.[19] A New Zealander brigadier wrote of the debacle:

> My opinion is that the senior generals who direct these operations are not conversant with the conditions, mud, cold, rain and no shelter for the men. . . . The Germans are not so played out as they make out. All the attacks recently lack preparation, and the whole history of the war is that when thorough preparation is not made, we fail. . . . You cannot afford to take liberties with the Germans.[20]

By now the dead and wounded lay in large numbers across the battle zone. A local truce on the afternoon of October 13 allowed parties from both armies to search for men half buried in the mud. Major G.S. Hutchison recalled: "The entry into the Salient had become nothing more or less than a plunge into a slough of filthy shell holes, amongst which hundreds of unburied dead grinned and gesticulated from

**An eighteen-pound field gun being hauled through the mud of Broodseinde Ridge, October 10, 1917. (A.W.M.)**

amongst miles of tangled wire and stunted trees."[21] The chronicler of the 7th Manchesters observed that "nothing green was visible anywhere. In fact the land looked as though it had been a very choppy earth-brown sea suddenly frozen to stillness."[22]

After the recent round of fighting, Crown Prince Rupprecht wrote gratefully in his diary: "Sudden change of the weather. Most gratifyingly—rain; our most effective ally." He added: "I am convinced that the British will continue to press home their attacks as long as they possibly can; that is to say for another four to six weeks. They certainly do not lack the troops. On the Somme they did not give up until the weather towards the end of November prevented a continuation of their attacks."[23] Rupprecht's thinking was on the right track. Field Marshal Haig was not ready to give up in Flanders; he recorded on October 14 that "the rain has upset our arrangements a good deal, but I still hope that the weather may take up before long."[24] At the heart of the BEF's misfortunes with the climate at Ypres in 1917 was the pattern of the rainfall. The dry weather of May and June greatly assisted the Messines operation; dry weather in September was of benefit to Plumer's set-piece attacks of that month. On the other hand, the heavy rains of August and October were an unmitigated disaster for British forces. In October 1917, 107 millimeters of rain fell; by comparison, the figure for October 1914 was 31 millimeters.[25]

General Home, the Cavalry Corps' chief staff officer, wrote on October 12 of the latest round of disappointments: "The weather has really broken and the luck is once more on the side of the Boche. I do not now think that there is a chance of using the Cavalry this year. I think if we get the Staden-Passchendaele Ridge we shall do well and cannot expect more."[26] The history of the Australians' 37th Battalion recorded:

Officers and men who were evacuated through Ypres to the casualty clearing hospital during the course of this battle, noted with amazement that the roads leading into Ypres were crowded with British and Indian Cavalry, awaiting orders to move forward to the battle zone. The battle orders had indicated that, in the event of complete success in this fight, the victory would be exploited by a dashing cavalry advance; but the actual situation was such that the presence of the cavalry seemed the height of absurdity. If both sides had ceased fire and invited the cavalrymen to use their best endeavours to reach the Passchendaele ridge, they could scarcely have crossed the sea of mud.[27]

Around this time Colonel Fuller of the Tank Corps was out driving with General Elles, the Tank Corps' commander. Out of the blue, they came upon a road crowded with cavalry. "At one place," wrote Fuller, "we pulled up for a few minutes to talk to some officers. We asked them: 'What do you imagine you are going to do? Have you any idea what conditions in front are like?' One answered: 'We are told there is a ridge of sand we can operate on.' I replied: 'Well, there was some sand three weeks back, but since then it has been blown off the map.'"[28]

On the morning of October 13, Haig, Plumer, Gough, and their senior staff met at the Second Army's headquarters. The conference decided to await an improvement in the weather before making further attacks. The next big push to seize the high ground at Passchendaele was to be spearheaded by the Canadian Corps, which was due to transfer into the salient.

The cavalry's chance to fight in Flanders had passed. Lieutenant Colonel W.T. Willcox of the 3rd Hussars recalled:

By 16 October it was evident that all hope of a breakthrough had been abandoned, for the division was ordered to march south. The weather was a steady downpour of rain, and the lines in an appalling condition, with the horses up to their hocks in mud. What the battlefield on the Passchendaele ridge must have been, Heaven knows![29]

The Cavalry Corps was earmarked to take part in a special and secret operation with the Third Army at the southern end of the BEF's front. Original plans were afoot for the cavalry in that army's sector. Fresh maps were set aside to be scored with arrows, markings, and timings in preparation for another flurry of blows.

By the middle of October, Plumer's Second Army lay bogged in the mud of Flanders, rather like Gough's Fifth Army in August. There was no longer any prospect of the Fourth Army's attack on the Belgian coast going ahead. General Rawlinson, the Fourth Army's commander, wrote in his diary for October 13: "Things have not been running at all smoothly—it is now clear that we shall do nothing on the coast here." Two days later, GHQ informed Rawlinson and Admiral Bacon that the amphibious landing was canceled.[30]

The 1st Division marched out of Le Clipon camp on October 21. Admiral Roger Keyes would soon succeed Bacon at the Royal Navy's Dover headquarters. Keyes was appalled by his predecessor's gung-ho plans for a descent upon the Belgian coast. "The attack, if it was ever delivered, would be a disaster, and the unfortunate division which was to carry it out would undoubtedly be annihilated."[31]

During the middle period of October, the press correspondent Repington visited France and spoke with Charteris.

> I find that he [Charteris] is strongly set upon continuing the Flanders offensive next
> year, and is most optimistic as usual. He has great ideas of the hurt that we have caused
> the Huns, and the number of divisions which we have "exhausted" as he terms it. I
> doubt whether they are much more exhausted than those which we take out of our own
> line after an attack. He believes that we can gain our present objectives, and next spring
> clear up to Ghent, and then be on the flank of the German line.[32]

All doors were open to Repington; after his interview with Charteris, he motored to Cassel—past horse lines, convoys of transport, and camps of white-stained tents—to speak with Plumer. Repington was informed that inclement weather had imposed a ten-day delay on further offensive operations. "I found Plumer," wrote Repington, "heart and soul for the Flanders offensive."[33]

On October 15, Repington visited GHQ. "I found Haig as firmly set upon the Flanders offensive as possible." Repington spoke at length with Kiggell, GHQ's chief of staff, who was of one strategic mind with Haig. "He [Kiggell] was convinced that the Huns must stand in Flanders and could not retreat elastically on the Hindenburg plan in this district. We should, therefore, be sure to find him, and, having gained the tactical mastery of him, should beat him." Kiggell brimmed with confidence:

> We [said Kiggell] should take the rest of the [Passchendaele] ridge and then continue
> next April, threatening the Hun coast defences on our left and Lille on our right. . . .
> The loss of the Belgian coastline would be a heavy blow to Germany, and no excuses
> could palliate it. He was prepared to stake his reputation that the Germans could not
> retreat without fighting foot by foot on the Flanders front, and that next year in from
> one or two months the operation would be concluded. Every attack which we made next
> year would draw more Hun divisions towards us and make the French task easier, so we
> must be ready to go on with blow upon blow as we are doing now, and for this strategy
> an assured supply of 500,000 drafts would be needed.[34]

Kiggell, whose place at GHQ granted him a unique angle of vision, discounted the possibility of a large transference of German forces from the eastern to the western front in the event of Russia's collapse.

In the meantime, Robertson's War Office did its best to support GHQ's interpretation of events. On October 17, General Maurice, director of operations at the War Office, provided the War Cabinet with the estimate that the Flanders offensive from

July 31 to October 5 had cost 255,000 German casualties to 148,470 British casualties.[35] Assessments of that kind helped to sustain Haig's belief that the Flanders offensive should be "the first and ruling feature of next year's general plan of operations on the Western Front." On October 17, Haig wrote: "I am decidedly of opinion that the British efforts [in 1918] should again be concentrated on the Flanders front. . . . In my opinion there is no other part of the Western Front where such great strategical results are obtainable by the forces available next year."[36]

The Canadian Corps was about to join the campaign at Ypres. The Canadians were an efficient, self-contained force and well able to perform the "corps" role in the Napoleonic sense of the term. Lieutenant Colonel Alan Brooke was a staff officer with the Canadian artillery. The perilous landscape to the east of Ypres was an appalling sight by this stage of the campaign. Brooke surveyed

> mile upon mile of mud and swamp with practically no roads. . . . I attended a conference which Douglas Haig ran at Canadian Corps H.Q. I could hardly believe that my ears were not deceiving me! He spoke in the rosiest of terms of our chances of breaking through. I had been all over the ground and to my mind such an eventuality was quite impossible. I am certain he was misinformed and had never seen the ground for himself.[37]

**Canadian troops passing the ruined Cloth Hall at Ypres. (A.W.M.)**

When the Canadians took over their new sector, an audit was made of the artillery they were to take under command. Of 250 heavy guns, only 227 were found, and of these, 89 were out of action. Of 306 field guns, less than half were in action, and these were dotted about the mudflats wherever a battery position could be found.[38]

The Canadians' commander was the forty-one-year-old Lieutenant General Arthur Currie. Before the war he had been a part-time militiaman pursuing a commercial career in insurance and real estate. On the western front Currie had commanded a brigade and then a division before his recent promotion to corps-level. A large, clean-shaven man, Currie would write: "Every Canadian hated to go to Passchendaele. . . . I carried my protest to the extreme limit . . . which I believe would have resulted in my being sent home had I been other than the Canadian Corps Commander. I pointed out what the casualties were bound to be, and was ordered to go and make the attack."[39] For better or worse, GHQ awarded pride of place to the Canadians for the next phase of the campaign.

Meanwhile, in the French sector of the western front, the preparations for Pétain's long-awaited attack in Champagne were now complete. On October 23 this operation went ahead, supported by 1,600 guns, almost two-thirds of which were of a heavy caliber. The German line in the Chemin des Dames sector was not strongly held given the relentless demands of the campaign in Flanders away to the north. The French Sixth Army attacked after a weeklong bombardment to make, in four days, a maximum advance of three and a half miles; 11,000 prisoners and 180 guns were taken. The Germans were driven behind the River Ailette, and on November 2 they evacuated their remaining positions on Chemin des Dames ridge.[40] The ridge and the full length of the road along its crest were now in French hands.

The French success in Champagne was swiftly overshadowed by some genuinely unexpected and dramatic events in the Italian theater of war. On October 24, Cadorna's army was attacked at Caporetto. An intense, six-hour bombardment of high explosives and gas was followed at 8 A.M. by a fog-covered infantry assault spearheaded by German divisions. A noteworthy and aggressive participant in the campaign was Captain Erwin Rommel of the Württemberg Mountain Battalion. By the third day of the offensive it was clear that Italian forces had collapsed in a tumultuous rout. In eighteen days Cadorna's troops retreated eighty miles through northeast Italy to the Piave River; the mouth of the Piave lay to the east of Venice. The Central Powers took 275,000 prisoners. The German divisions in Italy, however, were only on short-term loan to that front. Ludendorff had nominated the Piave River as their final objective.

When news of the debacle at Caporetto reached London, Lloyd George and the War Cabinet acted decisively to send aid to Italy. The prime minister wrote firmly to Robertson that an offer of assistance to Italy must be made at once. Robertson informed the prime minister on the 27th that orders had been given to send two British divisions to Italy "as soon as possible."[41] The French government also reacted quickly to the situation in Italy. In the weeks ahead, five British and six French divisions set out for the Italian front. The Caporetto disaster added weight to the argument that the Allies needed a more unified system of command to counter Germany's advantageous geographic position at the heart of Europe.

The sudden onset of disaster in Italy was swiftly followed by further unsettling news for the Western Allies. On the night of October 24/25, V.I. Lenin's Red Guards of the Bolsheviks launched a coup in Petrograd. On October 26 it was announced that a new government had been formed to lead the peoples inhabiting what had once been the Tsarist empire.

The weather in Flanders improved across mid-October. Fresh divisions came splashing into the wilderness of the salient, a place where Napoleon's "fifth element"—mud—had achieved supremacy. Instead of communication trenches, duckboard tracks were laid at ground level across the mudflats. Despite the dire state of the terrain, the next round of operations was due to commence on October 26.

The weather on October 25 was fine, but by midnight steady rain was falling. At 2:30 A.M. Gough telephoned Plumer's headquarters to request a cancellation. Harington, the Second Army's chief of staff, took the call and consulted Plumer. In turn, the Second Army's corps commanders were telephoned by Harington to ask their views.

> They all, with one exception, who did not express a definite opinion, agreed that it was impossible to stop the attack as the infantry had already been on the move for hours, and it would be impossible to get orders to them. General Plumer then took the telephone and I [Harington] remember his words so well: "Is that you, Gough? The attack must go on. I am responsible, not you. Good night and good luck."[42]

The rain that windy night fell on soldiers huddled under steel helmets and capes. The deep darkness of an overcast night was fleetingly lit up by the flash and glare of gunfire. The troops waited anxiously for the gray light of early dawn.

In the northern part of the salient, the Allied assault on October 26 went badly. The Germans were strongly posted in Houthulst forest, which loomed over that sector like a raised monument. In dire conditions, units of the French First Army edged a short distance closer to the southwest corner of the forest. To the south of the French, the battered Fifth Army's XIV Corps attacked with the 50th and 57th Divisions. The troops soon lost the creeping barrage's thin line of bursting shells in the heavy going; they were forced to ground in front of a line of pillboxes that spat scything machine-gun fire. Farther south, XVIII Corps attacked with the 58th and 63rd Divisions for a similar outcome.

On the front of Plumer's Second Army, the main thrust of the day was in the hands of the Canadian Corps. In the Canadians' left-hand sector, the 3rd Canadian Division attacked with two brigades. After zero hour, the assault began well behind an effective creeping barrage; the infantry swiftly crossed the broken-down wire entanglements that had held up previous attacks; German posts on the slopes of Bellevue spur were overrun. The war diary of the 43rd Cameron Highlanders of Canada recorded: "When dawn broke sufficiently our men could be clearly seen moving slowly over the skyline and round the two formidable-looking pillboxes on the crest of the ridge overlooking Battalion H.Q."[43] The situation seemed well in hand, but it transpired that only fifty men of the Camerons and two Vickers machine-gun crews were in position in front of the captured pillboxes near the vital crest line. In heavy rain the 52nd (Manitoba) Battalion was sent forward to help secure the position. About noon these troops reached Lieutenant Robert Shankland's isolated party and began to work southwards against those pillboxes still in German possession. Shankland would receive one of the three Victoria Crosses awarded to members of the 3rd Canadian Division that day. By nightfall the Canadians had established a firm footing on the high ground at Bellevue to the southwest of Passchendaele village; this was an important achievement given the setbacks of October 9 and 12.

In the Canadian Corps' right-hand sector, the 4th Canadian Division attacked on the southern side of the marshy Ravebeek stream, an obstacle that continued to blight the landscape. Some ground was gained in the morning and given up again in the afternoon; most objectives, however, were taken the following day with the aid of reinforcements. A detachment of Australian troops covered the Canadians' right flank to the south of the Ypres-Roulers railway.

In a subsidiary operation at the southern end of the Second Army's assault front, X Corps again attacked Polderhoek spur and Gheluvelt village in a bid to secure the elusive southeast corner of Gheluvelt Plateau. The 5th and 7th Divisions made few gains, if any; the survivors were demoralized and disillusioned. The silent corpses of the missing added to the litter of the battlefield.

On October 26, British forces suffered another twelve thousand casualties. Generals Cavan and Maxse of the Fifth Army advised Gough to postpone further offensive operations until the ground was hardened by frost. Ludendorff wrote of British methods in Flanders: "The enemy charged like a wild bull against the iron wall which kept him from our submarine bases. He threw his weight against Houthulst forest, Poelcappelle, Passchendaele. . . . He dented it in many places, and it seemed as if he must knock it down. But it held, although a faint tremor ran through its foundations."[44] General Birch, GHQ's artillery adviser, would report that October's Royal Artillery casualty toll was the highest monthly figure on record. He requested that the field artillery of the Second and Fifth Armies "at once be given the most sympathetic treatment possible, if it is to be an effective fighting force by the early Spring. In some cases batteries are much below establishment and the men are so tired and enervated that they have reached a state of listlessness."[45] On October 29, Captain M. Wheeler wrote of his battery's plight:

> I cannot attempt to describe the conditions under which we are fighting. Anything I could write about them would seem an exaggeration but would, in reality, be miles below the truth. The whole battlefield for miles is a congested mess of sodden, rain-filled shell holes which are being added to every moment. The mud is not so much mud as a fathomless, sticky morass. The shell holes, where they do not actually merge into one another, are divided only by a few inches of this glutinous mud. There is no cover and it

is of course impossible to dig. If it were not for the cement pillboxes left by the Boche, not a thing could live for many hours. The guns are all in the open and—most fantastic of all—many of them are in full view of the Boche. I must not say much about my own battery's position but to give you some idea of it, our gun was in water up to its breech and when it recoiled, the breech splashed under water.[46]

By late October the BEF had a sullen air. The unvarnished futility of the campaign rocked the foundations of faith of many soldiers. New drafts were soon infected by the prevailing mood of despondency. The flooded terrain and cooling weather caused rising rates of illness and tragic accidents. Detachments of military police actively performed their duties at Ypres in support of the policies of GHQ. From July to December 1917 there were 311 condemnations in British divisions and 45 executions; for those divisions in the salient, the figures were 264 and 43.[47]

On October 30 the Canadians attacked again on either side of the poisoned Ravebeek morass. A five-hundred-yard advance was made across the slope of slime. On the northern flank of the Canadians, XVIII Corps also lunged forward on lower and muddier ground for scant gain.

The weather leading up to November 6, the date of the next Canadian push, was relatively dry. The day itself, however, proved to be wet, windy, and cold. The objective of the 1st and 2nd Canadian Divisions was Passchendale village and an arc of ground farther to the east. Zero hour was 6 A.M., after which the troops advanced behind the usual rolling barrage; muzzle flashes flickered in the half-light; shells whined overhead; the ridge was again covered with bursting spouts of mud and black smoke. That morning the flattened village of Passchendaele was finally overrun. Low piles of rubble were all that remained of the village's housing. The capture of Passchendaele was in many ways an anticlimax: It crowned an advance of five miles after months of repeated slogging. Elsewhere on November 6, along the salient's southern shoulder, the 5th Division made another failed attempt to carry the ruins of Polderhoek Château.

By this time General Plumer had been ordered from Flanders to take command of British troops in Italy; he handed over the Second Army to Rawlinson, who was in need of employment given the retrenchment of the coastal operation.

On November 10, another day of rain, the Canadians made a further push northwards from the site of Passchendaele village; a short stretch of ground on the ridge was taken in the featureless waste; Westroosebeke village, however, remained in German hands.

In the engagement of November 10, the 1st Division covered the left flank of the Canadians. All autumn the 1st Division had been fattening up in camp at the coast, and from the viewpoint of GHQ, it seemed a shame not to involve the forgotten formation in the principal fiasco of the season. Instead of being sacrificed in a likely doomed descent on the Belgian coast, the 1st Division played the part of a forlorn hope on Passchendaele ridge.

As might have been predicted, the division's advance accomplished little; the 1st South Wales Borderers and 2nd Royal Munster Fusiliers plodded across a sea of mud behind an irregular barrage. A gap opened up, into which the Germans opportunistically counterattacked. A large part of the Munsters was lost; only 4 of 17 officers returned to British lines, and there were 400 other rank casualties. The South Wales Borderers lost 382 casualties, which was over two-thirds of the troops that went into action. A fresh crop of abandoned corpses was left behind in the mud and puddles of the crater fields. This careless massacre typified so much of what had unfolded over the futile campaign.[48] The Germans had been attacked unimaginatively at one of the strongest points of their strongest front.

Canadian casualties over the past month had reached 15,654. A member of the 16th Canadian Scottish wrote to a friend:

> I look back on the Passchendaele show as a nightmare. The ground was strewn with our dead. I have never seen anything to compare with the holocaust. When I think of shell-holes filled with water; the road leading up to the ridge heavily shelled day and night; wading through water, mud up to the knees; the stretcher bearers carrying out the wounded, eight men to a stretcher, and sometimes the whole party would be smashed up before they reached the dressing station, it makes me wonder how the troops stood it all.[49]

The final capture of Passchendaele village had created a fresh local salient that fingered eastwards from a narrow base. The BEF took only 2,135 prisoners from October 16 to November 12; many of these were secured by the Canadians.[50] Little more than a mile of ground was taken in the last month of bitter fighting.

The cost paid to gain parts of Passchendaele ridge was immense. Casualty statistics are often derived from government sources. Asquith said that the War Office "kept three sets of figures, one to mislead the public, another to mislead the Cabinet, and the third to mislead itself." Lloyd George once compared War Office statistics to sands of the desert, which were blown into an ever-increasing set of dunes depending on the direction of the wind.[51]

Officially, 244,897 British casualties were lost at Ypres from July 31 to November 12, 1917.[52] This figure, however, understates the Flanders toll by excluding the fighting at Messines, Nieuport, and in the Ypres salient during June and July 1 to 30 (excluding the 31st). According to official figures, for the whole of the western front the BEF lost 75,123 casualties in June and 84,695 in July.[53] A significant proportion of the losses for June and July were undoubtedly incurred in Flanders. A figure of 340,000 is arrived at when the excluded parts of the Flanders campaign are added into the calculation. And then there is the question of the French First Army, which lost 1,625 killed and missing and 6,902 wounded, to give an overall Allied toll in Flanders from the start of June to mid-November of 350,000.[54]

The Flanders campaign was also costly for the Germans. The waterlogged nature of Flanders made it difficult to dig the kind of deep dugouts that best protected troops from the attrition of shellfire. Pillboxes were often utilized to house machine-gun teams and unit command posts. Less fortunate troops had to trust to luck in shell holes and ditches. The German High Command's casualty figure for the Fourth Army was 202,000 for July 21 to November 10.[55] An estimate of 250,000 can be given if the period is cast back to the start of the Messines battle in early June. The Fourth Army's front stretched from the Lille-Armentières road, ten miles south of Ypres, to the sea.

The number of German prisoners taken in Flanders was 7,200 at Messines and 24,065 in the main Ypres offensive. The number of German guns captured by the BEF was sixty-seven and seventy-four for the two battle periods, respectively.[56] Incredibly, during the main three-and-a-half-month period of the Ypres campaign, the number of German guns captured was only marginally higher than the number taken at Messines in a matter of hours.

# 9

# The Switch to Cambrai

The heavy casualties at Ypres for little tangible gain was a blow to the Allied cause. Ministers in London were dismayed by what had transpired in Flanders. On the whole, Lloyd George's doubts about the venture proved to be well-founded. The prime minister confided to Hankey after a War Cabinet meeting that "he [Lloyd George] would not go on unless he obtained control of the war. He meant to take advantage of the present position to achieve this."[1]

Lloyd George had announced to the War Cabinet on October 30 that the need for an inter-Allied general staff was more urgent than ever. Field Marshal French and General Wilson had strongly supported that course of action in their recently submitted reports on future war strategy. The prime minister pointed out to the War Cabinet that, in the past, Allied conferences had been mere horse-trading exercises that reached down to the lowest common denominator when it came to planning strategy. On November 2 the War Cabinet agreed to support the policy of an Allied War Council. Lloyd George's negotiations with the French to create such a council were already well advanced.

On November 4, Haig and Lloyd George met in Paris. The prime minister was on his way to Italy for a conference of Allied leaders. Haig told Lloyd George that an Allied War Council and Staff would be "unworkable." In reply, Haig was informed that the matter was settled and he had best quickly adjust to the new situation.

Lloyd George, Smuts, Hankey, and Wilson arrived in Italy for the Rapallo Conference on November 5. Robertson was already at Rapallo, and he wasted no time telling Wilson of his opposition to the creation of an Allied War Council. Wilson, however, had lost patience with Robertson and wrote in his diary: "Since he [Robertson] has been C.I.G.S. we have lost Romania, Russia and Italy, and have gained Bullecourt, Messines and Passchendaele!"[2] The extent of the spectacular Austro-German success at Caporetto had brought into sharp relief the meager gains on the western front. The crisis in northeast Italy had been inflicted by the joint action of the Central Powers in a theater where the Allies had conspicuously failed to cooperate.

On November 6 the Rapallo Conference established the Supreme War Council "with a view to the better coordination of action on the Western Front" from the Channel to the Adriatic. It was hoped that an improved forum for debate and discussion might encourage more united and effective action when the next crisis arose. The safety and viability of the Italian front was now an integral part of strategy for the western front. The Supreme War Council was to comprise the prime minister and a member of government for France, Britain, and Italy, with meetings at least once a month. Each power was also to appoint a permanent military representative. General Wilson, given his knowledge of and sympathy for France, was appointed British representative. Lloyd George noted that Robertson was sullen and unhelpful at Rapallo.

In Paris on November 12, Prime Minister Painlevé publicly announced the establishment of the Supreme War Council. Lloyd George made a speech at the French War Ministry in which he emphasized the need to coordinate Allied policy-making; there had been too much "stitching" of plans together; there had been some Allied victories, but, he added: "When I look at the appalling casualty lists I sometimes wish it had not been necessary to win so many [Allied victories]."[3] A few days after this, Georges Clemenceau replaced Painlevé as France's prime minister. Clemenceau was the fourth French prime minister for the year of 1917. The building of effective relationships between Anglo-French leaders was continually undermined by the political game of musical chairs underway in Paris and London.

The first official meeting of the Supreme War Council opened at Versailles on December 1 with a delegation from the United States present. Cool heads felt that American reinforcements would cancel out the looming collapse of the Russian war effort. French leaders expected that Haig would be replaced as British commander in chief; Foch exclaimed to Wilson that Haig would "have to go owing to colossal losses and no gain."[4]

Once the muddy site of Passchendaele village had been secured, the battered Canadian Corps was withdrawn from the salient. The Germans were unsure whether or not the campaign in Flanders had run its course for the year. "Artillery fire remained lively," recalled Ludendorff, "the enemy's conduct was no different to that in the earlier pauses in the major assaults. The conclusion that the battle was at an end could not be drawn."[5] Haig, however, had decided to close down the Flanders campaign for the season. On November 15 the field marshal wrote to Robertson: "The positions already gained fell short of what I wanted to secure before the winter."[6] If left to his own devices, Haig fully intended to launch another grinding drive toward the Belgian coast in the spring of 1918; Passchendaele ridge would serve as the jumping-off point for that venture.

On November 14 the Fifth Army's headquarters was withdrawn into General Headquarters (GHQ) reserve; Gough's remaining stretch of front was handed over to the Second Army. The threat of a further attack at Ypres was maintained. In this critical sector, once dusk had fallen, a regular stream of flares headed skywards to shudder at the top of their graceful arcs before sinking back to earth. Lingering gas fumes made pillboxes difficult to inhabit. The British-held section of the ridge was partly overlooked from nearby Westroosebeke, to the north of Passchendaele village. Misinformed speculation that the Germans might retire from western Flanders of their own volition would amount to nothing.

Despite the extent of the disappointment at Ypres, the focus of Haig's ever-hopeful GHQ had shifted to another part of the British front, where preparations were underway for a tank-led attack by the Third Army. "The Passchendaele offensive had ended in mire and carnage," wrote Winston Churchill, "when suddenly there emerged from the British sector opposite Cambrai a battle totally different in character from any yet fought in the war."[7]

The German-held town of Cambrai, near the southern end of the British Expeditionary Force's (BEF) front, had a peacetime population of about twenty-eight thousand. The outskirts of Cambrai were eight to nine miles behind the German front, which in this sector featured the Hindenburg Line. Early in 1917, British troops had followed up the German retirement to the Hindenburg Line. On April 25, during the Arras campaign, GHQ ordered that a scheme for breaking the Hindenburg Line southwest of Cambrai be prepared by the headquarters covering that sector. The proposed attack front lay between the St. Quentin Canal and Canal du Nord. The works of the Hindenburg Line in this sector were substantial and featured fields of wire of an unprecedented depth. "Never before," wrote a British observer, "had such terrific barb-wire entanglements been encountered. A peculiarly heavy type of wire had been employed and there were several rows of entanglements of a thickness hitherto undreamt of."[8]

In accordance with GHQ's instructions, the staff of III Corps submitted a plan to the Third Army's headquarters on June 19 for an attack to capture the villages of Havrincourt and Flesquières. A force of six divisions was deemed necessary for the operation. The Third Army's commander, General Sir Julian Byng, did not take up the plan, though this preparatory work set the scene for the attack that eventually took place at Cambrai in terms of frontage and troop numbers.

Byng would play a central role in the Cambrai operation launched in late November. The fighting could not have gone forward in the shape it took without Byng's strong support and advocacy. Born in 1862 and the youngest of the 2nd Earl of Strafford's thirteen children from two marriages, Julian Byng joined the 10th Hussars after Eton and a spell in the Militia. Byng was a tall and self-sufficient young man; he saw active service early in his career in eastern Sudan at the 1884 Battles of El Teb and Tamai. Back in Britain, a period as regimental adjutant was followed by attendance at the Staff College.

In the Boer War, Byng led the South African Light Horse and larger mobile columns principally composed of colonial troops. In the Edwardian decade, Byng commanded cavalry brigades; this was followed by a posting to Cairo in 1912 to oversee

**General Sir Julian Byng. (A.W.M.)**

garrisons in Egypt and the eastern Mediterranean. On the whole, Byng was popular with his contemporaries, a capable public speaker, and pragmatic in his thinking.[9]

In the war against Germany, Byng's first appointment in France was with a cavalry division; command of a cavalry corps and then an infantry corps followed, including a stint at the Dardanelles. In May 1916, Byng's big break came when he was given command of the Canadian Corps, a cohesive and permanent set of divisions. The Somme campaign was followed by the impressive Canadian capture of Vimy Ridge in April 1917. Byng's promotion to the Third Army in early June was based on genuine achievement.

The initial bout of planning for a possible attack in the Cambrai sector did useful work, but after that was set aside, an outside intervention was needed to rekindle interest in the project. This intervention was provided by the Tank Corps and the deadlock in Flanders. On August 2, Colonel Fuller, the Tank Corps' chief staff officer, had toured the flooded Ypres battlefront, after which he wrote a memorandum for General Elles, the Tank Corps' commander, outlining the situation.

> From a tank point of view, the Third Battle of Ypres may be considered dead. To go on using tanks in the present conditions will only lead to good machines and better personnel being thrown away, but also to a loss of morale in the infantry and tank crews, through constant failure. From an infantry point of view, the Third Battle of Ypres may be considered comatose. It can only be continued at colossal loss and little gain.[10]

Fuller went on to propose that a tank-led attack be made in a more suitable sector. "In order to restore British prestige and strike a theatrical blow against Germany before the winter, it is suggested that preparations be at once set on foot to take St Quentin." The town of St. Quentin was near the southern end of the BEF's front, not far from the junction point with the French army. Elles pointed out to Fuller that GHQ was unlikely to welcome French involvement in a British-planned battle. Fuller recalled: "I then stepped up to a large map of our whole front which was pinned on the wall of my office, and having looked at it for a minute or so, I placed my finger on the area immediately south of Cambrai and said: 'Well, why not here?'" Elles agreed with that choice and suggested a large raid be proposed, as that was the type of venture most likely to win the approval of GHQ.[11]

Fuller briefly outlined a scheme in writing and gave it to Ellis on August 4. Four days later, Fuller produced a more detailed plan entitled "Tank Raids." This plan envisaged a hit-and-run raid of eight to twelve hours' duration. The aim was to inflict loss on the enemy, and not to capture ground. Fuller proposed using a force of three tank brigades each of two tank battalions, one or two infantry or dismounted cavalry divisions, and the usual quantity of artillery given the size of the force involved. The raid would take place on an eight-thousand-yard front and aim "to raid the reentrant formed by the L'Escaut–St Quentin Canal between Ribecourt-Crevecoeur-Banteux." This pocket opposite Cambrai was to be cleaned out by the assault force. "The spirit of such an enterprise," wrote Fuller, "is audacity, which should take the place of undisguised preparation. . . . We must abandon the obvious and rely on surprise and the unexpected."[12] Smoke barrages could be utilized to screen the advance of the tanks. The trailblazers of the Tank Corps had always been drawn to the idea of a tank assault en masse to create chaos in a sector favorable to that type of operation. The effective use of tanks had the potential to economize the expenditure of the lives of infantrymen, who were no longer in abundant supply. Under the right circumstances, tanks might crawl like giant beetles across no-man's-land, crush barbed-wire entanglements, and successfully enter a German trench system. The rolling chalk downland near Cambrai would provide firm terrain for a *coup de main* by tractored vehicles.

Meanwhile, Elles had wasted no time; on August 4 he took Fuller's scheme to GHQ, where it elicited some interest from General Davidson, the chief of operations.[13] Given that the proposed tank raid was to take place in the Third Army's sector, Fuller also wanted the scheme shown to General Byng to win his support. "That evening [August 4]," wrote Fuller, "I dined with Hardress-Lloyd [III Tank Brigade's commander] and discussed the Cambrai project with him. He was much taken with it and suggested that G.H.Q. should be urged to carry it out. I told him that it was useless the Tank Corps thinking of doing this; but that, should General Byng do it, it would stand a better chance. Hardress-Lloyd said he knew Byng well, and would see him the next day."[14]

On August 5, Hardress-Lloyd visited Byng and the two men discussed ideas for using tanks on the Third Army's front. Hardress-Lloyd and the Tank Corps were no strangers to the Hindenburg Line, as tanks had attacked it near Bullecourt during the spring offensive of 1917. (At that time Hardress-Lloyd had commanded the Tank Corps' D Battalion.) The attack of April 11 was a ghastly failure and involved a single company of D Battalion's tanks and infantry of the 4th Australian Division.[15] This failed attack on the Hindenburg Line made it abundantly clear that a greater mass of tanks was needed for success; the engagement also made clear that surprise was needed to give the tanks the best chance to cross no-man's-land unscathed. Fuller later stated: "Though the [first] battle of Bullecourt . . . was a complete failure, from a tank point of view it was one of those turning-points which are decisive in the history of an army."[16]

In addition to the Bullecourt precedent, the lobbying of Byng by Hardress-Lloyd fell on particularly fertile ground, as the Third Army's commander was already well acquainted with the Tank Corps. Byng's Canadians had worked with tanks during the 1916 Somme campaign. In the spring offensive of 1917, Byng had again been involved with tanks. A tank detachment of Hardress-Lloyd's D Battalion took part in the Canadian Corps' attack on the Vimy heights, though the rough ground at Vimy proved too difficult for them to be effective.

In respect to the Cambrai sector, Byng had the strength of perception to see that fresh life could be breathed into III Corps' plan of June 19 by the involvement of tanks. The armored vehicles of the Tank Corps were the ideal weapon to lead a surprise attack through the dense wire entanglements of the Hindenburg Line. Byng seems to have been genuinely excited by the possibilities of the scheme and enthusiastically supported it henceforward with all of his authority and power of personality.

Byng's main contribution to the detailed planning of the Cambrai battle was that he expanded Fuller's scheme for a raid into a much larger operation. On August 6, which was the day following the visit of Hardress-Lloyd, the Third Army's commander visited GHQ and suggested a tank-led attack south of Cambrai for September 20.[17] Byng recalled: "Sir Douglas Haig was much taken with the idea and was backed up by General Davidson. Then Kiggell came in and, when he heard of the project, he shook his head and said: 'The British Army cannot win a decisive battle by fighting in two places at once; we must concentrate every man in the Ypres area.'"[18]

There was now another pause in the planning of the Cambrai battle. This impasse was broken by the sheer weight of disappointment generated by the August stalemate in the Ypres salient. Shrewd observers could see that nothing much was likely to come from such a flawed campaign. In the meantime, Elles, the Tank Corps' commander, had visited the Third Army's sector to see for himself the places nominated by Fuller as ideal for tanks. On September 5, Byng, after meeting with Elles, again pressed GHQ to support a tank-led attack along the lines proposed in early August.[19] Byng remembered that Haig showed some interest in the scheme:

> But the fact remained that at this time it did not seem possible that our [Third] Army could undertake this; the difficulties of railway transport, and everything of that sort,

seemed so great that it was almost decided not to attempt it. However, the Commander-in-Chief told us to think it out and carry on with what few preparations we could make. And we did so.[20]

On September 16, Byng went to GHQ again with a more detailed plan. He spoke with Haig and asked for extra infantry drafts for the proposed attack. Byng also envisaged a dramatic role for the Cavalry Corps in the exploitation phase of the battle. Haig, though preoccupied by the Flanders campaign, sent Davidson, GHQ's chief of operations, to discuss matters further with the Third Army's staff.[21]

On October 13, with the push toward Passchendaele ridge reduced to a crawl, Haig gave permission for Byng to start the preparations needed for the Cambrai operation. Byng visited GHQ on October 15 to meet with Haig, who promised to provide the necessary additional troops required for the attack. Byng had hoped to use the Canadian Corps at Cambrai, but he would soon lose that formation to the voracious demands of Passchendaele.

On October 19, Elles informed Fuller "that an extensive tank operation was to take place on the Third Army's front on 20 November, and at the exact place selected by me on August 4, and outlined in my project of August 8." Elles and Fuller went on a reconnaissance of the Cambrai sector. "It was a wonderful sight from a tank point of view," recalled Fuller, "especially after Ypres; the ground was perfect 'going.'"[22] The final plan, as put together by the Third Army's staff, drew upon the work undertaken by III Corps earlier in the year, the ideas of the Tank Corps, and the desire of senior commanders to involve a large force of cavalry. Despite the enormous and profligate losses of the Flanders fighting, Haig determined to roll the dice and try his luck with a new battle at Cambrai. While the German front had not crumpled at Passchendaele, another sudden push elsewhere on the BEF's front might reap the territorial gains yet to be realized in Flanders.

On October 26 a Third Army conference was held at which corps commanders were told of the scheme to attack a stretch of the Hindenburg Line southwest of Cambrai on a frontage of ten thousand yards. Up until this time planning for the attack had been a closely guarded secret. Byng explained to his audience that a surprise attack led by tanks was to break the front, after which the cavalry were to pass through and roll northwards past Cambrai and Bourlon to the Sensee River. This would threaten the rear of the German defensive front in the Arras sector.

The Third Army's prospective assault frontage lay between the St. Quentin Canal and the Canal du Nord. These two canals were on the southeastern and northwestern flanks of the battle zone, respectively. The moat-like St. Quentin Canal was filled with water to a depth of six or seven feet, but the Canal du Nord was still under construction and there was no water in the excavated channel. The countryside thereabouts was firm, rolling meadowland broken by ridges and narrow valleys. The sector's pristine landscape of relatively undamaged villages and woods was "rather like Salisbury Plain, but somewhat less poor and bleak."[23]

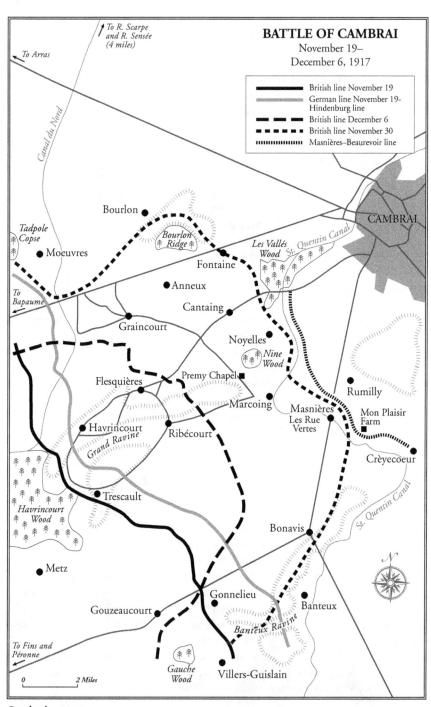

**BATTLE OF CAMBRAI**
November 19–
December 6, 1917

| | |
|---|---|
| —————— | British line November 19 |
| —————— | German line November 19-Hindenburg line |
| – – – – | British line December 6 |
| ▪ ▪ ▪ ▪ | British line November 30 |
| ▮▮▮▮▮▮ | Masnières–Beaurevoir line |

To R. Scarpe and R. Sensée (4 miles)

To Arras

Canal du Nord

Tadpole Copse

Moeuvres

To Bapaume

Bourlon

Bourlon Ridge

Fontaine

Anneux

Cantaing

Graincourt

CAMBRAI

Les Vallés Wood

St. Quentin Canal

Noyelles

Nine Wood

Premy Chapel

Flesquières

Marcoing

Rumilly

Masnières
Les Rue Vertes

Mon Plaisir Farm

Havrincourt

Grand Ravine

Ribécourt

Crèyecoeur

Trescault

Havrincourt Wood

Metz

St. Quentin Canal

Bonavis

N

Gonnelieu

Banteux

Gouzeaucourt

Banteux Ravine

To Fins and Péronne

Gauche Wood

Villers-Guislain

0    2 Miles

**Cambrai sector**

The deep and well-drained trenches of the Hindenburg Line's forward system were ten to twelve feet wide in places and designed with tank-proofing partly in mind. An outpost zone of disconnected trench lengths covered the forward system. Deep dugouts and well-built gun pits were features of the defensive layout. The vast aprons of still-unrusted barbed wire gave off a sinister blue sheen in the weakening autumnal sunlight. Two to three thousand yards behind the Hindenburg Forward System lay the Hindenburg Support System, which also comprised a front and support trench and belts of wire. Farther to the rear, a third system of less well-developed defenses formed a reserve line. Behind the stretch of front to be attacked, Flesquières Ridge was the principal feature in the middle distance; to the north of Flesquières, Bourlon Wood hovered like a dark cloud upon the ridge of that name and commanded the surrounding countryside.

The operation at Cambrai was due to be launched on November 20. Haig decided to proceed as scheduled even though the unfolding crisis in northeast Italy had compelled him to send troops to that theater. The field marshal understood, however, that it was necessary to proceed at Cambrai with circumspection. There was the distinct possibility that more British troops might soon be ordered to Italy by the War Cabinet. Byng was informed that the Third Army's attack would be halted after forty-eight hours unless the situation justified a continuation of the offensive.[24] A wait-and-see attitude, on this occasion, seemed appropriate. Haig reassured Robertson on November 15 that "the nature of this operation is such that it can be stopped at once if it appears likely to entail greater losses than I can afford."[25]

The Third Army's finalized plan of November 13 stated: "The object of the operation is to break the enemy's defensive system by a *coup de main*; with the assistance of tanks to pass the Cavalry Corps through the break thus made: to seize Cambrai, Bourlon Wood, and the passages over the Sensee River and to cut off the troops holding the German front line between Havrincourt and that river."[26] Two infantry corps—Lieutenant General Sir Charles Woollcombe's IV Corps on the left and Lieutenant General Sir William Pulteney's III Corps on the right—would lead the assault. The Cavalry Corps' full strength of five divisions and 27,500 cavalrymen would then be flung into action to exploit the breach created by the infantry. Behind the front, the three divisions of V Corps were held in reserve; these troops would enter the battle "as the action develops." V Corps was "allotted the task of advancing North and North-east to exploit success as far as the River Sensee and to push advanced guards across the Sensee River to gain and hold the heights north of the river."[27] The Third Army's specific instructions to the Cavalry Corps said that the main tasks on "Z-day" were to "surround and isolate Cambrai"; to "secure the crossings on the River Sensee between Paillencourt and Palluel (inclusive)"; and to secure the flanks of V Corps as it advanced northeastwards to the River Sensee. Toward the end of the instruction was the reminder that the "conduct of the Cavalry should be as actively offensive as possible."[28]

Of the Third Army's corps commanders to be involved in the main attack, Lieutenant General Woollcombe of IV Corps had commanded a division in the Somme campaign of the previous year; he was promoted to command IV Corps in January 1917 having proved himself a willing executive of GHQ's bludgeoning style of battle. Lieutenant General Pulteney had commanded III Corps since it was formed in August 1914; he had been passed over for promotion to army-level on every occasion such an appointment was made. As for the Cavalry Corps' General Kavanagh, he had started the war as a cavalry brigade commander, after which he moved up to a division and then a corps command. Given the importance of the cavalry branch to Haig, it can only be presumed that somehow Kavanagh had earned the commander in chief's approval. By this stage of the war, younger and more dynamic officers might have been given corps-level appointments. On the whole, however, it suited Haig to surround himself with obedient, aging, and mediocre subordinates; there was almost no risk that men such as Woollcombe, Pulteney, or Kavanagh would ever gain sufficient political support to topple the field marshal from his throne at GHQ.

The Third Army was the southernmost of the BEF's armies, which meant that the French sector was nearby. Haig informed Pétain of his intention to attack at Cambrai. The French, after all, were Haig's ally and could not be kept in the dark. In a bid to cooperate with the British, Pétain allotted two cavalry and three infantry divisions to take part in the exploitation phase of the battle; these troops were disposed within striking distance of the Cambrai sector. If the Third Army could establish a bridgehead over the St. Quentin Canal at Crèvecoeur, on the right flank of the projected battle front, that was Haig's preferred location for French involvement.

On November 19, Haig moved to an Advanced GHQ at Bavincourt, ten miles southwest of Arras, to keep a close eye on the Third Army's activities. Charteris predicted that Germany would not be able to transfer a significant number of divisions to France from the eastern front before winter set in. Haig later wrote: "To maintain his defences . . . [in Flanders] the enemy had been obliged to reduce his garrisons of certain other parts of his line to a degree which justified the expectation that a sudden attack at a point where he did not expect it might attain a considerable local success."[29] It might be added that the recent French success on the Aisne had also drawn in German reserves to patch up that part of the front.

All three of the Tank Corps' brigades and all nine tank battalions were concentrated in the Cambrai sector by rail to deliver a sledgehammer blow. Tank Corps staff would have preferred to use tanks at selected key points and hold back a reserve, but given the depth of the Hindenburg Line's wire entanglements, the infantry needed the support of tanks right across the attack front. No risks could be taken in that respect. I Tank Brigade was to lead out the infantry of IV Corps; II and III Tank Brigades would do likewise for III Corps. Each tank battalion had 36 tanks plus 6 more in reserve. There were available 378 fighting tanks, 54 supply tanks, 32 tanks for widening gaps in the wire, and 12 more tanks for sundry tasks to give a grand total of 476.[30]

Tank units were assembled close behind the British front at designated "tankodromes." Havrincourt Wood provided ample cover in that locality. Low-flying aircraft droned overhead at night to accustom the Germans to unusual mechanical sounds. The width of the main trenches of the Hindenburg Line was a potential hazard for tanks. To help the tanks cross particularly wide trenches, they were to carry fascines—compressed brushwood tightly bound by chains—on a giant pair of arms. The fascines could be dropped into any trench encountered that threatened to ditch a tank. This method was no guarantee of success, but anything that might prevent the nose of a twenty-seven-ton Mark IV tank plunging too deeply into the bottom of a trench was of value.

The infantry units earmarked to take part in the Cambrai attack conducted training exercises with tanks. Some units had previously worked with tanks, but others were not so familiar with the tank concept. Practice trenches were dug and belts of wire erected to prepare troops for tackling the fabled Hindenburg Line. Field Marshal Haig visited some of this training. He explained to a group of subordinates on November 13: "The object of the operations of the Infantry aided by Tanks is to break through the enemy's defences by surprise and so to permit the Cavalry Corps to pass through and operate in open country."[31] The infantry's training with tanks was hurried, though sufficient for what lay ahead; the infantry learned to follow tanks in files instead of advancing in waves behind a creeping barrage. A brigade commander of the 6th Division recalled that his units did their pre-battle training with tanks represented by soldiers carrying flags.

Colonel Baker-Carr's I Tank Brigade was to work with the 51st and 62nd Divisions of IV Corps. At a planning conference at corps headquarters, Baker-Carr found enthusiasm for the upcoming operation in short supply.

> Uncle Harper [Major General G.M. Harper of the 51st Division] plainly demonstrated by his attitude that he thoroughly mistrusted the entire plan. He actually said little during the meeting, but after it was over, he took me on one side and described the whole conception as "a fantastic and most unmilitary scheme." Up to the last moment he was completely lukewarm and, as I learned years later, had not hesitated to communicate his apprehensions to his brigade commanders.[32]

The 51st Division had worked with detachments of tanks in battle earlier in the year, but not on anything like the scale in prospect. Harper, a former GHQ staff officer who possessed a luxuriant crop of white hair, was concerned that the highly visible tanks might draw additional fire onto nearby infantry. The infantry of the 51st Division was instructed to advance in waves behind the tanks at a distance of 150 to 200 yards, rather than follow them in files more closely, as advised in the Third Army's training note on tank-infantry cooperation: "Infantry should keep from 25 to 50 paces behind the Tank as it enters the wire."[33] Fuller drew to the attention of Byng's chief of staff, Major General L. Vaughan, that Harper was tracing an unsound tactical tangent of his own devising, yet higher authority chose to let Harper run his own show.

In contrast to Harper, the 62nd Division's Major General W. Braithwaite soon "became a confirmed tank enthusiast." Braithwaite, who had been General Sir Ian Hamilton's chief staff officer at Gallipoli, was won over by the tanks' robust performance on a demonstration obstacle course built behind the front. Tank Corps personnel were accustomed to climbing their steel monsters "in and out of trenches like performing elephants" to win the approval of highly ranked onlookers.[34]

The 62nd Division had not taken part in the Flanders campaign. The 51st Division, however, had endured a lot of hard fighting across 1917. According to the division's history:

> The Division had not been long in rest in its new area [after leaving Ypres] before it transpired that it was again required to take part in active operations [at Cambrai]. The news that this was the case came rather as a shock, as the Division had already fought battles in the year 1917 on 9-12 April, 23-24 April, 16 May, 31 July-1 August, 20-23 September, and had lost in casualties since 9 April 457 officers and 9966 other ranks—a total of 10,523.[35]

The 51st Division was made up to strength for the Cambrai engagement with an influx of recruits and recovered wounded. Harper's division was not the only formation facing this predicament. Most of the BEF's infantry divisions had been rotated through the campaign for Passchendaele. The severity of the fighting over the past nine months meant there was only a limited pool of "fresh" divisions available in late November.

The recent Flanders offensive had been loudly advertised by a protracted preliminary bombardment. The artillery had treated the campaign as an exercise in static siege warfare. The Tank Corps' staff, however, wanted none of that, and insisted that surprise and undamaged ground was essential to maximize the prospect of success. The Tanks did not want a shell-cratered landscape, nor warning given of the approach of their slowly moving vehicles.[36] There would be no artillery fire prior to the operation's commencement; even shots to register the range were forbidden. The barrage would be fired "off the map" at zero hour. Colonel Gervase Thorpe of the Third Army's staff recalled that this notion was unpopular with artillery officers when it was proposed, yet Byng backed the viewpoint of the Tank Corps and insisted that surprise was of paramount importance.[37] The innovative requirements of the Tank Corps compelled the gunners to recant the clumsy methods of Passchendaele.

A thousand guns were assembled to support the Third Army's attack. Of these, 684 were field guns and the rest were of a heavier caliber, mostly sixty-pounders or six-inch howitzers.[38] Given the undoubted strength of the Hindenburg Line, the number of heavy guns allotted to the Cambrai operation was surprisingly low. At this time, however, guns were not plentiful in the BEF; artillery losses at Passchendaele had been unprecedentedly high and a strong force of artillery remained in Flanders in case of unforeseen developments.

The scale of the surprise barrage to be employed at Cambrai certainly posed novel problems for those artillery officers directly concerned. Nevertheless, it should be remembered that those batteries long-resident on the Cambrai front had the range already registered.[39] British forces had been sitting in front of the Hindenburg Line near Cambrai for a period of months. British gunners from a variety of units, formations, and headquarters knew a lot about the German defensive layout from day-today observation and aerial photography. When reinforcing artillery units arrived for the upcoming battle, they benefited from the technical advice of those units already in the sector.

A barrage fired off the map at zero hour was unlikely to be as accurate as a carefully registered barrage. To make allowance for that, the guns were hastily mapped by field survey teams to fire well clear of advancing tanks and infantry, which were not expected to closely follow the barrage. The opening bombardment would not be the usual creeping barrage; rather, the barrage would be "lifted" into the German front a set distance at timed intervals. The use of a "lifting" barrage was in some respects a step backward in gunnery technique to the flawed methods of 1915–1916. The main shortcoming of a lifting barrage was that the lifts forward often bounded over entire stretches of a defensive line. (Certain aspects of the opening bombardment have sometimes been attributed to Brigadier H.H. Tudor of the 9th Division, but neither Tudor nor his division took part in the Cambrai assault.)

The guns and supplies of ammunition were positioned ahead of time and left crouching under camouflage canvas and netting. After nightfall, batteries were pushed as far forward as possible to reduce the range and the difficulty of the opening shoot. In a bid to improve accuracy, the calibration of some guns was tested at a range behind the front. Meteorological information in respect to wind and air temperature was factored into gunnery calculations. On the morning of the attack, the British artillery would outnumber German guns opposite by an enormous margin.

The Royal Flying Corps' III Brigade was to support the attack with 289 aircraft.[40] In addition to this, the RFC Headquarters' Ninth Wing and units of I Brigade RFC would also take part in the battle. British air supremacy during the opening phase of the assault was more or less guaranteed. If the weather permitted, aircraft would strafe and bomb targets at low level. Squadrons designated to support the attack practiced low-level flying in the days leading up to the operation's commencement.

# 10

# The Tank Corps
# and the Hindenburg Line

Cambrai was a quiet backwater across the summer of 1917. The sector earned a reputation among German forces as a rest area—a sanatorium—from the savage fighting underway in Flanders. The German troops covering Cambrai belonged to General Georg von der Marwitz's Second Army, the left-hand army of Crown Prince Rupprecht's army group.

The countryside around Cambrai was firm and reasonably dry; ground mist and low cloud helped to shield British preparations from the eyes of German airmen, as did the longer, shrouding nights of November and the wide no-man's-land in front of the Hindenburg Line. Indeed, from November 12 onwards there was consistent foggy weather. Interestingly, on October 28 on the Cambrai front, the Germans recovered the body of a British soldier who had been killed two days earlier in a patrol clash. Upon examination, no badges or identification marks were discovered, but "when the contents of the man's wallet were examined, he was found to be carrying the insignia of a British tank unit."[1] In the absence of corroborating evidence, and given the ongoing campaign in Flanders, German intelligence staffs decided not to read too much into the incident.

On the ten-thousand-yard front that British forces were preparing to attack, the three systems of the Hindenburg Line were held by the equivalent of two German divisions. Lieutenant General Oskar Freiherr von Watter's 54th Division, a veteran of the August fighting at Ypres, held the middle portion of the front to be attacked—from Havrincourt to La Vacquerie. The division's headquarters was located at Cambrai. As the main defensive line was sited on a forward slope, observation into the British front was limited. The 54th Division's sector was divided into regimental sectors; as a rule, each regiment had one battalion in the forward zone, one in support, and one farther back in reserve. The first two systems of the Hindenburg Line were well constructed; the rear line, however, had received limited attention and was little more than marked out on the ground in places. A lot of laboring work was required of German troops to build up and maintain such an extensive set of defenses on a long front. Regular raids were made to identify British units opposite. The 54th Division was supported by only thirty-four field guns, a small number of heavy guns, and limited stocks of ammunition.

Somewhat surprisingly, General von Watter had trained his divisional artillery regiment to fight tanks. Watter's own background was in horse artillery, and he had studied the news of the tanks' debut in the Somme campaign with keen professional interest. Across the winter of 1916–1917 he had commenced training his 108th Field Artillery Regiment to engage a moving vehicular target over open sights. Artillerymen were taught how to use guns in a mobile role rather than the static positional firing that had become the norm. In April 1917 the 108th Field Artillery Regiment had engaged French tanks during the Aisne-Champagne campaign. In August in Flanders the gunners had added to their experience of fighting tanks, this time British.[2] Training and experience were important to mastering the challenge of switching from indirect to direct firing at short notice.

The 20th Landwehr Division was on the 54th Division's northern flank; the 9th Reserve Division was on the southern flank. Parts of those two flanking divisions would be caught up in the initial assault. These divisions all belonged to Caudry Group (XIII Corps), which was under the command of General Theodor Freiherr von Watter. (The Watters were cousins.) To provide Caudry Group with a reserve, the 54th Division's left-flank 27th Reserve Regiment was withdrawn from the line and replaced by a regiment of the 20th Landwehr Division and other Landwehr troops.[3] (Landwehr units were composed of older men and were generally regarded as less efficient than other German units.)

Cambrai was well served by railway lines should it prove necessary to quickly reinforce the sector. This was no accident: The Hindenburg Line had been sited with that requirement in mind. The German military's recent successes in Russia had made it possible to transfer troops to the western front. Flanders no longer needed urgent reinforcement; this meant that the sector covering the Cambrai rail junction could receive reinforcement instead. On November 19, General Otto Havenstein's 107th Division began arriving at Cambrai after a long journey from Russia that had lasted several days. It was intended to give the division a week to settle down in northern France, after which it would relieve troops in the line.

The Germans had received fragmentary hints of an impending offensive near Cambrai from prisoners and intercepted radio signals. Yet, in the event of a big attack, the defenders expected ample warning in the form of the usual drawn-out preliminary bombardment. The obvious strength of the Hindenburg Line's defenses may have lulled its garrison into a sense of security. Army Group Crown Prince Rupprecht issued an appreciation on November 17: "For the time being it is improbable that major attacks will occur anywhere. Minor operations in the 2nd and 6th Army sectors are still possible. . . . It is possible to envisage that the British, if they abandon their offensive in Flanders, may move to secondary operations in other areas."[4]

On the night of November 17/18, a German raid took six prisoners in the Cambrai sector. From these prisoners the Germans seem to have gained the impression that a local attack on Havrincourt village was imminent, but nothing more than that was learned. On the evening of November 19, the 54th Division was put on high alert by General von Watter given the accumulated signs of unusual activity opposite. The 27th Reserve Regiment was returned to the 54th Division from corps reserve. In the event of a local attack, the 54th Division would have the support of the 107th Division once that formation had detrained at Cambrai.[5]

The preparatory period for the Third Army's operation passed without giving away concrete news of the surprise attack. The war diarist of the 10th Rifle Brigade archly noted that "for the first time a serious attempt at secrecy is being made."[6] To keep the Germans in the dark, the assault divisions moved up to the line marching by night and then spending the day in villages, woods, or beneath camouflage canvas screenings. When reconnaissance parties of the 51st (Highland) Division visited the front, they wore trousers instead of kilts to avoid raising any suspicions that the division might be in the neighborhood. Mail back to Britain was halted for a brief period. The front trenches were held by troops from those units already in place. Troops of the 36th Division held the outpost line of all the divisions of IV Corps due to attack.

During the night before the assault the tanks were drawn up a thousand yards from the German wire. General Elles's order of the day to tank commanders on the eve of battle read:

> Tomorrow the Tank Corps will have the chance for which it has been waiting for many months—to operate on good going in the van of the battle. All that hard work and ingenuity can achieve has been done in the way of preparation. It remains for unit commanders and tank crews to complete the work by judgement and pluck in the battle itself. In the light of past experience I leave the good name of the Corps with great confidence in their hands. I propose leading the attack of the Centre division.[7]

This was a great opportunity for "a newer and less socially popular corps" to make its mark.[8] A resolute Elles boarded Lieutenant T.H. de B. Leach's "Hilda" tank. Fuller later wrote of this: "At first I remonstrated with him, pointing out that if he were badly wounded or killed, it would be disastrous for the Tank Corps. But he held out and persisted, and he was right and I was wrong. To lead his command was to give life and soul to all our preparations—it was spiritually the making of the Tank Corps, and in value it transcended all our work."[9]

The early morning of November 20 was dull, cool, and misty. A soft wind wafted across the countryside from the southwest. The Third Army's Artillery Instructions stated: "Before Zero hour the normal night firing programme will be carried out. It is necessary that there should be no increase of fire, and it is almost equally important that the night should not be abnormally quiet."[10] During the night before the assault it was unclear if the Germans had learned of the upcoming attack. Brigadier General A.T. Anderson of the 62nd Division recalled:

> The night of the 19th was a very anxious time and will long be remembered by all who took part in the battle. It was impossible to tell whether the enemy had any suspicions of what was in store for him. . . . If he did know, the enemy might wreck the attack before it began by bombarding the long line of guns, which had the most definite orders on no account to fire a round till 6.20 A.M., when the attack was to be launched. As it happened, the Boche showed great uneasiness and fired very heavily during the night, though fortunately not on any vital places.[11]

Six British infantry divisions and three tank brigades stood poised to attack. At 6:10 A.M., when it was still dark, the tanks began to drive forward in low gear to their start line, drivers peering through the narrow aperture of the slit that provided a restricted field of vision. By late November the hours of daylight on a typical northern European day were sharply reduced compared to high summer, and this necessitated a relatively late zero hour.

At 6:20 A.M.—zero hour—the German front line was struck by a thunderous bombardment; sudden flashes of gunfire rippled across the front. Amid the mass of bursting shells, showers of incandescent rockets rose up calling for help. A battery commander, Major E.F. Norton, wrote of the bombardment: "The batteries were literally flank to flank in two long lines as far as the eye could see, the rear tier firing over the front tier at 200-300 yards distance. The synchronisation was excellent and it was a most impressive sight to see the hillsides burst into a perfect sheet of flame."[12] As part of the attack's preparation, more than 4,000 gas projectiles were fired at Bourlon Wood.

The engines of the tanks roared as they moved out into no-man's-land; the machines gradually grew more visible as the dull light of early dawn strengthened. A tank battalion was divided into companies of twelve vehicles. A tank company could cover the advance of an infantry battalion. Each company was divided into sections of three tanks. In most instances, the sections advanced in a triangular formation, with one tank at the tip and the other two tanks at the points of the base followed by files of infantry. As was explained by one divisional historian: "The general principle on which sections were to work was for the two outside tanks to cross a trench, turn alongside it and help to clear it, while the centre tank carried on to the next trench, there to be joined by the two others as soon as the infantry had reached the first trench."[13]

For this engagement, British gunners had a large stock of smoke shells to build up a screen in designated places to shield the lumbering vehicles. In addition to that, the front was helpfully blanketed in dense fog, though this proved a double-edged sword insofar as it badly hampered the work of aircraft of the Royal Flying Corps. A fogbank might suddenly part to give a pilot a clear view of the ground below, only for mist to drift over again just as quickly.

On the southern flank of the attack front, III Corps' divisions—6th, 20th, and 12th—made rapid progress into the German front. Infantrymen strode out with rifles slung to traverse a no-man's-land that was hundreds of yards wide in places. Cigarettes were lit, and for the fortunate, the start to proceedings seemed like a very noisy training drill. The German defensive barrage was decidedly thin and fell on fixed areas, which the infantry was able to skirt around and avoid. For the Germans peering into the foggy twilight of dawn, the tanks were a terrible apparition that appeared with little warning; men in exposed outposts fled or surrendered when the clanking and throbbing line of mechanical tractors slowly lurched out of the gloom.

The 12th Division was the assault's right-flank formation. Two infantry brigades of the division attacked with tanks of two battalions. The first objective—the Hindenburg Forward System—was soon secured. As planned, the tanks crushed paths through the wire and rolled on to tackle machine guns threatening to shoot down the following infantry. When tanks reached the German trench lines, they raked the fleeing occupants with machine-gun fire. Where tanks broke down or ditched unexpectedly, the infantry had to regroup and fight their way forward regardless. By late morning the troops had advanced five thousand yards to take almost all of the Hindenburg Support System, which was the second objective. The 12th Division

"Hyacinth" tank of H Battalion ditched near Ribécourt on November 20, 1917. (Imperial War Museum)

152

*Chapter 10*

would now form a defensive flank for III Corps on Bonavis Ridge. Three hundred eighty-three prisoners were taken, mostly from the 19th Reserve Regiment of the 9th Reserve Division, along with twelve guns.

To the left of the 12th Division, the 20th Division attacked with a pair of brigades. Retaliatory German shelling was slow to start and generally ineffectual. The first objective was reached by 10 A.M. The advance to the second objective proved more difficult, and eleven tanks were knocked out by artillery fire. Nonetheless, both the 60th and 61st Brigades had completed their tasks by 11 to 11:30 A.M. The division's reserve brigade came forward to pass into the lead; the target for these troops—later in the day—would be the third objective, the Hindenburg Reserve System. Prisoners were taken from the 90th Reserve Regiment, the left-hand regiment of the 54th Division.

In the left-hand sector of III Corps, the 6th Division was to attack on a frontage dominated by the village of Ribécourt. The 71st Brigade was the division's left-hand brigade and the 16th Brigade the right-hand brigade. The 6th Division was near the center of the Third Army's attack front. For the sake of the entire operation, the assault in this sector needed to be a success. Ahead of the 6th Division, the Hindenburg Line's outposts were from 250 to 750 yards distant and hidden from view by the curve of the ground. Tanks of II Tank Brigade's B and H Battalions were to cooperate with the 6th Division. General Elles rode into battle in a vehicle of H Battalion, the Tank Corps' flag on prominent display. According to Major S. Foot: "Red, Brown and Green were the colours [of the flag]—red for fire, brown for mud, and green for the open country beyond."[14]

On the 71st Brigade's front, Lieutenant Colonel B.H.L. Prior of the 9th Norfolks watched the leading line of tanks

> starting across No Man's Land—a wonderful spectacle in the half light of early morning. Ponderous, grunting, groaning, wobbling, these engines of war crawled and lurched their way toward the enemy lines, followed by groups of men in file. Overhead our shells were pouring over . . . but the slowness of those tanks! It is at these moments that one itches for quickness and rapidity, and the slow, deliberate action of these monsters was exasperating.[15]

The thick belts of wire of the forward system were broken down by the tanks; German artillery fire was scattered, and British infantry following the tanks reached the second objective by 11 A.M. The most heavily defended point on the divisional front proved to be Ribécourt village. The 6th Division took prisoners from both the 387th Landwehr Regiment and the 90th Reserve Regiment. Landwehr troops in the Ribécourt sector had been shocked by the weight of the sudden assault.

> Spectral beings, which soon revealed themselves as the outline of tanks, loomed up out of the fog. Immediately our rifle and machine gun fire clattered against them. It was an extremely uncomfortable sensation to discover that our fire did not appear to have any effect at all on the tanks. The protective barbed wire was also a failure: the wires tore

apart and clung together in heaps. The tanks crossed the trenches, pouring fire down into them with their main armament and machine guns. They then pushed on into the depth of the position, leaving follow-up waves to complete the destruction of the trench garrison.[16]

The width of the main trenches proved insufficient to halt many tanks. One of the exceptions was Elles's "Hilda" flag-tank, which ditched in front of Ribécourt. The Tank Corps' commander returned to his headquarters on foot.

In the northern sector of the attack front, IV Corps' divisions—36th, 62nd, and 51st—began proceedings in fine style. In the center of the corps-sector, the 62nd Division attacked from the northern side of Havrincourt Wood with two brigades. Tanks of G Battalion and one company of E Battalion advanced with the 62nd Division. The troops had carried Havrincourt village by 10:15 A.M. The 2/6th West Yorkshire lost more than 150 casualties in the assault on Havrincourt Château.

Havrincourt village was held by German troops of the 84th Regiment (54th Division). Lieutenant Adolf Mestwarb of the 84th Regiment wrote that soon after the bombardment commenced

the sentry standing next to me suddenly made an extraordinary remark. His actual words were, "*Herr Leutnant*, something four-cornered is coming!" I looked and immediately recognised that it was a tank; the fascine perched on its roof did indeed give it a square appearance. . . . We opened fire immediately—unfortunately without making the slightest impression on this monster.

It carried on towards us, firing, then veered off to the left so as to make room for those following it, who were emerging one by one from the corner of the wood to our front. What a superb target this wood corner would have made for our artillery! But there was no sign of any such intervention; not a shot landed. From the minute the tanks first appeared I shot off flares. I eventually fired off every flare I possessed but nothing happened. The telephone had been put out of action immediately.[17]

Mestwarb was taken prisoner after being wounded by fragments of a hand grenade. Lieutenant Adolf Saucke of the 84th Regiment recalled that after the bombardment had passed through his position, "the entire area to the front was cloaked by fog. Behind us a yellowish-grey wall of smoke rose into the sky, caused by the incessant exploding shells. I was rather surprised about how little damage the enemy shelling had caused. The trench was almost untouched; there had been barely two or three direct hits." Saucke would also end the day as a prisoner. As he was trudging to a holding cage, "our accompanying guards told us that the British had occupied Cambrai. Worn down mentally and physically we could not bring ourselves to doubt their word and, heads hanging low, we trudged towards a dismal, inglorious future."[18]

On the northern flank of the 62nd Division, the 36th Division attacked successfully with the 109th Brigade; the other two brigades of the division were held in corps reserve. This attack, on the western side of the Canal du Nord, began at the later time of 8:35 A.M. The 36th Division had no supporting tanks, and the division's

**Infantry of the 51st Division crossing a trench at Ribécourt, November 20, 1917. (I.W.M.)**

task was to cover the flank of the main operation. It was counted upon that the German defenders of this stretch would be demoralized by tanks pushing behind their flank from the 62nd Division's sector. That proved to be the case. The local German garrison retired in haste, and the 109th Brigade secured five hundred prisoners.[19]

The main drama of the day involved Harper's 51st (Highland) Division, the right-hand division of IV Corps. This formation had the vital task of securing Flesquières Ridge. The 51st Division had orders to overrun a sector that expanded appreciably in width at each stage of the projected advance—fifteen hundred yards at the frontal system, twenty-seven hundred yards at the second system, and wider again at the reserve system. The infantry was to cooperate with the tanks of two battalions: D Battalion and two-thirds of E Battalion. The ground ahead of the 51st Division sloped down toward the first system of the Hindenburg Line, and then ran upwards to Flesquières village, round which snaked the double trench lines of the Hindenburg Support System. Beyond Flesquières the ground sloped gently downhill to the villages of Cantaing and Fontaine-Notre-Dame.

The attack of the 51st Division was launched on a two-brigade front, the 153rd Brigade on the left and the 152nd Brigade on the right. The divisional history noted that the opening bombardment was no more than "a light artillery barrage . . . just in front of our assembly trenches."[20] The tanks, shrouded by the blue-gray smoke of their exhausts, flattened the thick fields of wire to create paths for the infantry to pass through. Captain D. Sutherland of the 1/5th Seaforth Highlanders wrote of this phase of the attack:

> At 6.20 A.M. after a quiet and almost silent night, the tanks crossed our front line, waddled through our own wire, and then proceeded across an almost unshelled and grassy downland slope towards the Boche front line. Each lumbering monster flattened out in his track all the barbed wire he crossed over, leaving a path nine or ten feet wide, still rather prickly with the flattened wire, but quite passable, wherever they crossed. Some had dragged behind, on long chains, what might be called for want of a better term four-pronged anchors, and when these caught in a stretch of barbed wire and the tanks went on, scores of yards with iron posts and all complete followed, and the twisted up mass was dropped at one side, leaving a clear way of advance. Allowing the tanks a start of one or two hundred yards the first wave of infantry followed, and were soon in the first Boche trench.[21]

The Highlanders overran the front system of the Hindenburg Line in an exemplary fashion with a wave of four battalions and modest losses. Hostile machine-gun fire was "wild and harmless" and the defensive barrage scattered. For instance, the 1/5th Seaforths lost 4 killed and 21 wounded in exchange for more than 250 prisoners. The 1/5th Gordon Highlanders lost 6 killed and 56 wounded and claimed 400 prisoners. (Prisoners were from both the 387th Landwehr and 84th Regiments.)[22] Lance Corporal R. MacBeath of the Seaforths was awarded the Victoria Cross for capturing a battalion headquarters in a deep dugout.

A standing smoke barrage was kept in front of Flesquières Ridge to protect the tanks from hostile fire as they climbed the hillside. Major W.H.L. Watson of the Tanks' D Battalion wrote of the scene:

> Beyond the enemy trenches the slopes, from which the German gunners might have observed the advancing tanks, were already enveloped in thick white smoke. The smoke-shells burst with a sheet of vivid red flame, pouring out blinding, suffocating clouds. It was as if flaring bonfires were burning behind a bank of white fog. Over all, innumerable aeroplanes were flying steadily to and fro.[23]

To tackle the Hindenburg Support System, a second wave of four battalions leap-frogged into the lead. Twenty-four tanks had been specifically set aside to spearhead this phase of the attack; the railway line along the Grand Ravine was a well-situated forming-up point. The objectives of the second wave were Flesquières village and a section of the sunken Marcoing-Graincourt road beyond Flesquières. At 9:30 A.M. the tanks and following infantry headed uphill toward the Hindenburg Support System, which was hidden behind the crest of the ridge.

On the front of the right-flank 152nd Brigade, the 1/6th Seaforths and 1/6th Gordons led the way. The Hindenburg Support System comprised a well-built trench behind belts of heavy wire, with a second trench a hundred yards to the rear.

The village of Flesquières lay behind this system and featured a château at its south-west corner, complete with walls and wooded grounds. British heavy artillery had shelled Flesquières village at intervals during the morning.

The day seemed to be going well for British troops, only for a calamity to strike the attackers. In quick succession, the six tanks in front of the right-flank 1/6th Gordons were all hit by artillery fire soon after they appeared on the skyline of Flesquières Ridge. The guns that did the damage had been pulled out of pits on the slope behind the crest and opened fire at a range of five hundred yards or less. The infantrymen trailing behind the tanks were cut down by machine-gun fire as they hunted for gaps in the fields of wire. To make matters worse, the attackers were now at the limit of the protection of their own artillery barrage, which simply melted away once the range became too great.[24]

To the left of the 1/6th Gordons, the 1/6th Seaforths were led by seven tanks into the Hindenburg Support System. The tanks passed through the wire and enabled the infantry to get a foothold in the first trench, but the tanks were severely punished by artillery fire as they pushed onwards from there. A party of soldiers got near the southeastern corner of Flesquières village, covered by the fire of immobilized tanks, but the defenders were too strongly posted in the château and nearby houses to be dislodged.

Farther to the left, in the sector of the 153rd Brigade, ten tanks led the way uphill with the infantry in waves 150 yards behind. The 1/7th Gordons was the brigade's right-hand battalion. These troops entered the first trench of the German system, took one hundred prisoners, and, assisted by tanks, reached the next trench in spite of fierce resistance. A foray was made by British infantry into Flesquières village, only for the survivors to be driven out again. A German counterattack regained much of the second trench line.

On the left of the 153rd Brigade's front, the 1/7th Black Watch reached the Hindenburg Support System about 10:35 A.M.; two hundred prisoners were taken, many from the 27th Reserve Regiment. Beyond the front trench, however, the leading tanks were knocked out and the infantry halted by uncut wire and heavy fire from the village.

Several batteries of the German 108th Field Artillery Regiment contributed to the defense of Flesquières Ridge. In the Tank Corps' D and E Battalions twenty-eight tanks were knocked out by artillery fire.[25] A stalemate lasted in the Flesquières sector for the rest of the afternoon, despite local efforts by parties of British troops to fight their way forward. This was in no small measure because some of the 54th Division's reserve—the 27th Reserve Regiment—was committed to the battle for Flesquières Ridge in a timely manner. Major Erich Krebs of the 27th Reserve Regiment took over command at Flesquières after the commander of the 84th Regiment was killed.[26]

Across Flesquières Ridge the knocked-out tanks lay dotted about the landscape; the charred remains of incinerated crews littered the burnt-out wrecks. Supporters of the Tank Corps blamed the debacle at Flesquières on the infantry trailing too far behind the tanks, meaning they were unable to shoot down the crews of the German guns with rifle and Lewis gun fire. The Tank Corps' General Elles, who took part in the attack with H Battalion in an adjoining sector, later wrote that the use of "waves" by Harper's division, rather than "worms," was "very faulty" tactics and "in some degree" responsible for the failure at Flesquières. According to Elles:

> The "waves" took a long time to get through the gaps in the wire and, as a result, the tanks going up the hill were 150-200 yards ahead of their supporting infantry. I know this because I saw it. If the infantry had been in "worms" on the tail of their tanks I am quite sure we should not have had all our losses on the reverse slope and Flesquieres must have fallen very much more rapidly than it did.[27]

This engagement, however, also revealed just how vulnerable slow-moving tanks were to a well-organized anti-tank defense.

There were other reasons that contributed to the 51st Division's failure to carry the Hindenburg Support System. For instance, the artillery barrage covering the advance barely reached Flesquières, as the barrage depended upon the eighteen-pound field gun, which lacked the range needed to reach vital targets. In addition, the British heavy artillery seems to have made no impression on the German guns behind the crest of Flesquières Ridge. It was always likely that a significant body of German artillery would shelter behind Flesquières Ridge. The firing of British heavy artillery was undoubtedly hindered by indifferent weather during the morning; this prevented airmen from seeing much of what was taking place on the ground. Nevertheless, the British counterbattery effort at Flesquières was a near complete failure in a portion of the battlefront where it needed to be effective.

**The wrecked tank "Edinburgh II" of E Battalion on Flesquières Ridge. (I.W.M.)**

Another important reason for the daylong setback of Harper's division was that the division's reserve brigade was not committed to action on November 20. This was a remarkable blunder and gravely undermined the plan of the overall battle. The line of German defenders clinging to Flesquières was thin, and vulnerable to a concerted blow by fresh troops. Harper's division was the only one of the Third Army's five main attacking divisions to be held up by the Hindenburg Support System during the daylight hours of November 20. The 51st Division was also the only one of those divisions not to use its reserve brigade to help secure distant objectives. Harper's headquarters was four and a half miles behind the original front line and poorly located for making the relatively quick decisions needed during a mobile battle. To the immediate left and right of Harper's sector, the 62nd and 6th Divisions had all three of their brigades in action by late morning. These troops would bypass Flesquières on both flanks as the day wore on. If Harper had used his reserve brigade to support the attack on Flesquières, his division may well have made better progress. IV Corps headquarters seemingly left Harper to do as he pleased. The evidence suggests that Harper's lack of confidence in the Cambrai battle plan made him unwilling to throw his division wholeheartedly at Flesquières.

# 11

## Bring Forward the Cavalry

By late morning on November 20 the Cambrai attack seemed to be progressing well, apart from the holdup at Flesquières. It was now time for the cavalry to enter the fray and play their designated part in the battle. During the previous night the leading cavalry divisions had moved up to Fins, close behind the front. Fins was also the location of the Cavalry Corps' headquarters. For some days past the cavalry had been taking elaborate precautions to avoid detection by German aircraft while they gathered behind the Third Army's front.

Before the main body of the cavalry could be committed to action, III Corps needed to capture the Hindenburg Reserve System on the far side of the St. Quentin Canal. The reserve system was the third and final of the Hindenburg Line's systems. The St. Quentin Canal ran roughly south to north, but looped from east to west near the villages of Masnières and Marcoing to run parallel to the British front for three miles between the Hindenburg Support System and the Reserve System.

While the 12th Division, III Corps' right-hand formation, formed a defensive flank, tanks and troops of the rest of the corps set out for the St. Quentin Canal. The 20th Division's reserve brigade—the 59th—had moved forward from La Vacquerie after 9 A.M. The 59th Brigade was to seize crossings over the canal at Masnières and hold this bridgehead until reinforcements arrived to continue the advance. Ten tanks from the detachment working with the 20th Division were to assist the 59th Brigade's advance on Masnières. The 11th Rifle Brigade led the way, followed by the 10th Rifle Brigade, with the other two battalions of the brigade bringing up the rear.

German troops driven out of the forward systems fell back ahead of advancing troops of the 59th Brigade to avoid capture. The left-forward company of the 11th Rifle Brigade took 150 prisoners at a strongpoint to the south of Marcoing Copse after a brief struggle.[1] Meanwhile, Les Rues Vertes, on the south bank of the St. Quentin Canal, was entered by the right-forward company of the 11th Rifle Brigade.

A bout of street fighting was needed to clear the village. British infantry pressed on to the main bridge leading from Les Rues Vertes to Masnières, a village on the north bank of the canal. German troops, however, had the bridge covered by sufficient fire to prevent the British from crossing.

Meanwhile, on the left flank of III Corps, the 6th Division's reserve brigade—the 18th—made good progress toward Premy Chapel Ridge. The 1st West Yorkshire and 2nd Durham Light Infantry advanced over the ridge to capture a German battery at bayonet point. Ahead of British troops lay Marcoing, which was on the near side of the St. Quentin Canal; this village was taken by tanks and infantry in a brisk fight soon after midday. The rail bridge over the canal at Marcoing was mined, but a quick-thinking tank officer cut the detonator leads in the nick of time to prevent demolition. By 12:30 P.M. British infantry had taken possession of Marcoing station on the far side of the canal.

The day was a great success for the 6th Division. Casualties were about 650 in exchange for German prisoners of 28 officers and 1,227 other ranks, along with 23 captured guns and 40 to 50 machine guns. The 2nd Durhams lost only 23 casualties and the 14th Durhams had just 7 men wounded. The 1st West Yorks had 1 killed and 13 wounded.[2] These were the losses of a minor action in the Boer War or a brisk fight with a tribal raiding party on India's northwest frontier. Major General T.O. Marden, the 6th Division's commander, observed: "Everything had gone like clockwork."[3]

In order to give the thrust of III Corps the weight needed to carry the Hindenburg Reserve System, the Third Army had provided III Corps with an additional division. This division—the 29th—acting as the "nose of the bullet," was to pass through the 6th and 20th Divisions and "occupy the Masnieres-Beauvoir [Hindenburg Reserve] line from the eastern edge of Masnieres to Nine Wood (inclusive)."[4] One company of tanks of A Battalion was to support the 29th Division.

After zero hour, the 29th Division had tramped forward to occupy the original British front line. As the battle was unfolding well, at 10:15 A.M. General de Lisle had asked for permission to advance, which was granted by the staff of III Corps. De Lisle, a former cavalryman, was keen to swing into action given the long distances to be traversed on foot by his troops to reach the final objective, most of which lay beyond the St. Quentin Canal.

The 29th Division advanced with all three of its brigades—86th, 87th, and 88th—in line abreast. Training for the battle had placed an emphasis on maneuver and the need for all commanders to display initiative. The Vickers machine guns of the division went forward on the backs of mules. The two brigades on the flanks of the divisional line advanced "in diamond formation with a battalion at each point, so that if the leading battalion was unable to advance, the flanking battalions by continuing to advance would automatically turn the flanks of the defenders."[5]

On the right of the 29th Division's front, the 88th Brigade headed for Les Rues Vertes and Masnières with the 1st Essex and four tanks in the lead. On a low ridge they met a German field battery at two hundred yards, and three tanks were knocked out. British infantry swiftly captured the guns and took seventy prisoners. This engagement delayed the Essex unit, which was overtaken on the right by the 4th Worcesters. Upon reaching the St. Quentin Canal, the Worcesters put two companies across via a lock to the east of Masnières; these troops, however, were soon driven to ground by machine-gun fire.

At Les Rues Vertes, tanks and infantry of the 20th and 29th Divisions lined the south bank of the canal facing German-held Masnières. Tanks shelled Masnières with their six-pound guns. In a bid to break this impasse, about 12:40 P.M. a tank attempted to cross the canal by the main bridge leading into Masnières. F22 "Flying Fox II" was the first tank to test the crossing. When the tank lumbered onto the bridge, which was partly damaged by demolition, the weight of the vehicle caused the steel girders to give way, and the broken bridge and tank subsided. The tank gave off a cloud of steam, and the crew scrambled clear to safety.

Further efforts were made during the afternoon to get infantry over the canal by lock bridges suitable for foot traffic on either flank of Masnières. The 88th Brigade's Royal Newfoundland Battalion crossed the canal to the west of Masnières and dug in on the far side. By 10 P.M. elements of all four of the brigade's infantry units had crossed the canal.[6]

A battalion of the 20th Division's 59th Brigade was ordered to push eastwards from the vicinity of Les Rues Vertes to Crèvecoeur. Troops of the 11th Rifle Brigade moved out late in the evening. The bridge at Mon Plaisir farm and the nearby lock were captured. An attempt to approach Crèvecoeur, however, was repelled by heavy

**The broken bridge over the St. Quentin Canal at Masnières with the tank "Flying Fox II" stuck in the wreckage. (I.W.M.)**

fire. This put an end to tentative plans to establish a bridgehead over the canal at Crèvecoeur.

The central of the 29th Division's brigades was the 87th Brigade. A morning fog still hung in the air when the advance of that formation got underway. The 87th Brigade moved with its four battalions in a square formation and with each battalion in diamond formation. The advance through the wire and captured German fieldworks was relatively uneventful, though smoke, mist, and the sounds of firing nearby were evident. The 1st King's Own Scottish Borderers and 2nd South Wales Borderers led the way to Marcoing Copse and the St. Quentin Canal. The 1st Borders and 1st Inniskilling Fusiliers followed behind the leading pair of battalions. There were three bridges or locks on the 87th Brigade's canal frontage.

The 87th Brigade passed companies across the St. Quentin Canal by the railway bridge at Marcoing and the lock that led to the station. A few of the brigade's supporting tanks also crossed the canal at Marcoing. Farther to the right, infantry traversed the canal by a lock near Marcoing Copse. This lock bridge was taken after a machine-gun post on the far side was put out of action. The King's Own Scottish Borderers and South Wales Borderers formed a bridgehead over the canal. At 2:30 P.M. the Borderers and Inniskillings passed through and advanced up an open two-thousand-yard slope toward the Hindenburg Reserve System. These troops came under fire soon after leaving the shelter of the canal bank and worked forward by short rushes. Fifty German prisoners were taken, but the wire of the reserve system was unbroken and no further progress was made.[7] At nightfall, the 87th Brigade had the bulk of its troops in a bridgehead position between Marcoing and Masnières. British troops could see a distant image of Cambrai's landmarks some three miles away.

On the left of the 29th Division's front, the 86th Brigade's objective was a stretch running from the near side of the St. Quentin Canal to Nine Wood. The 16th Middlesex led the way to the wood with a section of tanks. Germans among the trees opened fire, but were suppressed and the wood secured. The 1st Royal Guernsey Light Infantry came up on the left of the Middlesex unit and connected with the 6th Division at Premy Chapel. On the right of the brigade's front, the 2nd Royal Fusiliers reached their designated objective at about 3:15 P.M. (The 1st Lancashire Fusiliers was the brigade's other infantry battalion.)

To the left of the 6th and 29th Divisions lay the assault frontage of IV Corps. The corps' right-flank 51st Division was held up at Flesquières throughout the afternoon. To the left of the 51st Division, the 62nd Division was the formation allotted the all-important task of securing Bourlon village and Bourlon Wood. After the 62nd Division's assault brigades had hacked a path into the defenses of the Hindenburg Line, the division's reserve brigade—the 186th—passed into the lead. The commander of the 186th Brigade was Brigadier General R.B. Bradford VC, who was twenty-five years of age and the youngest general in the army. The brigade was supported by a company of tanks and King Edward's Horse.

The advance of Bradford's force began well, though six tanks were put out of action by two guns at the edge of Graincourt. British infantry secured Graincourt by

**Captured German field guns at Graincourt. (I.W.M.)**

3:30 P.M., but wire and machine-gun fire slowed the advance, which stopped short of Bourlon Wood.

The failure to capture Bourlon Ridge on November 20 would prove costly. In hindsight, the set of tasks given the 186th Brigade was highly ambitious for a single brigade. A force of at least two brigades was probably needed to attack Bourlon Ridge with any prospect of success. As had been the case with Harper's 51st Division, the attack of the 62nd Division was the responsibility of IV Corps headquarters, which again showed itself in a poor light. An extra brigade might have been secured from the Third Army's reserves.

On the German side of the lines, concrete news of a large-scale British attack opposite Cambrai had reached Caudry Group headquarters during the morning. The three infantry regiments of the 107th Division was the only sizeable reserve close to hand when the crisis broke. At 9:40 A.M. the 107th Division was instructed to send two battalions of the 227th Reserve Regiment to Masnières and the regiment's third battalion to Crèvecoeur, farther to the east. The 232nd Reserve Regiment was sent in haste to positions covering the southwest and westerly approaches to Cambrai.[8] The 52nd Reserve Regiment was placed under the command of the 54th Division.

About midday Major Fruehling of the 52nd Reserve Regiment reported to General von Watter at the 54th Division's headquarters. Fruehling was ordered to send battalions to Cantaing and Fontaine. Motor lorries were used to move part of Fruehling's regiment. These troops emerged from Cantaing late in the afternoon and drove off a British cavalry patrol before occupying the site of the nearby Hindenburg Reserve System.

Nonetheless, there was a degree of confusion and delay surrounding the dispatch of the 107th Division's units. If the German front was to hold at Cambrai, much depended on the speed of the 227th Reserve Regiment's arrival in the Masnières sector. This regiment set out in late morning, and its commander, Major Buchholz, passed through the village of Rumilly, which was under artillery fire. Buchholz went on to Masnières, where he found the rear headquarters of the 90th Reserve Regiment. The telephone line to the regiment's forward command post was cut, and much of that unit had been overrun in the opening attack. After completing his reconnaissance, the self-reliant Buchholz set up an observation post behind Rumilly and ordered his troops to push through Masnières and secure the line of the St. Quentin Canal.[9] Yet when Buchholz's soldiers reached the canal, they were in for a surprise. *Oberstleutnant* D. Feuerheerd of III/227th Battalion recalled:

> We heard the characteristic noise of tanks on the other bank. Finally, four of them emerged out of the mist, after having passed through Les Rues Vertes. This was the first time our men, coming from Russia, had seen a tank. The impression was astonishing and almost comic. All stood up and looked at those monsters with the greatest interest, although they were only 500 yards away and were actually firing.[10]

To complicate matters, the right flank of the 227th Reserve Regiment was under threat from the British advance across the canal at Marcoing. As has been related earlier, from midafternoon German troops in the Hindenburg Reserve System to the west and southwest of Rumilly were attacked by British troops of the 87th Brigade. Lieutenant Horold of the 227th Reserve Regiment's 5th Company wrote of this engagement:

> Some of us clustered around the dugouts [of the Hindenburg Reserve System], some of which were ready, whilst others were unfinished, others sheltered in isolated sections of trench. It began to rain! Soon we heard a grinding roaring sound which was getting closer and a stink of petrol fumes was carried on the westerly wind. We knew what were on their way!—Tanks! Very shortly three of them appeared to our front, one of them in the wide gap by Flot Farm. Watching them crawling forward like great prehistoric monsters and crossing all obstacles with ease, sent unpleasant shivers up our spines. But they could not be permitted to get through![11]

One of the tanks was set on fire and immobilized by a machine gun firing armor-piercing ammunition. The other two tanks disappeared behind folds in the ground after a brisk exchange of fire. Lieutenant Quehl recalled: "As it went dark, a patrol moved forward to the crippled tank. They found it abandoned, but discovered all sorts of excellent booty within it: sparkling wine, cognac, chocolate and fruit cake; almost all luxury items which we had not seen for a very long time. That only increased our happiness further."[12] Meanwhile, German troops at Masnières had an open left flank facing the village of Crèvecoeur. During the evening, however, an improvised regimental group filled this gap, having arrived at Cambrai in the late afternoon. Overnight most German troops at Masnières withdrew a short distance to the shelter of the Hindenburg Reserve System.

In the late morning of November 20, after the main tank assault had burst into the German front, Major Stephen Foot of the Tank Corps' staff walked through the broken Hindenburg systems toward Marcoing. (This was on the front of the 6th Division.) Before reaching Marcoing, he stopped for lunch at the headquarters of B Battalion of Tanks.

> There on the hillside, right out in the open, Bryce had established his Headquarters. Stuck in the ground was the Battalion flag, its colour a flaming yellow; and seated round it, with the sun shining overhead, we had our lunch—chicken, *pate de fois gras* sandwiches and champagne, exactly as if we had been at Ascot instead of three miles inside the German lines.
>
> But where were the Cavalry? It was nearly eleven o'clock [A.M.]. All the tanks and Infantry had reached their objective in our part of the line. Marcoing had been captured. The Germans were in flight. When would the Cavalry arrive to exploit the success? I began to feel seriously alarmed. Bryce and I climbed up the hill towards Premy Chapel, from which point we could look back to our old front line; but no Cavalry were in sight. A signal Tank was not far off; I sent back a message to Tank Corps Headquarters giving an outline of the situation, so favourable for immediate exploitation. Another hour passed; still no sign of any Cavalry. The precious moments were slipping by and giving the Germans time to rally in front of Cambrai.[13]

Where, indeed, were the cavalry? The hopes for the exploitation phase of the Cambrai battle depended on the Cavalry Corps' timely participation.

The specific plan for the Cavalry Corps was complex. The 2nd and 5th Cavalry Divisions were allocated to III Corps. The 1st Cavalry Division was to work with IV Corps; the 3rd and 4th Cavalry Divisions were held in reserve.

A detachment of tanks had torn wide lanes in the captured wire entanglements of the Hindenburg Line so that the masses of horses and riders could cross into the captured defensive zone. A track for the cavalry was laid through the Hindenburg Front and Support Systems. The cavalry trotted forward, passing ditched tanks and German prisoners heading in the opposite direction. The snake-like columns of horses and men stretched back for miles into the original British front. The sun appeared briefly to cast its rays upon the horsemen. The Cavalry Corps' commander, General Kavanagh, remained at his headquarters, while the divisional and brigade staffs mounted horses and took to the road with their formations.

The task of the 1st Cavalry Division in IV Corps' sector was to advance to Ribécourt, push along the Grand Ravine to Nine Wood, and then move north on both sides of the St. Quentin Canal with the object of turning the villages of Noyelles,

Cantaing, and Fontaine. After all that was achieved, a detachment was to head for Sailly and Tilloy, northwest of Cambrai, and there gain touch with other mounted troops. Finally, the 1st Cavalry Division was to approach Bourlon village from the northeast and hold that place until the arrival of the 62nd Division's infantry.[14]

At 11:07 A.M., IV Corps received a message from the 51st Division that "many prisoners from Flesquieres" had been taken. The 1st Cavalry Division was then mistakenly informed that Flesquières was captured and the Trescault-Flesquières road open for cavalry. The 1st Cavalry Division set off into the systems of the Hindenburg Line led by its 2nd Brigade, followed by the 1st Brigade and with the 9th Brigade in reserve. The outskirts of Ribécourt was reached just before midday by the leading regiment. Bullets were flying about, and an officer of the 4th Dragoon Guards was wounded by machine-gun fire.[15] The commander of the 2nd Cavalry Brigade, Brigadier General D.J.E. Beale-Browne, was told there was some doubt as to whether Flesquières was in British hands. Beale-Browne ordered the 4th Dragoon Guards, the leading regiment, to investigate; this unit soon discovered that fighting was underway at Flesquières and the route through that place blocked. The march of the cavalry was diverted back along the Grand Ravine, the route originally intended, after wasting a lot of precious time. (If Harper's division had secured Flesquières in a timely fashion, it might have opened the way for cavalry to advance directly on Cantaing and into the gap between Bourlon Wood and Cambrai.)

By 3 P.M. the 2nd Cavalry Brigade had traversed the Grand Ravine and was approaching Nine Wood. The cavalry's march in a long column of regiments and squadrons drastically reduced the number of troops that could be quickly sent into action. Scouts saw Cantaing ahead through mist and fine rain. At 4 P.M. two squadrons of the 4th Dragoon Guards were sent forward, one to Cantaing and the other to Les Vallées Wood, which was north of Noyelles. Wire and machine-gun fire, however, held up the push on Cantaing. On a more resolute note, two troops rode beyond Les Vallées Wood to La Folie Château and threw a German detachment encountered into disarray. In particular, the leading troop of Lieutenant J.A. Aizlewood chanced upon a column of German horsed transport, drew swords, and charged. Not a shot was fired in reply, and twenty-odd prisoners were taken at sword-point. The following troop under Lieutenant L.F. Marson rounded up some German infantrymen and took them prisoner. Heavy fire from the direction of Cantaing and across the canal caused the squadron to retire to Noyelles. The squadron commander was subsequently killed by machine-gun fire, and both Aizlewood and Marson returned on foot after their horses were shot from under them.[16] The 4th Dragoon Guards spent the night alongside the 86th Brigade in the vicinity of Nine Wood and Noyelles.

Late in the afternoon the 5th Dragoon Guards, the second unit of the 2nd Cavalry Brigade's column, arrived at Marcoing. This regiment was to advance on the eastern side of the canal. Soon after 4 P.M. one squadron crossed the canal by the bridge at Marcoing, but was then halted by machine-gun fire. The regiment subsequently retired west of Marcoing for the night, not far from the main body of the 2nd Cavalry

Brigade. The 1st Cavalry Brigade bivouacked at Trescault overnight, and the 9th Cavalry Brigade remained within the original British front.[17]

While the 1st Cavalry Division was operating in the sector of IV Corps, the main body of the Cavalry Corps marched out through the sector of III Corps. At 11:40 A.M. the Cavalry Corps' headquarters ordered the 5th Cavalry Division to pass through the captured German front and head for the St. Quentin Canal. The cavalry advanced in two long columns in the direction of Marcoing and Masnières, respectively. After crossing the canal, the 5th Cavalry Division was to make a thirty-mile march, during the night of November 20/21, past the eastern side of Cambrai and northwards to the Sensee River. The railways and roads running toward Cambrai from the east and north were to be blocked and the town isolated. The 2nd Cavalry Division was also to cross the canal and advance in support of the 5th Cavalry Division. In addition to that, the Lucknow Cavalry Brigade of the 4th Cavalry Division was to cross the St. Quentin Canal at Crèvecoeur, to the east of Masnières, and from there launch raids against the German lines of communication. The cavalry loaded up with rations for man and beast for the next two days, and the transport carried a third day's ration.[18]

The captured Hindenburg Line defenses were traversed by the 5th Cavalry Division's leading regiments without major incident. At the head of the mounted column moving on Marcoing was the Indian Army's Secunderabad Cavalry Brigade, which was led by the 7th Dragoon Guards, followed by the 34th Poona Horse and 20th Deccan Horse. (The Ambala Cavalry Brigade followed behind the Secunderabad brigade.) The cavalry reached Marcoing, which was held by British infantry, soon after 2 P.M. The 7th Dragoon Guards' C Squadron crossed the canal by the bridge at Marcoing and came under machine-gun fire. The squadron dismounted and took up a position on the flank of nearby infantry.

In the meantime, D Squadron of the 7th Dragoon Guards under Captain C.W.T. Lane was sent in the direction of Noyelles, on the western side of the canal, in a bid to find another bridge. The squadron galloped into Noyelles and continued onwards, scattering groups of German soldiers encountered along the way. A broken canal bridge was found, though that was of no immediate value. The squadron retired from their exposed position as the light began to fail.

It was apparent to senior officers of the Secunderabad brigade that the infantry had yet to clear a path for cavalry into the countryside beyond the Hindenburg Reserve System. The Deccan Horse's Lieutenant Colonel E. Tennant would write: "As the Divisional Commander's orders were most explicit that the Cavalry Brigade must on no account be drawn into the infantry fight and that the work of the cavalry did not commence until the infantry had secured their final objective, the further advance of the Brigade was held up and once more hopes were dashed to the ground, just when success seemed to be within its grasp."[19]

The 5th Cavalry Division's column heading for Masnières was led by the Canadian Cavalry Brigade. Shortly before 2 P.M. the Canadians' Brigadier General J.E.B. Seely arrived at Les Rues Vertes. Seely spoke with the commander of the 88th

Brigade, who believed that tanks and infantry had crossed the canal successfully. Acting on this advice, Seely ordered his leading regiment to come forward to continue the advance as originally planned. Before long, however, it became clear that the main bridge into Masnières was broken and the cavalry could go no farther by that route. Seely was to comment:

> Will it be believed that at the point selected for attack there was the one obstacle on the whole of the Western Front which formed an insurmountable barrier to the cavalry—the Canal St Quentin. Horses can cross almost anything; they can even swim broad rivers, as they have often done in war. But the one thing they cannot get over, unless they can bridge it, is a canal with perpendicular banks. They can get in, but they cannot get out.[20]

The brigades of the 2nd Cavalry Division marched behind those of the 5th Cavalry Division. The 4th Cavalry Brigade followed the mounted column heading for Marcoing; the 5th and 3rd Cavalry Brigades took the Masnières route followed by the Lucknow Cavalry Brigade. The 4th Cavalry Division's Lucknow brigade was to have crossed the canal near Crevècoeur, but that plan was abandoned, as the Germans held that place.

Soon after 3 P.M., in drizzling rain, Major General W.H. Greenly of the 2nd Cavalry Division rode into Les Rues Vertes. (Major General H.J.M. Macandrew of the 5th Cavalry Division was on the road to Marcoing.) Daylight was already failing. The cavalry units outside Les Rues Vertes remained stationary, and to their rear a cavalcade of mounted troops stretched back into the old British front line. After conferring with his subordinates, Greenly ordered the Canadian Cavalry Brigade to assist the infantry facing Masnières. Any mounted troops on the north bank were to be recalled. (A wooden bridge, about sixteen hundred yards southeast of the main Masnières bridge, leading to Mon Plaisir farm, remained undiscovered at this time.)[21]

Meanwhile, a squadron of the Fort Garry Horse, the Canadians' lead regiment, had managed to cross the canal by a lock three hundred yards southeast of Masnières. By 4 P.M. B Squadron was ready to ride for a ridge two miles northeast of Masnières. The Canadians set off before messengers could arrive with instructions for their recall. Not far into the ride, the squadron commander was killed by machine-gun fire and, as a result, Lieutenant Henry Strachan took command. Strachan would write:

> The squadron now proceeded up to the high ground, east of Masnieres, and on gaining the ridge, came face to face with a German battery of four [field] guns about 300 yards away. Fortunately swords had been drawn . . . and the squadron charged the guns, each troop column converged on them. It is interesting to note that one gun continued to fire until the last and those gunners probably escaped owing to the difficulty of reaching them, whereas the remaining gunners, who ran away as soon as we appeared, were satisfactorily accounted for almost to a man.[22]

Parties of German soldiers fled in all directions as the cavalry rode on. The squadron reached a sunken road about a thousand to fifteen hundred yards east of Rumilly.

"A hurried inspection," wrote Strachan, "was made and the squadron was found to have suffered severely, more so than had been anticipated. Only forty-three men and horses were left, all the pack horses were lost, several men had minor wounds and all the horses but seven were found to be wounded, many were exhausted and several actually dropped dead while we were going around looking at them."[23] (The squadron had started the day with 4 officers, 129 men, and 140 horses.) There were further skirmishes with German troops nearby, but more importantly, darkness was falling and a large force of Germans was seen moving from Rumilly toward the Canadian squadron's line of retreat. Strachan added: "In addition, long columns of motor lorries (which, incidently, had no tyres and made a terrific din) were moving down the road from Cambrai to Rumilly all loaded with troops." The surviving horses were released, and the Canadians headed back to the St. Quentin Canal on foot. The canal was recrossed in the early hours of a rainy morning after further brushes with hostile troops. Three officers and forty-three other ranks returned with eighteen prisoners; Strachan would be awarded the Victoria Cross.[24]

During the afternoon, while the Fort Garry Horse's foray was in motion, Major Buchholz and the staff of the 227th Reserve Regiment was posted by the Cambrai-Masnières road. Buchholz was given the news that British cavalry had overrun a nearby battery and were threatening to turn behind Rumilly. An improvised group of soldiers was hastily assembled to drive the cavalry off. Lance Corporal Albert Mueller, who belonged to a reinforcement draft, recalled:

> We were off loaded in open country and formed up into companies. After a tough forced march, we were met by a German artillery officer: "The British cavalry has broken through and is operating in rear of a German division which is heavily engaged in battle. They will be here any moment!" We had to deploy and moved forward a bit in extended line, then we took up position in a sunken road and received the advancing British cavalry with murderous small arms fire. The attack withered away, we took many prisoners. Dead horses, men and fine leather equipment lay around in tangled heaps. We also seized numerous riderless horses. Our casualties were slight.[25]

Darkness had fallen by 5 P.M. to bring down the curtain of night on proceedings. It had been a disadvantage for the Third Army to mount such an ambitious attack a month from the shortest day of the year.

The Canadian Cavalry Brigade bivouacked for the night a thousand yards south of Marcoing Copse. Of the other Cavalry Corps formations heading for Masnières and Marcoing, the 3rd, 5th, Ambala, Lucknow, and Secunderabad Cavalry Brigades also spent the night inside the captured German front. The 4th Cavalry Brigade retired back into the original British front.[26] In addition, two of the 1st Cavalry Division's three brigades bivouacked in captured territory. In total, nine cavalry brigades entered the German front during November 20 and eight remained in situ overnight. The extent to which masses of cavalry clogged up the battlefield should not be understated.

III, IV, and the Cavalry Corps were not the only Third Army troops to be in action that day. To the north and south of the main battle zone, divisions of VI and VII Corps had carried out diversionary and feint attacks to occupy the attention of German troops in those sectors. The largest of the diversionary attacks was carried out by the 16th (Irish) Division and a brigade of the 3rd Division on either flank of Bullecourt. The number of prisoners taken was 718, in exchange for casualties of 805.[27]

# 12

## The Drive for Bourlon

November 20, 1917, was one of the western front's most dramatic days: A three- to four-mile advance into a heavily fortified defensive system was achieved on a six- to seven-mile front. In just four hours a bridgehead in the formidable Hindenburg Line was established at a modest cost, especially when compared with the cataracts of blood spilled during the grisly crawl to Passchendaele. More than four thousand Germans were made prisoner, and that figure would almost double by the following day after the motley influx was counted more carefully. More than a hundred guns were captured, which again highlights how little was achieved at Passchendaele. A company commander in the Tanks' F Battalion described November 20 as the "happiest day of my life." The Tanks had at last, seemingly, come into their kingdom.[1]

Not everything, however, had gone to plan. On the front of III Corps, the cavalry had not crossed the St. Quentin Canal; on the front of IV Corps, Bourlon Ridge remained in German hands, not least because the cavalry had failed to turn the flank of Bourlon from the northeast. Of the 378 fighting tanks that started the day, 179 had been put out of action: 65 by hostile fire, 71 by mechanical trouble, and 43 by ditching or other causes.[2] The tanks had processed into battle with a terrific vitality, but this new type of fighting equipment was riddled with technical fallibility.

During the opening day of the Cambrai battle, the possibility had existed of French troops moving forward to support the attack. At 1 p.m., however, Pétain was informed that French involvement was not yet advisable. Haig confirmed this when he visited Byng's headquarters at Albert late in the afternoon.

The French detachment was not the only idle body of Allied troops behind the Cambrai sector on November 20. The three divisions of V Corps were also waiting in reserve twenty miles behind the front. And within IV Corps, as mentioned earlier, the 51st Division's reserve brigade had not been committed to action.[3] Indeed, the quantity of British and French infantry standing in reserve behind the Cambrai front was not far short of the quantity of infantry actually sent into battle. Charteris would later claim: "It was the absence of the British divisions which had been sent to Italy that prevented Haig's pressing his success at Cambrai after November 20th, and achieving fuller success."[4] That was clearly not the case: There were plenty of troops near to hand. The reason why the reserves of infantry were not used to exploit the success of the tanks was that this opportunity was handed to the cavalry. Captain C.R.M.F. Cruttwell observed of the Cambrai fighting:

> The inaction of the two [leading] cavalry divisions has never yet been intelligibly explained. They had been brought close up on the morning of the battle but, to the satirical derision of the foot-soldiers, stood all day idle. . . . Doubtless it was a grave risk to use cavalry . . . yet if the risk was not to be taken on a favourable opportunity, why thrust them ostentatiously forward as the only "reserve of exploitation"? The infantry were constantly pushed remorselessly on the forlornest of hopes. The cavalry were kept for the impossible event of every detail of the schedule being performed with clock-like exactness.[5]

The packing of a large part of the Cavalry Corps into the Cambrai sector crowded out the infantry. The cavalry were especially voracious in their monopolization of roads, which made it hard to pass quickly forward follow-up infantry units and teams of horses hauling field guns and ammunition wagons.

Captain Sutherland of the 1/5th Seaforth Highlanders recorded: "It was a fine sight to see an apparently endless succession of men and horses wending their way across the valley toward Ribecourt and Flesquieres, but to the infantrymen it was a maddening sight to see them come wending back next morning having accomplished nothing."[6] Sutherland had scant regard for the "antediluvian fossils" of the cavalry's leadership. Lieutenant Aizlewood of the 4th Dragoon Guards wrote that "a fleeting opportunity was missed due to poor communications, and the fact that [Cavalry] Commanders authorised to make quick decisions were too far back. Possibly this can be blamed on two years of trench warfare and comfortable chateaux. I think the Duke of Wellington would have been up forward at the Bois des Neuf."[7] The staff of cavalry formations seem not to have properly studied the maps and air reports of the ground they were to cover. Colonel Fuller would bluntly write that General Kavanagh, the Cavalry Corps' commander, was "surely the worst Cavalry general in all history."[8]

Field Marshal Haig was also deeply disappointed by his cavalry's lack of aggression when given such a fine chance to get the rust off their spurs. He wrote: "They [cavalry officers] must be blind. . . . They fail to realise that the horse is our weapon, that we can do anything if we use it, and that the German is the feeblest of foes if pushed. . . . Risks must never be considered and the objectives must be obtained no matter what the losses are."[9] Regimental cavalry officers, however, were in no hurry to repeat the drama of the famous Charge of the Light Brigade (at Balaclava in 1854).

The surprise attack by tanks at Cambrai was a sensational contradiction to what had taken place at Ypres. German accounts speak of panic at the appearance of large, slow-moving machines that were impervious to small-arms fire. Ludendorff would write: "We were expecting a continuation of the attacks in Flanders and on the French front, when on the 20th of November we were surprised by a fresh blow at Cambrai."[10] German commanders were slow to fathom what had occurred in the front line. A heavy mist kept reconnaissance aircraft grounded for long periods. Crown Prince Rupprecht wrote of the events of November 20:

> The attack on Group Caudry of Second Army came as a total surprise. The fog during the past few days completely camouflaged the enemy offensive preparations and the attack was not preceded by an increase in artillery fire; rather large numbers of tanks cleared the way forward for the infantry. . . . The speed at which the tanks were able to advance due to the dryness of the going was almost unbelievable. Even more unbelievable was the way that they made child's play of breaking through the barbed wire, which before both the Main Defensive Line and the Intermediate position, was no less than one hundred metres deep—more formidable than anywhere else.[11]

The 54th Division was shattered by the onslaught; parts of neighboring divisions were also destroyed. Once the extent of the crisis was better understood, units were ordered to Cambrai from adjoining sectors of Marwitz's Second Army. Three divisions from other armies were ordered to entrain for Cambrai that first day.

There was alarm at German headquarters that a further tank attack might take place the following morning. General von Watter of Caudry Group informed the Second Army's headquarters: "It cannot be denied that, if the enemy continues the tank battle before more artillery arrives, an expansion of the break in and, therefore, possibly a real breakthrough will hardly be preventable. Even after this crisis is overcome, the situation will remain serious."[12] The energy and novelty of the massed tanks was a noteworthy landmark in the history of warfare in the Western world.

After news of the success at Cambrai had reached London, the War Office arranged for the church bells of the metropolis to be rung in celebration. Hopes were falsely raised that deliverance from a blood-soaked conflict was near at hand. Charteris wrote with glib satisfaction that the tank attack was a "fine answer to Lloyd George's carping criticism of the soldiers."[13] At Cambrai on November 21 the fighting continued as British forces sought to secure those objectives not taken the previous day. Half of the Tank Corps' armored vehicles had been put out of action on November 20, and confusion and exhaustion of crews and machinery further reduced the number of tanks available to continue the battle. Detachments of tanks would support the infantry on an ad hoc basis in the days ahead. The direction of those detachments was primarily in the hands of the Tanks' brigade and battalion commanders. Henceforward the task of Tank Corps headquarters in the Cambrai sector's operational planning was circumscribed and General Elles and Colonel Fuller had a limited influence on events.

On the front of IV Corps, German troops had evacuated Flesquières during the cold, rainy night of November 20/21. After this was discovered, troops of the 51st

Division pushed forward into the village during the early hours of the morning. Beyond the crest line of Flesquières Ridge, some of the guns that had dealt out destruction to the tanks the previous day were captured. Three miles to the north, a mist-shrouded Bourlon Wood lay across an open plain. The 51st Division's reserve brigade—the 154th—belatedly came forward in drizzling rain and renewed the advance at 10:30 A.M. The 154th Brigade was led by the 1/7th Argyll and Sutherland Highlanders and 1/4th Gordon Highlanders; the gentle breeze carried the sound of bagpipes into the distance.

In the path of the 154th Brigade lay the villages of Cantaing and Fontaine. During the night, troops of the German 107th Division had hastily taken up positions around Cantaing. The Hindenburg Reserve System in this sector ran from Nine Wood to Bourlon Wood, and comprised trenches that had only been traced out, though numerous dugouts, wire entanglements, and machine-gun emplacements were completed.

The advance of British troops on Cantaing was at first held up by machine-gun fire and a double belt of wire. Shortly after midday, however, thirteen tanks came over Premy Chapel Ridge and approached Cantaing from the southeast. The tanks were joined by an infantry detachment of the 6th Division and cavalry of the 2nd Dragoon Guards (Queen's Bays). Meanwhile, the 1/4th Gordons successfully attacked Cantaing from the west, and by midafternoon the village was in British hands. Four hundred prisoners were taken, mostly from I/52nd and I/232nd Reserve Regiments. The infantry now stood on rising ground, and stretched out before them in the distance was a postcard-like vista of Cambrai's picturesque spires and factory chimneys.

On the left front of the 154th Brigade, the 1/7th Argylls could not advance until 11:20 A.M. due to cross fire from Anneux on the left flank. After Anneux had fallen to the 62nd Division, the Argylls made some progress, only to be halted by fire from Bourlon Wood and Cantaing. About 3 P.M. six tanks arrived and helped to restart the Argylls' advance. The infantry and tanks continued onwards to the village of Fontaine. The small German garrison of that place hastily evacuated their posts and retired to a safer locality.

Fontaine was a sleepy village, still undamaged by shellfire. The civilian population, taken unawares by the sudden onset of battle, had hidden in their cellars and emerged again once the sounds of firing had slackened. A soldier wrote: "Our reception in the village was a very cordial one. Men, women and children came out of the houses, and recognizing us, they made a great fuss. They called us 'Scotchia,' and many of the men were kissed by the womenfolk. The men were well treated, receiving beer, wine, coffee and various kinds of food. The people could not do enough for us."[14] At 8 P.M. the 154th Brigade's commander ordered the 1/4th Seaforth Highlanders to take over the defense of Fontaine; the Argylls were pulled back to a position on the left flank facing Bourlon Wood. The Seaforths had only four hundred men to defend the village, which was sited in the tactically important bottleneck between Bourlon Wood and Cambrai. If the battle was to develop as British commanders intended, it was vital that Fontaine remain in British possession. Cambrai was only four thousand yards by road from Fontaine. During the night ahead a great deal of feverish activity could be heard in Cambrai; trains were arriving with regularity, likely carrying German reinforcements.

On the left flank of the 51st Division, the 62nd Division's task for November 21 was to overrun Bourlon Wood and Bourlon village. The 186th Brigade, with the support of nineteen tanks of G Battalion and some cavalry, successfully captured the German-held village of Anneux in front of the wood, but the exhausted troops made little further progress and the advance halted near the sunken Bapaume-Cambrai road. German troops were strongly posted in Bourlon Wood, and machine-gun and rifle fire from its slopes proved damaging. Throughout the day the work of the Royal Flying Corps was handicapped by fog and low cloud.[15] That evening the 186th Brigade was relieved; this formation had done its utmost and had taken more than twelve hundred prisoners across the previous two days. Meanwhile, west of the Canal du Nord, the 109th Brigade of the 36th Division advanced a further half mile to cover that open flank.

On the front of III Corps, hopes still prevailed on November 21 that a path might be cleared for cavalry through the Hindenburg Reserve System on the far side of the St. Quentin Canal. During the previous night, troops of the 29th Division's 88th Brigade had worked into Masnières from the eastern flank. In the morning, once Masnières was mostly cleared of Germans, British troops edged northwards to the wire of the reserve system. On both flanks of Masnières, additional infantry reinforcements crossed the canal to help build up the bridgehead garrison. Farther to the east, German troops retained possession of the near-side bank of the canal facing the 20th Division. On the whole, the German front remained unbroken in the Masnières sector.

To the west of Masnières, in the bridgehead near Marcoing, the 87th Brigade of the 29th Division mounted another attack up the slope toward the German line. The 1st King's Own Scottish Borderers and 2nd South Wales Borderers led the mid-day assault. A detachment of tanks had crossed the canal at Marcoing and advanced with the infantry. The regimental history of the South Wales Borderers noted that "the artillery support was almost negligible, for touch had not been established with the artillery and very few guns had come forward."[16] The slope ahead was a veritable glacis. The tanks were greeted by machine-gun fire that included armor-piercing ammunition; the infantry was held up by mostly intact wire entanglements. Footholds were gained in the German position, but the intruders were driven out again and the attack had failed by midafternoon. The defenders in the sector had been reinforced by units newly arrived at Cambrai. The tanks lost three vehicles in the fighting, and numerous others were damaged.

The 86th Brigade, the 29th Division's left-hand brigade, remained around Noyelles, on the near side of the canal. These troops, supported by units of the 1st Cavalry Division, skirmished with parties of Germans during the course of the day.

By afternoon of November 21, it had become apparent at Third Army headquarters that III Corps' advance had stalled. There was no longer any prospect of

**Highlanders in Flesquières, November 23, 1917. (I.W.M.)**

large-scale cavalry action beyond the St. Quentin Canal. This was a grave blow to the original battle plan. The 5th Cavalry Division had spent the day waiting within striking distance of the canal, but that night orders were received to withdraw behind the original front. During the afternoon orders were also given for the 2nd Cavalry Division to retire, along with the 4th Cavalry Division's Lucknow Cavalry Brigade. French commanders were again informed that their troops would not be needed that day on the Cambrai front.[17]

The push across the St. Quentin Canal was stalled, yet on the evening of November 21 there persisted at General Headquarters (GHQ) a sense that the Germans were in difficulty and might give ground if pressed by IV Corps at Bourlon. Haig had requested of Robertson "that the two additional Divisions now warned for Italy may be placed at my disposal." Robertson replied that the War Cabinet had agreed that the 2nd and 47th Divisions should be made available as Haig wished provided two other divisions were put on standby for Italy instead.[18] The addition of these troops to the three uncommitted divisions of V Corps meant there were now five "fresh" infantry divisions on hand to stoke the fires of battle at Cambrai.

On November 21, German commanders were fearful of further large-scale tank attacks. The 107th Division, the principal local reserve, had been committed to action and was fighting a decentralized battle on a wide front against odds. Battered companies belonging to the 54th Division and the division on its southern flank continued in action in places. On the front from Bourlon to Moeuvres, the remnants of the 20th Landwehr Division were exhausted. Two regiments of the 214th Division and that division's artillery arrived in the nick of time to shore up the line in that sector.

At this point in proceedings, on the evening of November 21, Haig fatefully intervened to extend the Cambrai operation beyond the forty-eight-hour period originally authorized. The battle had begun as a giant raid, but would now start to develop the tortured features of a campaign more typical of Haig's tenure as commander in chief. The field marshal instructed Byng's Third Army to capture Bourlon and roll up the German line in a northward direction. III Corps was to consolidate a defensive flank facing the St. Quentin Canal, while IV Corps attacked Bourlon with the support of those tanks that were battle ready. Byng spoke to Generals Pulteney and Woollcombe by telephone and informed them of the revised plan. Haig later explained:

> The possession of Bourlon Ridge would enable our troops to obtain observation over the ground to the north, which sloped gently down to the Sensee River. The enemy's defence lines south of the Scarpe and Sensee Rivers would thereby be turned, his communications exposed to the observed fire of our artillery, and his positions in this sector jeopardised. In short, so great was the importance of the ridge [Bourlon] to the enemy that its loss would probably cause the abandonment by the Germans of their carefully prepared defence systems for a considerable distance to the north of it.

Haig also made the dubious claim that he needed to continue the fighting at Cambrai to relieve pressure on the Italian front.[19]

This turn of events was not without its critics. "Douglas Haig was quite obstinate," remarked Colonel Thorpe of the Third Army's staff, "and determined the battle should go on, when it should have been obvious that the failure to get a footing over the Marcoing [St. Quentin] canal made the main objective unobtainable." General Davidson at GHQ thought likewise: "It was clear, after the first two or three days, that substantial German reinforcements were being brought up."[20] On November 20 and 21, Haig had let Byng fight the Cambrai battle as Byng wanted to fight it. From November 22, however, Haig placed himself firmly in the driver's seat, which would enable him to lay a larger claim to the laurels of what seemed to be a successful venture.

In an uncharacteristic outburst of curiosity, on November 22, Haig toured the Cambrai sector's battlefield. The field marshal's staff and escort amounted to a cavalcade of about sixty men on horseback. He visited the headquarters of the 51st Division and afterwards met Major General R.L. Mullens of the 1st Cavalry Division. Haig later wrote:

> I then got on to [a] . . . horse and rode with Mullens and Butler [deputy chief of staff, GHQ] to a point overlooking Ribecourt from which I got a good view of Flesquieres,

Bois du Neuf, etc. Mullens explained all that his Cavalry Division had done, and said that this experience had been worth very much to them and they were all as pleased as possible. On the ridge about Flesquieres are a dozen or more Tanks which were knocked out by Artillery fire. It seems that as the Tanks topped the ridge and began to descend the ridge into the village they came under direct Artillery fire. An eyewitness stated that on the appearance of the first Tank all the personnel of a German battery fled. One officer, however, was able to collect a few men and with them worked a gun, and from his concealed position knocked out Tank after Tank to the number of eight or nine. The officer was then killed. This incident shows the importance of Infantry operating with Tanks, and at times acting as skirmishers to clear away hostile guns and reconnoitre. The holding up of the 51st Division at Flesquieres on the 20th had far-reaching consequences because the Cavalry were also held up and failed in consequence to get through.[21]

In the next phase of the battle, Haig would again look to involve cavalry. Robertson signaled GHQ that in continuing the battle Haig was to be mindful of "probable Italian demands and to a very unsatisfactory manpower position."

In the front line on November 22, the village of Fontaine, which lay to the east-southeast of Bourlon Wood, was subject to German counterattack. The day was cold and misty; rain would fall in the afternoon. The 1/4th Seaforth Highlanders was the solitary infantry unit in Fontaine. After first light, the Seaforths were greeted by German aircraft circling overhead. This was an ominous sign, and they "swooped and circled over the village for three hours, like gulls waiting for the nets to be emptied."[22]

Shelling of the eastern end of Fontaine began at 9 A.M. and half an hour later extended to cover the whole village. Part of the civilian population was hurried to the rear, but others fled back into hiding in their cellars below ground. By 10:30 A.M. the garrison was under German attack; before long both flanks and the north face of the village were threatened with envelopment. The thick mist made it difficult to call down effective artillery support, which was lacking for much of the engagement. There were no tanks present to aid the defense.

By midafternoon the German counterattack had pushed the Seaforths out of Fontaine. The German attack was made by the 46th Regiment of the 119th Division. Possession of Fontaine had been central to British plans to advance northwards in the Bourlon sector, yet Harper of the 51st Division and Woollcombe of IV Corps had left a single understrength battalion to hold that village in an isolated local salient.

In accordance with Haig's revised intentions, IV Corps was ordered to make a fresh attack on November 23 in the northern part of the Cambrai sector. From right to left, the 51st Division was to recapture Fontaine and push northwards; the 40th Division was to clear Bourlon Wood and Bourlon village; and the 36th and 56th Divisions were to advance a short distance to cover the western flank. Ninety-two tanks were available to support the attack, which was a sharp reduction of strength when compared to the several hundred tanks used during the opening day's fighting.[23] Replacement tank crewmen had to be found for those unable to continue. After Fontaine was secured by the 51st Division, the 1st Cavalry Division was to pass through that subsector and threaten Bourlon from the northeast. The 9th Cavalry Brigade would lead the way for the rest of the cavalry.

The 40th Division relieved the 62nd Division during the night of November 22/23. The 62nd Division had lost casualties of 75 officers and 1,613 other ranks over the previous three days. The 40th Division, a formation of V Corps hitherto held in reserve behind the front, comprised a mix of Welsh, English, and Scottish infantry units. The division had landed in France in June 1916, and the upcoming action would be its most significant battle thus far. The 40th Division's headquarters and reserve brigade was situated at Havrincourt; the other two brigades took over the front line facing Bourlon Ridge. The roads and tracks behind the new front line were crowded and muddy. The 40th Division took over a sector still strewn with the dead and debris of earlier fighting.

A strong force of artillery was assembled for the assault on Bourlon Wood, which was a thickly timbered six hundred acres situated on a ridge. The highest point of the ridge rose 150 feet above the level of the Bapaume-Cambrai road.[24] Zero hour on November 23, another cold, wet morning, was at the untypical time of 10:30 A.M. The barrage came down at 10:10 A.M., after which it lifted two hundred yards at 10:30 A.M., and jumped forward in similar lifts at set intervals. The 40th Division directly attacked Bourlon Wood with Brigadier General F.P. Crozier's 119th Brigade and sixteen tanks of G Battalion. (The tough-minded Crozier would

**Bourlon Wood. (I.W.M.)**

produce the memoir *A Brass Hat in No Man's Land*.) To the left of Crozier's force, the 121st Brigade and thirteen tanks of D Battalion was to secure Bourlon village and the western shoulder of the ridge thereabouts. The 40th Division had scant experience of working with armored vehicles; the infantry was instructed to follow the tanks through whatever wire entanglements were encountered.

After dawn on November 23, in preparation for the attack, flights of Royal Flying Corps aircraft swept low to machine-gun Bourlon Wood. When the barrage lifted at 10:30 A.M., the tanks and the 119th Brigade's mostly Welsh infantry streamed across a mist-covered stretch of ground before plunging into the wood, which was a confusion of trees, undergrowth, and forest tracks that all looked alike. Crozier's brigade fought their way to the wood's northern edge. German counterattacks lasting into the night regained some ground, but British troops maintained a firm grip on the crest of the ridge within Bourlon Wood.

To the left of the wood, the 121st Brigade advanced on Bourlon village across ground swept by machine-gun fire. The Tank Corps' Major Watson recalled:

> At 10.30 A.M. the barrage fell and we could see it climb, like a living thing, through the wood and up the hillside, a rough line of smoke and flame. On the hillside to the left of the wood we could mark the course of the battle—the tanks with tiny flashes darting from their flanks—clumps of infantry following in little rushes—an officer running in front of his men, until suddenly he crumpled up and fell, as though some unseen hammer had struck him on the head—the men wavering in the face of machine gun fire and then spreading out to surround the gun—the wounded staggering painfully down the hill, and the stretcher-bearers moving backwards and forwards in the wake of the attack—the aeroplanes skimming low along the hillside, and side-slipping to rake the enemy trenches with their guns.
>
> We watched one tank hesitate before it crossed the skyline and our hearts went out to the driver in sympathy. He made his decision, and the tank, brown against the sky, was instantly encircled by little puffs of white smoke, shells from the guns on the reverse slope. The man was brave, for he followed the course of the trench along the crest of a hill. My companion uttered a low exclamation of horror. Flames were coming from the rear of the tank, but its guns continued to fire and the tank continued to move. Suddenly the driver must have realised what was happening. The tank swung towards home. It was too late. Flames burst from the roof and the tank stopped, but the sponson doors never opened and the crew never came out.[25]

The infantry was driven to ground by heavy fire in front of Bourlon village, but the surviving tanks pressed boldly into the village and were greeted by a destructive hail delivered at close range. According to *Unteroffizier* Hetschold of Lehr Infantry Regiment (3rd Guards Division):

> Suddenly from our left half rear came the clank of metal. A British tank was steering for us and was firing. Our comrades yelled and leapt for the sunken road. I heaved my gun round and loaded "K" [armor-piercing] ammunition. There was no time for thought; the monster was within twenty metres of me. I fired at the place where I had

been taught. . . . There was a whirring noise and smoke appeared. Men jumped out of the monster and raced away. Driverless, it came past us burning. It ran into a concrete block and jammed there.[26]

The Germans repelled the attack on the village and thereby maintained a footing on Bourlon Ridge, though they had lost most of the nearby wood.

To the left of the 40th Division, troops of the 36th Division struggled to make worthwhile progress when they advanced. The 107th and 108th Brigades attacked on either side of the Canal du Nord. Those units committed to the attack lost heavily and made only minor gains of ground. The leading wave of tanks was pulverized by intense and accurate artillery fire.

During the day, the cavalry waited in vain for the chance of mounted action. The 9th Cavalry Brigade concentrated behind Flesquières. Captain A.F. Lascelles of the Bedfordshire Yeomanry wrote of the scene:

November 23rd remains in my mind as one of the few picturesque days in the whole war. . . . In the plain to the south-east of Bourlon Wood, squadrons were manoeuvring in line, Generals cavorting about with orderlies carrying pennons, and the whole scene like an eighteenth-century battle-print, with only a few strong puffs of shrapnel to mar the harmony. We were all elated by the feeling that at last something was doing in the cavalry world.[27]

That did not turn out to be the case, though Byng did his best to get cavalry into the picture. At 2:05 P.M. IV Corps received a signal from Army headquarters stating that the 1st Cavalry Division was available to be used in a dismounted capacity. Then at 2:30 P.M. Byng informed Cavalry Corps headquarters that airmen had reported the capture of Bourlon Wood. It might now be possible to pass cavalry northwards to "operate against Cambrai from the west."[28] Later in the afternoon, however, once it was apparent there had been no breakthrough, the 9th Cavalry Brigade formed a dismounted battalion and reinforced the 40th Division that evening.

Meanwhile, the 51st Division had attacked the village of Fontaine with the 152nd Brigade. The attack was led by the 1/6th Seaforths and 1/6th Gordons. There were no smoke shells available to build up a screen to cover the advance of the tanks and infantry. The Highlanders were driven to ground by machine-gun fire in front of Fontaine. The tanks that drove on to enter the strongly garrisoned and barricaded village lost heavily; armor-piercing bullets fired at close range were able to drill holes in the tanks. A tank commander reported that desperate German soldiers physically wrestled with one of his tank's guns.[29]

During the night of November 23/24 snow fell, then rain. The Guards Division was brought forward from V Corps to relieve the 51st Division, which had lost casualties of 68 officers and 1,502 other ranks for November 20 to 23. The historian of the Grenadier Guards observed that the relief was made more difficult by the presence of a host of cavalry, which "stood about in large numbers and blocked the road."[30]

Severe fighting continued in Bourlon Wood during November 24. German attacks in the morning were beaten off, but another attack at 3 P.M. from the northeast was more effective. A British counterattack from 4 P.M. pushed the Germans back onto the northern slopes of the ridge. While this was taking place, troops of the 40th Division had again attacked Bourlon village. The main result of this effort was that a large part of the 14th Highland Light Infantry was cut off and trapped within the village.

Field Marshal Haig had visited Byng at Albert on the morning of November 24. Haig again insisted that Bourlon Ridge be taken. He also wanted the cavalry to be involved in the battle once open country was reached. When the Third Army's headquarters issued IV Corps orders to continue the Bourlon battle into the following day, contingency was made for cavalry action on a large scale "if the capture of Bourlon village enables the cavalry to get through."[31] If that happened, General Kavanagh of the Cavalry Corps was to assume command of operations north of Bourlon and use all five of his cavalry divisions.

On the morning of November 25, the 13th East Surrey (of the 40th Division's reserve brigade) endeavored to link up with the Highland Light Infantry (HLI) unit stranded in Bourlon village. Contact was made with the HLI's headquarters and one company, but the other three companies in the northern part of the village were compelled to surrender about 9:30 A.M. The East Surreys and remainder of the HLI formed a rough-and-ready perimeter near the southeast corner of the village; these troops were later brought back into British lines to avoid falling victim to friendly shelling. In the meantime, the 2nd Cavalry Division had arrived at Ribécourt at 11 A.M. By noon it was clear there was no prospect of mounted action, and the division formed three dismounted battalions to assist the infantry.

Another round of German attacks on Bourlon Wood in the midafternoon of November 25 added to the confusion and tumult that had blighted that patch of disputed terrain for the past three days. German commanders were determined to fight hard to retain a footing on Bourlon Ridge.

By November 25 a stalemate had settled upon the front at Cambrai. Field Marshal Haig's plan for a deep advance beyond Bourlon Ridge to the Sensee River had amounted to precious little apart from heavy losses. Haig ordered Byng to at least complete the capture of Bourlon Ridge. A deadline of November 27 was given for this task. Haig informed Robertson at the War Office: "My orders to Byng are to complete the capture of Bourlon position and such tactical points on its flanks as are necessary to secure it. The positions gained are to be held and troops to be ready to exploit any local advantage and follow up any retirement of enemy. Nothing beyond above to be attempted."[32] The political value of the Cambrai success would rapidly turn sour if the ground recently gained was not properly consolidated. Throughout the war communiqués issued by GHQ had placed enormous value on any real estate captured, however small in extent. The prevalence of that doleful political standard was an ever-present factor in operational decision-making.

The 62nd Division relieved the 40th Division after darkness had fallen on November 25. The 40th Division had lost upwards of four thousand casualties in the sustained dogfight to capture and hold most of Bourlon Wood. "The success had been achieved," recorded the division's history, "against a resolute and enterprising enemy. There had come into fashion . . . by 1917 a tendency to depreciate the fighting worth of the enemy. Those who were in the front line knew better. The Hun had many objectionable qualities, but lack of 'guts' was not one of them."[33]

Improved flying weather saw the Royal Flying Corps constantly in the air over the Bourlon sector. British aviators were opposed by Richthofen's "Circus," which had arrived on the Cambrai front from Flanders to bolster German fighter strength. On the evening of November 26, Freiherr von Richthofen was a dinner guest of the officers of Arras Group. General Otto von Moser wrote:

> I had the pleasure of the company of Rittmeister von Richthofen at dinner—despite all his fame he is of exemplary modesty and a good companion. He explained to us in simple terms, that the entire secret of his success was his firm decision in aerial combat to approach enemies so closely that he both pressured them psychologically and was certain of hitting them with his machine guns. In other words the same principles apply in the air as on the ground! When our First Adjutant remarked to him at the table that he had now done his duty and could in future restrict his contribution to the important task of training newcomers, he replied, without a trace of bitterness, "I am not numbered amongst those whose primary concern is to survive the war and to preserve their valuable lives for the post-war world."[34]

While the Germans were building up their air strength at Cambrai, the British were starting to do the opposite. On November 26, aircraft of I Brigade RFC were withdrawn from the Third Army's front to rejoin the First Army.

On the morning of November 26, a IV Corps conference was held at the advanced headquarters of the 62nd Division, which was situated in a hut in the grounds of Havrincourt Château. A dawn attack was arranged for the following day to secure a tenable line on Bourlon Ridge for the coming winter. Major General G. Feilding of the Guards Division believed that this proposed operation had no prospect of success; he put his views in a written appreciation for his corps commander, General Woollcombe.[35] Feilding pointed out that the Germans overlooked much of the country from Bourlon Wood to Flesquières. Fontaine was covered by the fire of German batteries sited on higher ground. Feilding went on to advise that if the resources were not available for a more powerful attack, the line should retire to Flesquières Ridge. Woollcombe said the matter must be referred to General Byng. Nothing came of this, as Field Marshal Haig had given Byng firm instructions to complete the capture of Bourlon Ridge.[36] The Third Army's commander ordered the attack to go ahead. The Guards and twelve tanks were to assault Fontaine; the 62nd Division and twenty tanks would attack Bourlon village and a strip of ground beyond a shell-shattered Bourlon Wood.

Snow fell during the night of November 26/27. The snow had turned to cold, drizzling rain by 6:20 A.M., which was zero hour for IV Corps' assault. The Guards Division attacked Fontaine with the 2nd Guards Brigade. The right-flank 3rd Grenadier Guards advanced on both sides of the Bapaume-Cambrai road, and fought their way into the village despite heavy losses from machine-gun fire. The left-flank 1st Coldstream Guards advanced into the gap between Fontaine and Bourlon Wood. Farther to the left, Lieutenant Colonel H.R. Alexander's 2nd Irish Guards fought their way through the northeast part of Bourlon Wood. A strong counterattack, however, by the 60th Reserve Regiment and other German troops retook Fontaine and forced the Guards back to their original start line. The 2nd Guards Brigade lost more than a thousand casualties in the engagement. A senior officer subsequently observed: "It was criminal to have launched this attack—I know Feilding did his best to avoid doing so, but got little backing from the Corps Commander."[37]

Meanwhile, the 62nd Division's 186th and 187th Brigades attacked in the adjoining sector. British troops entered Bourlon village, but were cast out again. The detachment of tanks involved lost heavily; the battle had failed by late morning.

That afternoon Byng ordered IV Corps to consolidate the front. The highest part of Bourlon Ridge within the wood was held by British troops, yet the Germans had retained observation across the British front from the shoulders of the ridge. During the night of November 27/28 the Germans shelled Bourlon Wood with gas, "in order," wrote General von Moser, "to make life as difficult as possible for the British who were occupying it."[38] There was further gas shelling of the wood the following night, during which the Guards and 62nd Divisions were relieved by the 59th and 47th Divisions, respectively. Haig informed the French that their assistance was no longer needed in the Cambrai sector; the troops made available by Pétain packed up and prepared for departure to other parts of the western front.[39]

Haig wrote in his diary for November 27: "Charteris reported no change in Enemy on Cambrai battle front since yesterday. His troops are very thin on this front except at Bourlon. In fact the situation is most favourable for us but unfortunately I have not got the necessary number of troops to exploit our success."[40] By November 28 a salient four miles deep and nine miles wide had been created in the German front. Haig's scheme to advance northwards beyond Bourlon had amounted to nothing more than an awkward enlargement to the piece of territory taken in the attack of November 20. As the 6th Division's General Marden was to put it: "While smashing in the enemy's salient we ourselves were making a salient, extending our front, as far as the Third Army was concerned."[41] The "sides and hinges" of this new salient were vulnerable to counterattack.

# 13

## The Tide Turns at Cambrai

The initial tank assault at Cambrai had been a rude shock for German commanders. In response to the crisis, a stream of divisions was rushed to the sector under threat, thirteen divisions from November 20 to 30 and four more by December 2. No fewer than 1,163 trains were hastily unloaded at Cambrai across this period.[1] The Cambrai rail junction was ideally situated for the rapid arrival of reinforcements in the event of a sudden emergency.

Once the situation had stabilized, German staffs began making plans for a riposte to restore the Hindenburg Line to its original undented condition. Marwitz's Second Army headquarters issued a preliminary order outlining a scheme on November 24. Three days later Ludendorff and Rupprecht met at Le Cateau to discuss matters further. The plan agreed upon was for the corps of Generals von Watter (Caudry Group) and Hugo von Kathen (Busigny Group) to attack the southern shoulder of the new salient pressing into the German front. General von Moser's corps (Arras Group) would attack the salient's northern shoulder to the west of Bourlon Wood. The point of the British salient would not be attacked. The operation had the support of 1,240 guns. The Second Army's general intention was for British forces in the Cambrai salient to "be cut off along the baseline of the salient and destroyed."[2]

The planned infantry assault was designed to deeply and rapidly penetrate the British front. The success of this "storm troop" approach would rely on the willingness of unit leaders to locate gaps in an enemy's front and bypass or envelop centers of resistance; the notion of "infiltration" best expresses the concept. The attack was to be preceded by a short bombardment of high explosives supplemented by large quantities of gas and smoke shells. There would be little time, however, for German troops to practice these revised tactical methods.[3]

The assembly of such a large force did not go unnoticed on the British side of the front. On November 28 and 29 there were reports at British headquarters of unusual

German rail and road transport movements opposite the southern part of the Cambrai salient. By day troops also noted an increase in German aerial reconnaissance.

Nevertheless, the state of play at the front was uncertain given the misty weather. This kind of weather had been of benefit to the British prior to the tank attack of November 20, but now the Germans would enjoy that advantage. In addition, the air superiority the Royal Flying Corps had possessed a week earlier had been carelessly put aside. The number of aircraft available to the Third Army was steadily reduced on the assumption that the Cambrai battle was winding down. For instance, on November 28 the Ninth Wing departed for routine operations elsewhere. This took place at a time when the Germans were increasing their air strength in the sector.

The 55th Division was the left-hand formation of VII Corps, the Third Army's southernmost corps. The unit history of the 1/10th Liverpool Scottish recorded that on November 28 German artillery fire fell across the 55th Division's sector with a suspicious regularity. "The fire appeared to come from batteries which had not been previously active and the type of fire—airbursts with high-explosive shell—could mean one thing only, registration. A number of low-flying enemy aeroplanes, too, persistently reconnoitred the whole of the Divisional area."[4] The following day there was more registration by guns and trench mortars of different calibers. The 55th Division's commander, Major General H.S. Jeudwine, made an inspection tour of the line and subsequently issued an order to his division warning that the Germans were preparing to attack. Jeudwine recalled: "On the evening of 28 November as a result of personal reconnaissance from the front line trenches, I made a report to the Brigadier-General General Staff [of VII Corps, J.T. Burnett-Stuart] stating definitely that I considered an attack probable and giving full reasons. He said that the [VII] Corps commander [Sir T.D. Snow] was thoroughly aware of the situation and that it had been reported to the Army."[5]

On the left flank of the 55th Division was the 12th Division. Officers of the 12th Division's right-flank 35th Brigade believed that a German attack was brewing. Some local precautions were taken in respect to the 35th Brigade's sector, but the trench routine of the center and left-flank brigades of the division went on as usual. On the afternoon of November 29, Jeudwine met with Major General A.B. Scott, the 12th Division's commander, to exchange views.

Lieutenant General Snow of VII Corps had only two divisions to cover a long front. He could do little to prepare for a major German attack without reinforcement. At 7 P.M. on November 28, VII Corps' chief staff officer—Burnett-Stuart—telephoned the Third Army's headquarters and spoke with Major General Vaughan, Byng's chief of staff, to warn of unusual enemy activity opposite the front of the 55th Division. Vaughan's record of the conversation read:

B.G.G.S. [Brigadier General General Staff] VII Corps rang up regarding unusual enemy activity opposite their front. G.O.C. [General Officer Commanding] 55th Division thinks enemy is going to attack. Discussed question and agreed that an attack from the north and south was a good and likely operation from enemy point of view. VII Corps are in touch with III Corps about it and are on the alert. Told VII Corps we would arrange to keep Guards handy to help if required. Cavalry also could move up if wanted. 61st Division coming down on 30th.[6]

No explicit action was taken by the Third Army in the wake of Burnett-Stuart's message; no warning order was issued or reserves repositioned.

The dogma prevailed at Third Army and General Headquarters (GHQ) that the Germans on the western front were exhausted and discouraged by the year's campaigning. That was a comforting and cheerful conclusion. An attack on Bourlon Wood was considered possible, but that place was heavily manned given the recent heavy fighting in the sector. The speed of the improvisation behind the upcoming German attack made it hard to tell whether German reinforcement of the Cambrai sector was for defensive or offensive purpose. The kaiser's army had not attacked in strength on the western front for a considerable period of time.[7] In defense of the Third Army's staff, however, it should be pointed out that the warnings passed up the chain of command did not anticipate the scale of the attack that was poised to strike. Nor was the situation felt to be sufficiently urgent to warrant personal representations at Byng's headquarters. After the event, the warnings would acquire a persuasiveness that was lacking when it actually mattered.

The storm in prospect soon descended. Six divisions of Busigny and Caudry Groups stood ready to attack III and VII Corps on the southern flank of the Cambrai salient. On the cold morning of November 30, in thick fog, the Germans advanced after a brief, drenching bombardment of high explosives and gas. The opening blows fell upon the 55th Division, which held an extended nine-thousand-yard front just south of the hinge where the salient reconnected to the old British front line. The length of the 55th Division's partly wired and poorly fortified sector was almost as long as the original attack front of ten days' before.

German guns opened the bombardment of the 55th Division at 6 A.M., when it was still dark. The division's defensive positions were on the forward slopes of the spurs running eastwards toward the St. Quentin Canal, which was about one thousand yards from the British front line. As the bombardment grew heavier, telephone wires were cut and warnings could not be sent rearwards by that method. The most exposed posts were deluged by the bombs of heavy trench mortars. A thick mist kept the morning dark when the German advance got underway at about 7 A.M.; warning flares flew skywards the length of the 55th Division's front. (There was no infantry attack on the division of VII Corps on the southern flank of Jeudwine's formation.)

The 165th Brigade was the right-hand brigade of the 55th Division. All of the brigade's infantry units belonged to the King's Liverpool Regiment. The brigade's right-hand battalion was not attacked, and the center battalion repelled those German troops to appear out of the mist; the left-hand battalion, however, had its defenses crushed by mortar bombardment, and the survivors were driven back to a reserve line.

The 55th Division's left-hand 166th Brigade felt the full force of the German blow. The weight of the thrust smashed in the patchwork defensive front. The left-hand battalion—1/5th South Lancashire—was holding a two-thousand-yard front that included the Banteux ravine. This unit's extended line of platoon and section posts was engulfed by German infantry emerging out of the fog. The whole of the South Lancashire battalion was overrun: 21 officers and 540 other ranks were lost.[8] In the center of the brigade front, the 1/5th Loyal North Lancashire had three companies in the front line; few men of those companies avoided capture after their positions were taken in a fight lasting upwards of an hour. The brigade's right-flank Liverpool Scottish (1/10th King's) was also heavily attacked and lost more than 500 killed, wounded, and missing. The brigade's support battalion, 1/5th King's Own Royal Lancaster, was drawn into the fight as the front caved in.

A British officer wrote of the desperate onslaught: "My first impression was that of an earthquake. Then it seemed to me that an endless procession of aeroplanes was grazing my head with their wheels. On recovering from the first shock of my surprise the Germans were far behind me."[9] Once through the left half of the 55th Division's front, the Germans pressed on for the village of Villers-Guislain. A German regiment reported that no more formal defenses were encountered from about that place. "It reminded one of the mobile warfare of 1914."[10] British artillerymen in Villers-Guislain lost fifty-eight guns of all types when German troops overran the village. The front gave way sufficiently for the Germans to reach Gouzeaucourt, three to four miles behind the original line, preceded by a stream of fugitives from a variety of British units. In Gouzeaucourt another five batteries of heavy howitzers were surprised and captured. By now the German advance was halfway to Metz, a village to the south of Havrincourt Wood. If the pincers attacking the Cambrai salient could converge on Metz, the salient might be collapsed.

The 55th Division's reserve brigade—the 164th—hastily took up positions to the south of Villers-Guislain. Two battalions of the neighboring 24th Division were sent to reinforce this line. The 55th Division had faced units belonging to three divisions of Busigny Group.

To the north of the 55th Division, III Corps' 12th Division held almost five thousand yards of front with all three of its brigades in the line. In this sector, German troops of Caudry Group were able to mass out of sight of British outposts due to the configuration of the St. Quentin Canal. The attack by Caudry Group to the north of Banteux ravine started an hour later than the attack of Busigny Group south of the ravine.

The 12th Division's front was heavily shelled from about 6:45 A.M. The attack fell at 8 A.M. with a sudden and devastating impact; the Germans came pouring on like a bank holiday crowd. The right flank of the 35th Brigade—the right-hand brigade of the division—was already under threat given the German drive down Banteux ravine. The 12th Division's forwardmost battalions were overrun. The nearby reserve brigade of the 20th Division—the 60th—was drawn into the desperate fight. The 12th Division lost thirty-five hundred casualties, which was over half its strength in infantry given the losses suffered in the earlier phase of the Cambrai campaign and a lack of reinforcing drafts.

Worse was to come for British forces. Beyond the 12th Division's left flank, waves of German infantry came swarming up the western bank of the St. Quentin Canal to fall upon the understrength 20th Division, which was in the canal bend south and southeast of Masnières. From left to right, the 61st and 59th Brigades held the division's poorly fortified front. In the 59th Brigade's sector, the forward line was held by two battalions of the King's Royal Rifle Corps (KRRC). These troops were overwhelmed by the sudden onslaught. Only 4 officers and 16 men of the 10th KRRC escaped rearwards; the fate of the 11th KRRC was similar and resulted in casualties of 385.[11] The brigade's support battalion, the 10th Rifle Brigade, suffered almost as badly. The brigade's reserve battalion (11th Rifle Brigade) managed to hold a position upon which the remnants of the units further forward rallied to fight off their attackers.

The left-hand 61st Brigade had the 7th Somerset Light Infantry and 12th King's in the forward zone. The Somersets reported that a heavy mortar barrage from across the canal was falling on their posts.

> Immediately behind the trench-mortar barrage the enemy's infantry could be seen advancing in great strength. It was indeed a sight which almost made men gasp. Line after line, in massed formation, the Germans advanced to the attack, providing splendid targets for Lewis guns, machine guns and rifles. . . . Swarms of low-flying aeroplanes, the observers using machine guns, crossed from the enemy's side and flew up and down above the British trenches at an altitude of from fifty to one hundred feet. Above the Somerset men, at least forty-five hostile machines were counted.[12]

Low-flying German aircraft were protected from a higher altitude by the Red Baron's wing of four fighter squadrons. The forward zone of the 61st Brigade was swamped and the remnants pushed back pell-mell. An officer wrote of the lively scene: "The whole of the high ground in our rear . . . was covered with men like Epsom Downs on Derby Day, and we realised some great disaster had taken place. The men we saw were . . . coming back from their front line in full retreat!"[13]

The German thrust burst through the 20th Division's front. The attackers fell upon the rear of the 29th Division, the commander of which, General de Lisle, had to make a rushed departure to safety with his staff after it was realized that hostile troops were only three hundred yards away. At the height of the crisis, the 29th Division, which was in Masnières and the bridgehead over the St. Quentin Canal, hastily formed a defensive flank to parry the German tide lapping against Les Rues Vertes and heading for Marcoing. The 29th Division's reserve brigade counterattacked at about 11:30 A.M. to stabilize the situation and secure the battery positions of the divisional artillery, which expended a prodigious number of rounds across the day. III Corps' left-hand division—the 6th—was not directly attacked in any great strength. The line near Cantaing was approached by German troops, but this tentative probe was driven off by defensive fire.

British reserves behind the Cambrai salient were assembled to shore up the front. About 12:30 P.M. the 1st Guards Brigade advanced from Metz toward Gouzeaucourt while troops of broken units headed in the other direction. A well-organized attack swept the German force at Gouzeaucourt out of that place and secured one hundred prisoners. During the afternoon British, Indian, and Canadian regiments of the Cavalry Corps arrived to prolong the line to the south of the Guards. As many tanks as were mechanically ready for action were set in motion back toward the firing line. The 3rd Guards Brigade took station on the left of the 1st Guards Brigade. The 6th Division's reserve brigade—the 16th—came up on the northern flank of the Guards. A series of brisk encounter actions were fought with German troops to patch up the front wherever that could be managed. Gonnelieu, on the eastern side of Gouzeaucourt, remained in German hands.

Caudry and Busigny Groups had waded into the British front with a force of six divisions supported by additional reserves. A high level of surprise and fog had helped German infantry make rapid progress in the first few hours of battle, but casualties among leaders, hard fighting, and the long distances traversed thoroughly disorganized units. By afternoon, despite the successes of the morning, the advance had faltered.

After receiving news of the German assault, Haig had hastened to the Third Army's headquarters. Reinforcements were ordered to the Cambrai sector from other

**Lieutenant H. Strachan at the head of a squadron of the Canadians' Fort Garry Horse. (I.W.M.)**

parts of the British Expeditionary Force's (BEF) front; Pétain made several divisions available to support the right flank of Byng's army.

In the meantime, the northern arm of the German offensive had commenced. The attack of Moser's Arras Group fell upon the right-hand division of VI Corps (56th Division) and IV Corps (2nd and 47th Divisions). Arras Group attacked with three divisions, which passed through two divisions holding the front. The German 221st Division attacked with its left on the western side of Bourlon Wood. The 214th Division was on the right flank of the 221st Division. Farther to the west, the 49th Reserve Division attacked on both sides of the Canal du Nord. Surprise was hardly possible given the open ground to the west of Bourlon and a midmorning start time. (The German attack did not involve IV Corps' right-hand 59th Division.)

Moser's artillery began firing at dawn and a heavy bombardment began at 8:50 A.M., shortly after which infantry advanced across the ridge running westwards from Bourlon to Moeuvres. A patchy smoke barrage was laid in a bid to obscure the view of the defense. Waves of soldiers in full marching order with packs swarmed over the skyline and moved down a gentle slope devoid of cover. Three German observation balloons ascended to float over Bourlon village; the crews had a panoramic view of the pitched battle in progress.[14] Overhead, German aircraft swarmed like angry bees.

The attack was greeted by a heavy fusillade of rifle and Lewis gun fire. Vickers machine guns fired steadily across open ground at the enticing targets on display. Two German field batteries that rode forward in close support of the infantry were quickly shelled to silence when they attempted to come into action. Late in the morning, near the junction of the 2nd and 47th Divisions, the Germans reached the posts of the 1st Royal Berkshire, but with the assistance of the 23rd Royal Fusiliers, the attackers were driven out again and lost heavily as they retired over the crest of the ridge.[15]

Early in the afternoon Arras Group attacked again. About 2 P.M. a flank and frontal assault pushed the bulk of the 1/6th London Regiment off some elevated ground outside the western fringe of Bourlon Wood. This thrust exposed the left flank of the 47th Division; reserves were rushed into place to form a defensive flank to combat the threat. The 1/6th London suffered casualties of 13 officers and 369 other ranks.[16] The 47th Division's right-hand brigade was not directly attacked in any strength, though within Bourlon Wood the 1/19th London was severely gassed to a point where only 70 of all ranks remained fit for duty. (The 47th Division's commander, Major General Sir G.F. Gorringe, had commanded Tigris Corps during the final phase of the ill-fated attempt to relieve Kut al-Amara in Mesopotamia in 1916.)

Farther west, the 2nd Division's left-hand 6th Brigade was astride the Canal du Nord. These troops were heavily attacked during the course of the day from the ruins of German-held Moeuvres. The 56th Division held the front southwest of Moeuvres and was also attacked without much success.

By midafternoon the northern arm of the German offensive was fought to a standstill; by evening a darkened sky had swept a veil over the masses of dead and wounded littering the battlefield. Arras Group took four hundred British prisoners, which was a disappointing haul and in no way commensurate to the effort made.[17]

The following day of December 1 the combatants renewed the unfinished struggle at Cambrai. British formations undertook counterattacks on the front of III and VII Corps. In particular, the Guards Division was ordered to attack eastwards at 6:30 A.M. in cooperation with units of the 4th and 5th Cavalry Divisions. Twenty tanks were to assist the Guards, though some of the vehicles did not arrive on schedule for this improvised operation.

In the left flank sector of the Guards Division, the 3rd Guards Brigade attacked Gonnelieu village. A spirited advance by the 4th Grenadier Guards was halted by machine-gun fire about two hundred yards from the outskirts of the village. To the right of the Grenadiers, the Welsh Guards lost heavily rushing a ridgeline southwest of Gonnelieu. In the right-flank sector of the Guards Division, the 1st Guards Brigade attacked Gauche Wood successfully.

On the southern flank of the Guards, the 5th Cavalry Division's Ambala Cavalry Brigade closed on Gauche Wood from the southwest. Dismounted cavalrymen entered the wood to find the Guards already in possession of this undamaged thirteen acres of forestry. Meanwhile, to the right, dismounted units of the Lucknow Cavalry Brigade attacked Villers-Guislain without success.

Farther to the south, the 4th Cavalry Division assembled near Peiziere with the object of seizing Villers Ridge. General Kavanagh, the Cavalry Corps' commander, "insisted" that troops of the 4th Cavalry Division advance mounted given the relatively fluid state of the front.[18] The division's lead formation, the Mhow Cavalry Brigade, massed near Peiziere from 6:30 A.M. behind a railway cutting. The cavalry was drawn up in formation and exposed to intermittent shelling for the next two hours.

About 8 A.M. Brigadier General Neil Haig, the Mhow brigade's commander, got news that the Lucknow brigade's attack to the north was stalled. When Kavanagh telephoned Major General A.A. Kennedy of the 4th Cavalry Division for news of the Mhow brigade's attack, he was informed that it had not started, as the Lucknow brigade was held up on the northern flank. In reply, Kavanagh said that the attack of the Mhow brigade was to get underway without any further delay. Haig felt that the decision was unwise, and Kennedy, the divisional commander, thought likewise. There was no artillery support available apart from the Royal Horse Artillery batteries usually attached to a cavalry division.

The Mhow Cavalry Brigade attacked at 9:35 A.M. The 2nd Lancers (Gardner's Horse), one squadron of the 6th Inniskilling Dragoons, and a section of the brigade's Machine Gun Squadron rode through Epehy. Captain D.E. Whitworth noted that "we passed through the trenches of our own very astonished infantry."[19] Fortuitously, instead of proceeding northeast directly toward their designated objective, the commander of the leading Lancer squadron, Major G. Knowles, chose a more easterly route down a valley leading toward Catelet Copse. The four squadrons of the Lancers galloped down the grassy valley, one behind the other. Bursts of machine-gun fire rang out, but there were few casualties. German troops in the vicinity may have been taken by surprise, in addition to which the valley afforded a degree of cover.

After a ride of two miles, C Squadron came to strands of fenced wire covering a defended sunken road known as Kildare Trench. Gaps in the wire were found, and the riders and horses forced their way onto the roadway.[20] Lieutenant Colonel H.H.F. Turner was killed by machine-gun fire passing the wire. After a flurry of hand-to-hand fighting with a small German detachment, Kildare Trench (or Lane) was occupied, though no further progress was possible. A number of Germans were killed in the melee, and two prisoners and three light machine guns taken. The attached squadron of Inniskillings and the machine-gun section joined the Lancers in the new position. Some of the horses were sheltered in the sunken road, but the rest had to be sent back up the valley again and suffered heavy losses on the way.

Kildare Trench was held by troops of the Mhow brigade for the rest of the afternoon. Darkness had fallen by 5 P.M., after which the cavalry abandoned their untenable outposts and retired southward to a position held by British infantry of the 55th Division. Total casualties for the 2nd Lancers were 9 killed of all ranks, 3 died of wounds, 53 wounded, and 48 missing (of whom 36 were killed and the rest prisoners).[21]

Meantime, soon after the charge of the 2nd Lancers, the main body of the Inniskilling Dragoons had advanced toward Villers-Guislain from Peiziere by a direct route. The strongly defended approaches to Villers-Guislain lay across rolling downland. The leading squadron of the Inniskillings and a machine-gun section were swiftly destroyed by machine-gun fire and sent crashing to the ground in heaps of horses and riders; the survivors were taken prisoner. The commanding officer of the Inniskillings ordered a retreat, and the remaining squadrons of the regiment returned back whence they came. The Inniskillings lost casualties of 6 officers and 108 other ranks; the machine-gun section lost 2 officers and 53 other ranks.[22]

During the morning, the Mhow Cavalry Brigade's commander sent squadrons of the 38th Central India Horse to the aid of the 2nd Lancers; these troops advanced dismounted, as hostile fire had grown too persistent to risk further mounted action.[23] This movement, which was renewed in the afternoon, was checked by cross fire and the troops driven to cover. About noon General Kavanagh ordered the 4th and 5th Cavalry Divisions to again attack their objectives, but little resulted from this.

Elsewhere on December 1, the 29th Division came under renewed attack. At 7:15 A.M. heavy German shellfire fell on Masnières and Les Rues Vertes; an hour later an assault by two regiments of the 30th Division on the south side of the canal was repelled. In the afternoon a further attack on Les Rues Vertes was only held with difficulty. During the night of December 1/2, Masnières was given up on the authority of the 29th Division's leadership. Marcoing remained in British hands. The tank "Flying Fox II" was abandoned in Masnières forlornly wedged in the collapsed wreckage of the bridge over the canal it had tried to cross on November 20.[24]

On the front of IV Corps, December 1 was marked by a heavy gas bombardment of Bourlon Wood in the early hours of the morning. During the day V Corps headquarters relieved IV Corps headquarters; Lieutenant General Sir E.A. Fanshawe took over at 6 P.M. Fighting continued in the sector of the 2nd Division's 6th Brigade, astride the Canal du Nord.

On December 2 the 61st Division began to take over the line covering La Vacquerie from the exhausted troops of the 12th and 20th Divisions. (The 21st Division had relieved the 55th Division the previous night.) Local fighting continued across the Cambrai front for the next couple of days, especially about the canal bend near Marcoing.

Crown Prince Rupprecht decided to close down the battle at Cambrai and ordered that the line be consolidated. The austere crown prince observed that "if the success is not so great as we hoped, it has nevertheless given the British a blow."[25] General von der Marwitz conceded that the battle had "run itself out." General von Kuhl wrote: "We ought to have been able to achieve much more on 30 November. The situation was so favourable and we can expect no such opportunity again. Along the [St. Quentin] canal the British presented a virtually open flank. They had been careless, over confident and were surprised."[26]

The Germans had worked out how to break rapidly into an opponent's front using artillery and infantry, but how to sustain an advance on foot for any appreciable distance was a problem still awaiting a solution. The army of Imperial Germany was not well prepared for an offensive style of warfare on the western front after three years mainly on the defensive. The headquarters of Army Group Crown Prince Rupprecht concluded:

> The Cambrai counter-offensive of 30 November has shown that the current organization and equipment of our Army on the Western Front does not in all respects correspond to the demands of mobile warfare. The deficiencies would have been brought into even sharper relief if our operations had been pressed forward over a larger area for days at a time. . . . The mobility of all formations and resupply of ammunition are of prime importance. All the accumulated ballast of trench warfare must be reduced or even—at least temporarily—be dispensed with.[27]

The railways had speedily delivered a large force of troops and their equipment to Cambrai, but a reliance on horse-drawn transport forward of that place restricted what an offensive could achieve. It would be difficult, however, to find the additional "horse-power" needed for hauling a larger stock of supply wagons and guns. The demands of the eastern front for horses, given its vast distances and weather extremes, had been exorbitant throughout the war, and remained high at the close of 1917, even though the fighting in the east had largely ceased.

Upon review, German commanders felt that the troops leading the attack were not sufficiently trained in the principles of an infiltration assault. The linear tactics and centralized control of operations that had been the norm on the western front were hard to suddenly cast aside.[28] There was also the thorny question as to whether or not a densely held defensive zone could be "infiltrated" on a broad front in any but the most favorable circumstances.

At the very least, German staffs realized that in the future they would need to be more watchful in any sector where tank attack was practical. Rupprecht wrote that "there can be no more mention of quiet fronts."[29] Nevertheless, the quick reversal of the result of November 20 tended to reduce the impact of the lesson of that day. The German High Command did not initiate a crash program to build armored vehicles. Marwitz wrote after the battle:

> I was back in Bourlon today. In one place five [knocked-out] tanks were right next to each other and three or four [more] were quite close by. Two had caught fire and the men within them were burnt to death—a dreadful sight! I cannot help it, I do not regard these things in their current form as battleworthy. Of the approximately 300 which attacked us, seventy-five were knocked out and are still within our lines and a further thirty are located to our front. A large number also ditched, but were subsequently towed away.

Marwitz concluded that the loss rate of the tanks was "unsustainable."[30]

British forces in the Cambrai sector commenced a retirement to a more defensible winter line on the night of December 4/5. This decision was made by Field Marshal Haig. The sector from Bourlon to Marcoing was given up. This included a number of places for which a great deal of blood had been shed by British troops. In some localities the Germans did not realize that the British had departed until the following afternoon. Additional adjustments of the line were made over the next couple of nights. Flesquières village was retained at the head of a reduced salient. Haig wrote to Robertson to explain that the withdrawal was regrettable, but necessary because of a lack of reserves.

In total, the BEF used fifteen infantry and four cavalry divisions in the Cambrai fighting. The Third Army's losses from November 20 to December 8 were 44,207. On November 30, 6,000 prisoners, 103 field guns, and 55 heavy guns were lost. German casualties for the battle were 41,000, which included 11,000 prisoners, along with 98 field guns and 40 heavy guns.[31] Given that both armies did their share of attacking in the brief campaign, it is credible that the casualty toll for each army was similar.

In spite of the campaign ending in renewed stalemate, Cambrai helped to vindicate the embattled tank arm and held out the prospect of an eventual return to a more open style of warfare. "That half an inch of steel will keep out half an ounce of lead," noted Colonel Fuller, "is a fact that cannot be disputed." At Cambrai, tanks "had performed the star turn of the war."[32] Colonel Baker-Carr wrote that "a new era in warfare had dawned, but only a few deep-thinkers were aware of it."[33] At the Munitions ministry, Churchill was impressed by the performance of the Tank Corps. He would assert with vigor that a more inspired army leadership ought to have made greater use of tanks. "This in many variants," Churchill wrote of Cambrai, "this in larger and better forms ought to have been done if only the Generals had not been content to fight machine gun bullets with the breasts of gallant men and think that was waging war."[34] In contrast, at GHQ, General Kiggell had not been converted by the recent spectacle; he would subsequently say to Elles of the tank attack: "A splendid show, but one that can never be repeated."[35] The tank, for Kiggell at least, remained a "stunt" weapon.

In London the Cambrai tank attack had caused considerable excitement. The advance made in the first couple of days was not far short of all the gains recently made at Ypres in several months: forty-two square miles at Cambrai as against fifty-four square miles in Flanders.[36] Reports of the German counterattack, however, caused grave displeasure. The War Cabinet was appalled that Haig's staff had failed to detect large German troop movements in a sector that was already the focus of attention. Such a blatantly poor display of staff and intelligence work did not bode well for the future. The Germans were clearly far from the end of their resources, notwithstanding the claims of GHQ that very heavy casualties had been inflicted earlier in the year. The claims of GHQ that German morale was weak and subject to deterioration had little foundation. Lloyd George was incensed and labeled Charteris, Haig's intelligence chief, a "public danger." At a December 4 War Cabinet meeting it was suggested that Haig was "not well-advised on the intelligence side of his staff."[37]

General Wilson wrote in his diary on December 5: "Whew! This will be a big shock at home. Also I suppose we have had heavy losses. Personally I am glad Haig came out of that salient [at Cambrai]. We ought never to have tried to hold it. It is an awfully expensive thing to teach a stupid man his business and really there was no excuse for Haig first making and then trying to hold another Ypres salient."[38] Haig had snatched defeat from the jaws of victory. The Cambrai battle had started as a tank operation, only to mutate into an attempted advance by masses of cavalry, before finally becoming just another installment of infantry attrition. For Haig the tanks were a useful engineering tool best utilized to create opportunity for a host of horsemen lugging saber and lance. The field marshal's shortsighted rejection of French involvement at Cambrai also makes explicit that he was seeking to gain personal prestige from the operation to shore up a sagging political position.[39]

General Byng threw fuel on the fire when he reported to GHQ that the German attack on November 30 had not been a surprise, nor was any senior officer to blame for the loss of ground. "I attribute the reason for the local success on the part of the enemy to one cause and one alone, namely—lack of training on the part of junior officers and N.C.O.s and men."[40] The Cambrai court of inquiry demanded by the War Cabinet proved to be a whitewash. Lloyd George would characterize the inquiry as "an utter sham." (There was no inquiry into Passchendaele.) Nonetheless, all three of the infantry corps commanders principally involved at Cambrai—Pulteney, Snow, and Woollcombe—were replaced in the weeks after the battle's conclusion.

The Cambrai fighting had begun well, but ended sourly. The main shortcoming of the tanks at Cambrai had been a lack of numbers. In less than a week, perhaps a few days at most, the Tank Corps had worn out or lost the bulk of its vehicles and there had been many casualties among tank crews. The battle had proved that field guns made effective anti-tank weapons.

On a brighter note, the success of the tanks had expedited discussions at the War Office, hitherto at a standstill, to expand the Tank Corps from nine to eighteen battalions. On November 27 sanction was given to provide the manpower for this fresh leap forward into the uncharted realm of armored warfare. It would be quite another matter, however, to find the new tanks required for this expansion, given the sharp restrictions on production laid down by Robertson earlier in the war. A long period of time would be needed just to replace the tanks that existing units had lost at Cambrai. Alas, tank production for 1918 would be only 1,359, which was not much higher than the 1,100 built in 1917.[41] Much more might have been done to mass-produce tanks, but their building remained a low priority. The High Command's attitude to tanks was riddled with doubt and qualification. In the aftermath of the Cambrai campaign, the Tank Corps embarked upon a lengthy period of refitting behind the lines; in some respects, the Tanks vanished from view like a child's forgotten toy buried at the back of a toy cupboard.

In Flanders, while the Cambrai battle raged, the front remained stationary. During the later part of November and early December the French First Army was relieved by British and Belgian troops. Two French divisions were sent to Nieuport to relieve the British force on the coast. In the meantime, pressure had mounted for the BEF to extend its front southwards to relieve a significant body of French troops. Anglo-French leaders had already agreed to this step. As the promised relief of French troops had not taken place, an irritated Prime Minister Clemenceau asked the British government for an explanation. Haig informed Robertson that sufficient troops were no longer available to relieve the French, as a number of British divisions had been sent to Italy or used up at Cambrai. The French military did not accept that line of argument. The French had also sent a force to Italy. Clemenceau, now doubly irritated, strongly supported the representations of his commanders; he also pressed for an additional extension of the BEF's front on top of that already promised.

The British government agreed with Clemenceau that the overdue line extension should be carried out. The French prime minister was persuaded to refer the question of an additional extension to the adjudication of the Military Representatives of the Supreme War Council. This news was given to Haig on December 15. The field marshal met with Pétain two days later. "I told him," wrote Haig, "exactly how tired the British troops were, and the shortage of drafts. I told him I could relieve two Divisions on January 10th and extend to the Oise [River] by the end of January."[42]

In Flanders, German commanders were unsure if the British intended to launch further attacks. The situation remained unclear until drum fire broke out again in the salient at the start of December. On December 2 and 3, British troops advanced once more in a bid to seize additional parts of Passchendaele ridge. Desultory progress was made. The New Zealanders unsuccessfully attacked Polderhoek Château and spur at noon on December 3. General Rawlinson, now in command in the salient, as Plumer was with British forces in Italy, concluded that Passchendaele was "at present a really untenable position against a properly organized attack."[43] Months of bitter fighting had exhausted a large part of the BEF merely to expand the Ypres salient and make it a positive liability.

By late December things were relatively quiet at Ypres. The primary strategic objective of the Flanders campaign—namely the clearance of the Belgian coast—was a distant and faded memory. In the front line, near the muddy, leveled site of Passchendaele village, troops peering over the sandbagged lips of shell holes were confronted by an eerie landscape. The haunted bog, laced with mist, was beyond the pale of civilization; reflections off dark clouds cast a strange light over the desolation below. The ruined salient was a scene of damnation fit to bring tears to the eyes of an Angel of Mons. Philip Gibbs, the press correspondent, recalled that, by the close of the Passchendaele campaign, "for the first time the British Army lost its spirit of optimism, and there was a sense of deadly depression among many officers and men with whom I came in touch. They saw no ending of the war, and nothing except continuous slaughter, such as that in Flanders."[44]

General Ludendorff wrote of the Flanders campaign: "Enormous masses of ammunition, such as the human mind had never imagined before the war, were hurled upon the bodies of men who passed a miserable existence scattered about in mud-filled shell holes. The horror of the shell-hole area of Verdun was surpassed."[45] A special order of the day was issued to the soldiers of Army Group Crown Prince Rupprecht on December 5:

> The major battle in Flanders appears to be over. In consequence the moment has arrived for me to express my thanks and recognition to all commanders and troops who participated in the Battle of Flanders. . . . Despite the deployment of immense quantities of men and material, the enemy achieved absolutely nothing. A narrow, utterly smashed strip of ground represents his entire gain. He has bought this outcome at the cost of extraordinarily heavy casualties. . . . Each individual man may be assured that he has the thanks of the Fatherland. It was only because our Flanders front withstood every attack that was launched at it, that we were able to conduct massive blows against the Russians in the east and the Italians in the south.[46]

Rupprecht's chief of staff, General von Kuhl, later wrote: "It would be quite wrong to deny the British credit for the courage with which they fought and for the obstinate way they brushed aside the heaviest casualties and kept renewing their assaults. It would be equally wrong to suggest that there was any possibility that they might have broken through." Kuhl described Flanders as "the greatest martyrdom of the war."[47]

Field Marshal Haig claimed in his dispatch that "it was the immense natural difficulties, accentuated manifold by the abnormally wet weather, rather than the enemy's resistance, which limited our progress and prevented the complete capture of the ridge."[48] The state of the ground at Ypres in the autumn of 1917 has been a matter of enduring controversy. Captain B.H. Liddell Hart later published an account of a senior staff officer's first visit to the Ypres salient at the conclusion to the campaign.

This highly placed officer from General Headquarters was on his first visit to the battle-front—at the end of the four months' battle. Growing increasingly uneasy as the car approached the swamp-like edges of the battle area, he eventually burst into tears, crying, "Good God, did we really send men to fight in that?" To which his companion replied that the ground was far worse ahead.[49]

This account is remindful of St. Paul's conversion on the road from Jerusalem to Damascus. The general in the grip of emotion at Ypres was subsequently identified as Haig's chief of staff, Kiggell.[50] The witness for the incident was Brigadier General C.F. Aspinall, chief staff officer of VIII Corps.[51] The incident was relayed to Hart by Brigadier General J.E. Edmonds, who was a GHQ staff officer and later the BEF's official historian. Edmonds could hardly publish such material in an official account, but he cooperated with Hart to ensure the information reached the general public.

Throughout the war, senior staff at GHQ led an existence remarkably divorced from the tumultuous experience of front-line soldiers. During the Passchendaele campaign there were periods—especially during August and October—when GHQ lost touch with the situation at the front.

# 14

## Aftermath

In the closing weeks of 1917, news of the final collapse of the eastern front reached London and Paris; this was a devastating blow to the Allied cause. A successful end to the war now seemed distressingly distant. The new regime in Russia appealed to Berlin for an armistice. On December 3, 1917, delegations of the Central Powers met Soviet representatives at Brest-Litovsk, a Polish fortress town. An armistice was put in place for the eastern front, though negotiations for a final settlement dragged into the new year. The main sticking point was the German demand for large annexations at Russia's expense.

To accelerate the stalled negotiations, German forces attacked eastwards beyond the armistice line in mid-February 1918. This caused the Soviet delegation to hastily cave in to German demands and concede Poland, the Baltic states, and large tracts of western Russia and Ukraine. The Treaty of Brest-Litovsk of March 3, 1918, ended Russia's involvement in the war. The bulk of German forces on the eastern front could now be transferred to northern France, though a large force of lower-grade troops was left behind to garrison the kaiser's expanded eastern empire.

The Russian collapse changed the circumstances that had governed the western front since the close of 1914. The initiative had passed into the hands of the Central Powers.[1] Allied commanders had strong suspicions that the Germans were already making plans for an offensive somewhere on the western front. Those suspicions were well-founded. As long ago as November 11, prior to the Cambrai campaign, a staff conference had been held by Ludendorff at the Mons headquarters of Rupprecht to set in train some dramatic events. By this stage of the conflict Hindenburg and Ludendorff had sufficient domination over the civilian government to draw up their own strategy.

At the Mons conference, assuming that final victory in Russia was imminent, Ludendorff proposed the launching of a major offensive in France early in 1918. He

assessed that a fresh campaign in Italy by German troops had no prospect of decision. The reinforcement of other theaters was barely considered. Ludendorff wanted
to make a single big attack on the western front without a simultaneous diversion. A
defensive strategy was rejected, as the Central Powers expected to have a manpower
advantage in the west after reinforcements arrived from Russia. The notion that an
offensive brand of warfare was the superior alternative was deeply ingrained in the
psyche of OHL (Army General Headquarters). To some extent, the opening campaign of 1914 and the various layers of prewar planning were to be revisited. The
ghosts of Schlieffen and Cannae continued to haunt the Prussian General Staff.[2]

Where exactly should the blow fall on the western front? Verdun? Flanders?
Ludendorff preferred a sector somewhere between those two places. No final decision was taken at Mons, though Ludendorff concluded that "our general situation
requires an attack as early as possible, at the end of February or start of March, before
the arriving American forces tip the scales."[3]

German planners proceeded to study the situation. The High Command decided
on January 21, 1918, to attack on a front between the Rivers Scarpe and Oise. The
ground on that stretch offered relatively few difficulties, and was near to the junction point of British and French forces. If this ambitious offensive began well, the
intention was to roll up the British Expeditionary Force (BEF) in a northwest direction toward the Channel. The German divisions that were to spearhead this attack
undertook intensive training in "storm troop" tactics, an approach that had been
given a thorough trial at Riga, Caporetto, and Cambrai.

The political aim of Ludendorff's offensive was to batter the Western Allies to
a point where they would fall into line with Imperial Germany's ambitious world-
view. This would include an acknowledgment of the expanded empire Germany
had gained in the east at the expense of Russia. There were expansionist goals for
Western Europe as well. If Berlin could take control of Belgium's industry and
coastline, and perhaps regain its prewar colonies, this would cement a commanding international status. There was the distinct possibility of Belgium and Luxembourg—in altered forms—becoming federal states of Germany.[4] Defeat, or even
stalemate, would be a disaster for Imperial Germany, which had been established
in 1871 off the back of military triumph. For the sake of its ongoing legitimacy,
the kaiser's regime needed a resounding victory over the Allied armies assembled
in France and Flanders.

In London, after three years of bitter conflict, Lloyd George was more discontent
than ever with the war's progress and Field Marshal Haig's steady consumption of
the nation's manpower in order "to gain the next shell-shattered hill top."[5] Despite
holding the office of prime minister, Lloyd George's personal power remained circumscribed by his political and constitutional circumstances. The War Cabinet's
approval was needed to dismiss commanders or alter strategy.

It was high time, though, to put the shoulder more firmly to the wheel. The setbacks of the Passchendaele campaign, and the shock of the Cambrai counterattack,

steeled the War Cabinet into a degree of action. In the naval sphere, Admiral Jellicoe was removed as First Sea Lord on December 24, 1917. By this time he was worn down and overdue for relief. Haig escaped dismissal, not least because Robertson would not advise that course of action; instead, an effort was made to restock General Headquarters' (GHQ) staff in the hope of improving their performance. Lord Derby, the War Office minister, had written to Haig on December 7 in respect to his intelligence chief: "For a long time past he [Charteris] has appeared to me and many others to take a quite unjustifiable view of the fighting value of the enemy." Haig replied that he objected to Charteris being made "the whipping boy for the charge of undue optimism brought against myself." Derby insisted again in stronger terms that Charteris had become a liability.[6] Haig was accused, Charteris would write, "of allowing himself to be unduly swayed by his Staff. To anyone with any knowledge of the man the suggestion can only appear ludicrous. There was no individual either on his Staff or elsewhere to whom Haig would—even in unimportant particulars—subordinate his own judgement."[7]

In mid-December the pressure on Haig was indirectly stepped up when a bout of press commentary publicly questioned the quality of his subordinates and the veracity of the stream of communiqués claiming a sagging enemy morale. Haig managed to retain the services of Gough, who had attracted his share of criticism in London, but he agreed to move Charteris from intelligence to a less high-profile administrative billet. Charteris was replaced at the intelligence branch by Major General H.A. Lawrence, a 17th Lancer, son of a viceroy of India, and, most recently, commander of the 66th Division. Like Bonar Law, Lawrence had suffered the loss of two sons killed in action. The deferential Kiggell was targeted as well; he was in poor health and had consistently given the outward impression of being a chief clerk rather than an executive decision-maker. Lawrence, who was still settling in at intelligence, was shifted again to replace Kiggell on January 24, 1918.[8] After this latest round of musical chairs, the new chief of the intelligence branch was Brigadier General E.W. Cox, who was thirty-five years of age when appointed. He had previously held a post at the War Office.

At the end of December 1917, Haig returned to Britain on leave. On January 6, 1918, he met with Repington, the ubiquitous pressman. Repington was briefed that the BEF was short of 114,000 infantrymen, with few drafts in sight. Haig, wrote Repington, "declares that the continuation of the Flanders offensive is the best way he knows of attracting and using up the Boches, [but] he cannot go on with it if he is not adequately supplied with drafts."[9] On January 7, Haig attended a War Cabinet meeting at which he expressed similar views.

> As regards the enemy's action, I stated that I thought that the coming four months would be the critical period of the war. Also that it seemed to me possible that the enemy would attack both the French and ourselves. . . . In my opinion, the best defence would be to continue our offensive in Flanders, because we would then retain the initiative and attract the German Reserves against us.[10]

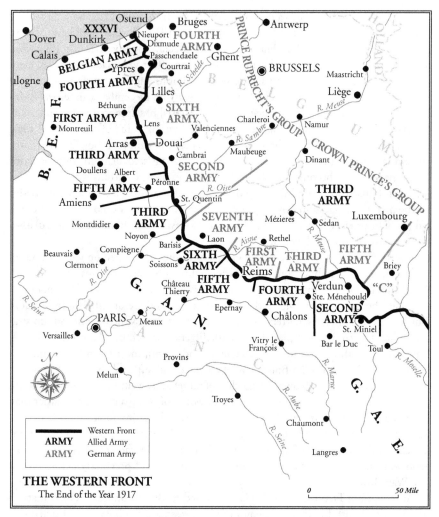

**THE WESTERN FRONT**
The End of the Year 1917

Western front, 1917, the end of the year

Two days later, after lunch with Lloyd George and Derby at Ten Downing Street, Haig wrote that a major German offensive in the upcoming spring to summer season would be "a gambler's throw."[11]

By this stage, however, the manpower consequences of Haig's own reckless gambling at Passchendaele and Cambrai were finally coming to a foreseeable fruition. On January 10 the Army Council ordered all British divisions of the BEF to reduce by three battalions; the recruiting shortfall could not be made up, and 20 percent of Haig's infantry battalions vanished at the stroke of a pen. (Dominion divisions retained their existing strength of twelve battalions.) The reduction of the number of infantry units per division would necessitate a more lightly held front, just at a time when the Germans were preparing for a large-scale offensive. Haig and his staff could have reined in the infantry shortage by restricting the self-imposed losses of the Passchendaele folly. There is no question that GHQ had imposed an unacceptable rate of casualty on British forces. From now on British infantry brigades would have three rather than four battalions, which would adversely compromise their performance whether attacking or defending. Throughout Haig's tenure at GHQ, there was an impenetrable quality to his dull-witted disregard for the limits to a finite supply of manpower; resources were squandered with little regard for the future.

The government's ability to raise recruits had been reduced by the discovery that an alarming number of the youths and men medically examined were either allocated to noncombatant medical categories or were entirely unfit for service. This problem had already come to official attention during the Boer War, though the flood of fit volunteers in 1914–1915 masked the issue. After the introduction of conscription, the Ministry of National Service was able to medically examine a cross section of the entire male population. The Ministry later reported in detail on the health of the pool of men examined from November 1917 to October 1918. Those examined were placed in four grades, of whom only 36 percent were in the highest grade and 22.5 percent in the second-highest grade. The report commented that the 31.5 percent of examinees in the third grade could "be described with justice as physical wrecks." An individual of the bottom 10 percent was typically "a chronic invalid with a precarious hold on life."[12] Conscription caused the floorboards of society to be ripped up for a close inspection of the populace's living conditions. "Mr Lloyd George," wrote Churchill, "viewed with horror the task imposed on him of driving to the shambles by stern laws the remaining manhood of the nation. Lads of eighteen and nineteen, elderly men up to forty-five, the last surviving brother, the only son of his mother (and she a widow), the father the sole support of the family, the weak, the consumptive, the thrice wounded—all must now prepare themselves for the scythe."[13] The pressure of a war of national attrition brought the bottom of the manpower barrel into sight faster than expected. It should be emphasized that Lloyd George and his ministers did not hold back replacement drafts for the BEF. Across the year of 1917 the British government was unstinting in its efforts to ship soldiers across the Channel.

Britain's manpower shortage struck with a vengeance at a difficult time. During January 1918 the BEF finally took over in stages an extra twenty-eight miles of front from the French south of the Somme River. Up to that time the BEF had held almost 100 miles of front and the French 325 miles; those figures became 125 and 300, respectively, after the adjustment. The extension of the British front, and a refortification of the stretch newly taken over, might have been undertaken the previous autumn, as the French had wished, instead of the repeated futile slogging against Passchendaele ridge in October and November. The Cambrai battle had provided a further excuse for procrastination. Field Marshal Haig was entirely responsible for the repeated delays to the extension of the BEF's frontage.

Given the shrinking manpower supply available to French and British forces, much now depended on the level of American participation on the western front. At the close of 1917 the American Expeditionary Force in France was 175,000; this figure was projected to grow substantially in 1918 and 1919. The prospect of the arrival of a third large Allied army on the western front made the proper coordination of Allied strategy a matter of urgency. The Supreme War Council met at Versailles from January 30 to February 2. Allied leaders agreed to a defensive strategy for the period ahead. Discussions were held regarding the formation of a "general reserve" that was to be presided over by the Military Representatives of the Supreme War Council. The executive committee to control the general reserve was to be chaired by General Foch. Neither Haig nor Pétain liked the notion of turning over a number of divisions to a rival commander; they preferred a mutual assistance arrangement of their own devising in the event of a crisis. Further discussions followed, but the opponents of the general reserve managed to wreck the scheme.

The deliberations of the Supreme War Council had infringed upon the status of the chief of the Imperial General Staff (CIGS) in London. To shore up his influence, Robertson wanted the posts of CIGS and British Military Representative at Versailles amalgamated. This scheme of Robertson's threatened to disrupt an agreement between the British and French governments. Faced with blatant obstructionism, the War Cabinet decided that Robertson's time at the War Office should be brought to a close. On February 17, Lloyd George met with Haig and made clear to the latter that Robertson had gone too far. The field marshal carefully indicated that he was willing to work under the Versailles machinery. Haig refused to offer Robertson an army commander's post in France; he also advised Derby not to resign as War Office minister in support of Robertson. Haig, who was no stranger to fancy political footwork, dropped Robertson like a weighted corpse committed to the darkened depths of the deepest ocean.

On February 18, Bonar Law announced in Parliament that Robertson was appointed to Eastern Command (a regional command in Britain). A few weeks later he was made commander in chief, Home Forces.[14] Haig explained his attitude to Robertson's professional demotion in a letter to Lady Haig: "I, like you, am sorry for Robertson, but then it seems to me . . . that he has not resolutely adhered to the policy of 'concentration on the Western Front.' He has said that this is his policy, but has allowed all kinds of resources to be diverted to distant theatres at the bidding of his political masters."[15] The news of success in Palestine during the winter season of 1917–1918 had confirmed Haig's clouded view that the BEF's manpower shortage was at least partly caused by sending too many troops to theaters far from the western front. This assessment by Haig, however, was unfair, as Robertson had consistently fought the cause of GHQ in Whitehall.

Once Robertson had been deposed, a new CIGS was needed who could work with both Lloyd George's ministry and the Supreme War Council. General Wilson, the British Military Representative at Versailles, was the obvious man for the job; he was already an adviser of the prime minister. (Rawlinson replaced Wilson at Versailles, and in due course Plumer was recalled from Italy to replace Rawlinson in Flanders.) After his appointment, Wilson did not recommend Haig's relief, which permitted the latter to cling to his position at GHQ. Nonetheless, from this point in time Lloyd George's position as prime minister was relatively secure. For much of 1917 he had been on shaky ground, but in 1918 he acquired that indispensable quality that has impressed itself on posterity. It did, however, take over a year for Lloyd George to achieve this position, given the complex nature of his coalition and the setback of Nivelle's campaign. The bitter experiences of Passchendaele and the German counterattack at Cambrai were needed to persuade Lloyd George's ministers—some of whom were long-standing former opponents—that the prime minister's instincts in respect to military affairs were more right than wrong.

In the early weeks of 1918, preparations for Luddendorf's great offensive gathered pace. On October 1, 1917, there had been 140 German divisions on the western front, 88 on the eastern front, and 6 en route to Italy.[16] By March 1918 the figure for the western front had risen to 192, to give the Germans a marginal numerical superiority over the 178 Allied divisions available.[17]

In early March 1918, Field Marshal Haig distributed the divisions of the BEF with a bias toward Flanders. The protection of the Channel ports was later put forward as the main justification for packing so many troops into the northern end of the British front, but there was also the need to garrison an enlarged Ypres salient. Haig still had hopes of using Passchendaele ridge as the jumping-off point for a renewed offensive toward the Belgian coast, once the Allies had regained the initiative.

The long-expected German offensive in northern France was finally unleashed on March 21. Three German armies attacked the BEF on a fifty-mile front that stretched from the Sensee River to the Oise River. The assault was aided by a dense fog that had gathered during the night and lasted well into late morning. On a day of intense fighting, and despite high levels of local resistance, German forces smashed through the Fifth Army's thinly held front. In the first twenty-four hours of the offensive, German troops captured 140 square miles of land; by comparison, only 98 square miles were captured by Allied troops in the whole Somme offensive lasting four and a half months.[18]

In the days ahead, the Fifth Army was bundled rearwards. The usually circumspect official history would relate that by the end of March 23, "eight out of the eleven divisions of the Fifth Army originally in the front line, and three brigades of the remaining divisions, had suffered such heavy losses that they were only 'remnants' of their former selves."[19] On the northern part of the attack front, German troops did not make such dramatic headway against the Third Army, which swung back its southern flank to keep touch with Gough's Fifth Army. The French-held stretch of the western front was not attacked. Confronted by a genuine crisis in the British sector, Pétain began moving his carefully hoarded reserves northwards to prevent the tearing of a permanent breach in the Allied line.

In London, disconcerting reports of a crisis had winged their way to ministerial hands. After a War Cabinet meeting on March 23, Lloyd George asked Lord Milner to set out for France to investigate the situation. General Wilson, the CIGS, departed for France on the morning of the 25th. Wilson met Haig that day and noted that the field marshal was "cowed. He said that unless the 'whole French Army' came up we were beaten and it would be better to make peace on any terms we could."[20]

On March 26, Allied leaders hastily gathered at Doullens town hall to assess the crisis. After preliminary discussions, Milner and Prime Minister Clemenceau agreed that General Foch should be made responsible for the coordination of the British and French armies on the western front. After the Doullens meeting, Wilson spoke with Haig and insisted that Gough be dismissed. Haig conceded that point, and Rawlinson was transferred from his appointment at Versailles to take over what remained of the Fifth Army.

With Foch now firmly in the saddle, the ability of Haig and Pétain to make strategy was markedly reduced. In all likelihood Haig faced speedy dismissal if he tried to undermine the new Allied command structure. In light of Robertson's recent sacking as CIGS, the politically savvy Haig toed the new line to save his professional skin.

Foch took up his post at the end of March 1918 with the Germans advancing on a broad front. The patch of ground taken in the Passchendaele campaign was abandoned when the main battle line was withdrawn to the eastern fringe of Ypres. Anglo-French forces were badly battered by Ludendorff's set of offensives that lasted from March to July, yet the Germans also suffered heavy losses in order to gain possession of a longer and relatively unfortified front. The quick-witted Foch pounced on the opportunity to regain the initiative. He exclaimed: "I am the conductor of the orchestra. Here is the American tenor, the French baritone and the British bass. I make them play together."[21]

Foch's plan for a coordinated Allied offensive on the broadest possible front was dependent on the full participation of the large American army that had recently arrived in Western Europe. The fighting of 1917 on the western front had made it crystal clear that Anglo-French forces could not take much ground from the Germans. Without the United States Army, the Anglo-French armies faced the likelihood of being stranded on a stalemated front for an indefinite period.

At the start of 1918 the American Expeditionary Force was relatively small, but it grew to 873,000 by June and would be two million by November.[22] By late summer of 1918, the American Expeditionary Force had profoundly changed the strategic landscape of the western front. Thanks to the arrival of the Americans, the Allies quickly regained the manpower lead lost during the previous winter. There were now three large Allied armies to share the load instead of two.

Under the direction of Foch, a series of ambitious Allied offensives commencing in late July successfully ended the war by November. A staggered set of rolling attacks by all three of the principal Allied armies in most sectors between Ypres and Verdun prevented the Germans from massing reserves against a particular thrust. By this stage of the war, the force of heavy artillery available to the French was devastating when used against improvised fieldworks. The BEF's most striking success in this period was a tank-led attack by the Fourth Army near Amiens on August 8. The Amiens battle was a Cambrai-type operation launched under more propitious circumstances.

The armistice between Germany and the Allies was signed at 5:15 A.M. on November 11, 1918. The order to stand fast at 11 A.M. was received with relief by troops in the firing line. During the night of November 10/11, the Canadians had cleared German rearguards from the Belgian town of Mons; this was near where British troops began the war in late August 1914. The prominence of Mons to the BEF's first and last battles of the war highlights the conflict's static nature. The entire war was spent fighting to regain the ground lost during the "Retreat from Mons" of August and September 1914.

The armistice signaled a defeat for Germany, yet the Allies were unwilling to prolong the war's duration to secure a more decisive victory. Allied troops did not reach German soil under combat conditions. The Belgian coast fell to Allied forces, but Brussels and the Ardennes forest remained in German hands. At the time of the armistice, the armies of both France and Britain were in the grip of a full-blown manpower crisis. The consequences of many wasteful battles fought earlier in the war hit home with a vengeance. The extent to which the Anglo-French armies were self-cannibalizing created a mounting political pressure to close down the war. The armistice avoided the need to fight another campaign on the western front in 1919. The failure to invade Germany, however, preserved that nation's military potential to fight again another day.

The suddenness of the armistice of November 1918, after Germany had enjoyed victory on the eastern front earlier that year, made it hard for German society to accept defeat. The political system of Wilhelmine Germany did not survive the war, but the social system of militarism was deep-rooted and stretched back many generations. German militarism—or "Prussianism"—remained defiantly unreconciled. In January 1919, Colonel von Thaer discussed the future with General Walther Reinhardt, who was the last Prussian minister of war. Thaer was gloomy about the future, but Reinhardt assured him that "the goal is and remains a free Germany, hopefully restored to its former borders, with [the] strongest, most modern army with [the] newest weapons." Thaer felt that was a very long way off. Reinhardt replied that the Allies would rest on their laurels "and in fifteen years all their weapons and equipment will be scrap iron."[23]

The strategic balance of the western front in 1918 was transformed by several new factors. Ludendorff's grand offensives, Foch's appointment as supreme commander, and the influx of American troops were the most noteworthy of those new factors. By contrast, in 1917 the Germans had sat firmly on the defensive on the western front and successfully withstood Anglo-French attack.

What in particular went wrong for British forces on the western front in the later part of 1917? To start with, throughout the war the British Army labored under a prior history of colonial warfare that had culminated in the blundering of the Boer War. More immediately, though, the BEF in 1917 was burdened with the poisoned inheritance of 1915–1916, which had featured the same sort of flawed battle fought on an ever-larger scale, almost as if that was a virtue in itself. The defeat of the Dardanelles campaign and siege of Kut al-Amara, far from Western Europe, suggest that the army's problems were not just confined to France and Flanders, but the magnitude of the western front drastically raised the stakes. At such a difficult time, the elevation and retention of General Haig as the BEF's commander in chief was a dangerous innovation. The performance of Haig is central to any meaningful discussion of British forces on the western front; he made so many of the command decisions, especially during 1916–1917.

The battles of the Somme campaign set the standard for Haig's tenure as commander in chief. By background Haig was essentially an administrator-politician; he was out of his depth when faced with the military problems of the western front. The Somme fighting featured a lot of crude bashing to inch forward the front line on the map; this was then claimed by GHQ as a hard-fought victory in a twisting of logic worthy of Alice in Wonderland. This style of thought became both communiqué propaganda and the internal interpretation of events that the army laid before the government.

The Asquith government fell at the close of 1916. The new prime minister, David Lloyd George, lost considerable support among his doubtful ministers by backing the plans of France's General Nivelle in the spring offensive of 1917, a campaign that failed to live up to its promise and did a lot of damage to the French army. This created the conditions for Haig to opportunistically take the lead in the making of strategy for the western front.[24] Haig's preferred strategy was an offensive in Flanders to capture the Belgian coast. The support of the Royal Navy was important to Haig getting sufficient political backing in London for his scheme. War Cabinet Secretary Hankey observed that "the campaign in Flanders in 1917, with its appalling losses, would probably never have been sanctioned but for the anxiety which the German submarines and destroyers at Zeebrugge were causing to the Admiralty."[25] An offensive in Flanders would require only a minimal level of direct French involvement.

Nevertheless, the campaign in Flanders began well at Messines Ridge on June 7. The stealthy sowing of the mines under the slopes of the ridge had been long underway. This was a definite display of British ingenuity and had its origins in the civilian mining industry. The Messines battle showed that the BEF was capable of carrying out a well-planned, localized operation at army-level. Success at Messines, however, was followed by a campaign of prolonged failure in the Ypres salient. On the eve of the offensive, Haig nominated Passchendaele ridge to the War Cabinet as the first objective of the campaign. This otherwise unremarkable low ridge thus acquired a political importance from the outset beyond its military significance. The capture of Passchendaele ridge became vital to Haig's reputation.

The assault of July 31 was long expected by the Germans, given the visibility of the prolonged buildup. The attack was well held, and II Corps in particular was badly mauled at the vital southern end of the attack front. The fighting in August featured poor weather and a doomed set of operations. The offensive plowed on despite a worsening manpower situation. As British forces pushed farther and farther into a preexisting salient, this gave the Germans the upper hand in the artillery duel. The principal British highlight in August was a local tank battle on the 19th. This "surprise" attack revealed that the thinking of the Tank Corps' leaders was ahead of much of the army.

In the dry weather of September, the three Plumer-led attacks of Menin road, Polygon Wood, and Broodseinde were better-organized battles than the August fighting, but more heavy losses resulted, along with advances too shallow to threaten the overall integrity of the German front. The best day in the campaign for the BEF was October 4, but even this was a Pyrrhic victory that lured British forces into a further series of ruinous engagements. The battles of October 9 and 12 were fiascos amid fields of mud. The Cavalry Corps stood ready to surge through a yet-to-be-broken German front. The final Canadian-led drive to secure a large section of Passchendaele ridge was undertaken to provide a springboard for a renewed campaign in Flanders in the spring of 1918, but it was also a political gesture intended to shore up the standing of GHQ in Whitehall. By the close of the offensive in mid-November, British troops had managed to advance five miles from the outskirts of Ypres to Passchendaele ridge, which left them sixty-five miles from the German submarine bases on the coast of Flanders.[26] The BEF's campaign in Flanders was so strategically ineffective that the Germans were able to send troops to the eastern front to defeat the Russians at Riga in September, and then repeat the blow against the Italians in October at Caporetto. The Germans never had any intention of attacking the French sector of the western front in 1917.

Why was the disappointing campaign at Ypres so prolonged in duration? The War Cabinet had explicitly authorized only the opening phase of the offensive. In practice, however, it was hard to stop an operation when no precise criteria had ever been set to determine its success or failure. As Hankey would point out, the generals remained optimistic and there was a considerable lag between events and the arrival of unofficial reports critical of official communiqués. If Lloyd George had secured the War Cabinet's agreement to halt the offensive, he would have laid himself open to accusations of preventing the army "from reaping the fruits of months of successful fighting."[27] Robertson explained that the Third Battle of Ypres continued as long as it did due to "the belief at G.H.Q. that the strain imposed upon the enemy was being so severely felt that it might soon reach breaking-point."[28]

The gloomy close to the Flanders campaign was quickly followed by the Cambrai operation. The Tank Corps was in a relatively pristine condition and available for battle at Cambrai, as it had played only a small part in the fighting in Flanders. The availability of the Tank Corps was due to happenstance and not design. If the ground in Flanders had permitted a more wholesale use of tanks, the Tank Corps would very likely have been consumed by that campaign and the Cambrai battle might not have happened in the form it took. It was General Byng who saw that tanks could penetrate the fields of wire of the Hindenburg Line near Cambrai and persuaded Haig of that. The field marshal had a limited technical horizon, but he was alive to the political possibilities of a fresh battle at Cambrai given the unsatisfactory conclusion to the Flanders campaign.

The tank attack at Cambrai on November 20 began well, as it was a surprise for the defenders. The main contribution of the artillery was its exclusion from participation until zero hour. The unregistered shoot of the opening bombardment was accurate in the sense that gunners avoided hitting their own tanks and troops. The British infantry rolled through the German front after the massed tanks. There was a fleeting chance to tear the German front open in the Flesquières sector, but this opportunity was lost when tanks were blown to flaming wreckage by artillery sheltering behind the ridge of that name. The pivotal failure of Harper's 51st Division at Flesquières was due to heavy tank losses, poor counterbattery fire, poor infantry-tank coordination, and the failure to commit the division's reserve brigade.[29] This was a long list of misfortunes, and all the more disheartening given that Harper's division had a fine reputation. (Harper was promoted to corps command-level early in 1918.) The sheer scale of the casualty rate on the western front, however, made it difficult for units and divisions to learn from past experience. The high tempo of combat that Haig negligently and callously imposed on his army seriously reduced its ability to learn and improve.

The introduction of the cavalry was the next phase of the Cambrai battle. Instead of using another wave of infantry divisions to exploit the success of the tanks, the reserves of infantry available were held back and masses of cavalry pushed forward. The thinking of Haig seemed to be trekking backwards to the days of the massed French cavalry at Borodino in 1812 and Waterloo in 1815. The advance of Haig's Cavalry Corps at Cambrai, however, achieved little. The march of the cavalry in long columns towards the St. Quentin Canal clogged up the front.

The pivotal role given the Cavalry Corps at both Passchendaele and Cambrai—two quite different battles—underlines the extraordinary extent of Haig's "cavalry-mindedness." Why was it necessary to use cavalry for the exploitation of the tanks' success? The straightforward answer is that Haig was increasingly desperate to involve the Cavalry Corps in operations, come hell or high water, given the failure to get the mounted arm into action in the slough of Passchendaele. Haig was relentless in his distracting devotion to the cavalry and a perceived need to keep alive the equine methods of the nineteenth century.

Haig's dispatch on the fighting at Cambrai would later record of the attack at Flesquières: "A number of tanks were knocked out by direct hits from German field batteries in position beyond the crest of the hill. . . . Many of the hits upon our tanks at Flesquieres were obtained by a German artillery officer who, remaining alone at his battery, served a field gun single-handed until killed at his gun. The great bravery of this officer aroused the admiration of all ranks."[30] The resolute officer mentioned in Haig's dispatch may have been Lieutenant Karl Mueller, or, more likely, he was

*Unteroffizier* Theodor Krueger.[31] Colonel Baker-Carr, I Tank Brigade's commander, would acidly remark:

> Nobody could help admiring the great courage of the German artillery officer, but to us it appeared somewhat tactless, to put it mildly, for the British C.I.C. specifically to mention him in dispatches. We all regarded this commendation as a direct incentive to others "to go and do likewise," a consummation sincerely to be deprecated at any rate by the Tank Corps. I feel sure that hundreds of German officers would have gladly laid down their lives if, by their self-sacrifice and devotion, they could merit the distinction of being mentioned in enemy dispatches.[32]

There seems little doubt that Baker-Carr thought it swinish of Haig to commend an enemy for killing soldiers of the Tank Corps. Why did Haig do this? It is likely that the field marshal was clutching at an excuse for his cavalry's failure to make meaningful progress on November 20. The interbranch politics of the army reared its head on this occasion in a particularly ugly fashion.

Bourlon Ridge was not taken in the tank attack of November 20. Haig's decision to keep hammering against Bourlon for the next week was futile and possibly political in motivation. On the whole, the Cambrai battle proved to be as centralized in its command arrangements as preceding offensives. The engagements fought by tanks after November 20 involved piecemeal detachments pitched against rapidly strengthening anti-tank defenses. The Germans were able to rapidly reseal the front at Cambrai, given the proximity of the town's rail junction. For the Germans, the railway system of northern France and Belgium was vital to their defensive effort across 1917. This point was especially obvious at Cambrai, as the railway delivered reinforcements directly into the rear of the battle zone. The German counterattack of November 30 undid much of the good work of the original tank attack and gave the Germans a trial of their offensive methods for the following spring.

During the 1920s work was begun in Britain to compile an official history of the "Great War." The "official" historian of the BEF in France and Flanders would be Brigadier General Sir James Edmonds, a Royal Engineer who had spent most of the war on the staff at GHQ. The official history series laid out some relevant material, but it followed the line of interpretation given in Haig's published dispatches. Edmonds, however, had known Haig for many years and harbored few private illusions about the field marshal. Edmonds told Liddell Hart on December 8, 1930: "I have to write of Haig with my tongue in check. One can't tell the truth. He was really above the average—or rather, below the average in stupidity." Haig was "unable to grasp anything technical" and had "no comprehension of siege-war matters."[33] Robertson's predecessor as CIGS, General Sir Archibald Murray, summed up Haig as "a man of mediocre ability, slow to absorb, tenacious of what he had learnt; not a very pleasant man to deal with, though he tried to be pleasant."[34]

The rich variety of Haig's blundering holds a strange and enduring fascination. The eighteen-month period from July 1916 to December 1917—the journey from

Thiepval to Passchendaele—squandered resources with little regard for the future. All too often, the field marshal was like King Canute seeking to command the tides with his most sycophantic followers in attendance. Army commanders were dependent on Haig's ongoing favor, and corps and divisional commanders lacked influence given their hasty and recent promotion. In practice, the BEF's corps headquarters were given a stretch of front and then allocated a revolving set of divisions, to be thrown into the fire as per instructions from on high.

The Prussian general Carl von Clausewitz wrote of the fog and confusions of war; Helmuth von Moltke the Elder counseled that no plan survives with certainty the first clash of arms in a campaign. In defiance of those notions, Haig's generalship was defined by a blunt determination to undertake the same sort of operation over and over again in the expectation of a different and improved outcome. The field marshal's willingness to keep pounding away to gain objectives of doubtful value whatever the cost comes close to defying reasonable explanation in strictly military terms. It is important to bear in mind, however, that these objectives—such as Passchendaele ridge or Bourlon Ridge—also had a political value to Haig. It should come as no surprise that a man whose prewar career had relied so heavily on politics and patronage for advancement should assiduously practice those things in time of war.

Apart from shortcomings of command, technical shortcomings were also a consistent drag on GHQ's ambitions on the western front. There was no lack of determination to push the Germans back on the Rhine, but the technical means to break through a defensive front were lacking. A significant ongoing problem in the field of British artillery was the underdeveloped design of the eighteen-pound field gun. This weapon was a piece of light artillery introduced in the aftermath of the Boer War; it lacked the range needed to push a barrage deep into an enemy's defensive front. A lack of artillery penetration meant that British offensive pushes at Ypres were too shallow to have strategic significance and invited tactical failure. The unmodernized eighteen-pounder of 1917 was well suited for the fighting in Palestine and Mesopotamia, or for chasing Afghans out of the Khyber Pass, but it was an unimpressive gun by the standards of Western Europe.[35]

Just as importantly, the BEF went to France in 1914 with little heavy artillery and spent the rest of the war trying to redress that handicap. This handed the Germans, who had a sizeable force of mobile heavy artillery, a tremendous operational advantage that was magnified on a static front. The deep, probing fire of the German five-point-nines was a consistent menace to British troops.

The battles for Passchendaele ridge starkly exposed the mediocrity of the equipment used by British forces, something that had already been made stunningly clear on the Somme campaign's opening day. At the very least, a mediocre stock of artillery meant that Haig's BEF was unsuited to a strategy that came to rely on attrition. Firing an increased quantity of munitions was a step in the right direction, but the quality of the guns doing the firing also mattered. GHQ and Robertson's War Office blithely assumed their equipment was qualitatively equal to that of Germany despite the prevailing stalemate suggesting that was not the case. In the British Army the technical arms were perennial bridesmaids. The creation of the Tank Corps was the exception that proved the rule. The army was dominated by senior officers drawn from units that valued private wealth and social prestige ahead of technical knowledge. In the Royal Navy, the need for an organizational capacity to develop new types of technology and weaponry was acknowledged to be important. The army's approach to such matters was sketchy and ad hoc.

The western front was invariably a costly theater of war whatever operation was attempted, yet an overreliance on that style of apologetics breaks down in the case of Passchendaele, which might have been reduced in duration or not fought at all. The protracted and expensive offensive campaigns developed by Haig's BEF in 1916–1917 compare poorly with Pétain's brief and efficient attacking strokes of August and October 1917. There was an obvious alternative strategy available. In the later part of 1917, Pétain was inclined to wait for the Americans to arrive in strength—and to see what transpired in Russia—before embarking on any rash ventures of the Passchendaele type. The preservation of an army is part of a commander's task; the "fleet in being" concept of naval warfare is also relevant to land warfare. The winter of 1917–1918 was marked by Russia's withdrawal from the war and the transfer of large German forces to the western front. In the spring campaign of 1918, the direct support of Pétain's French was needed to help save the situation in Haig's sector.

After the war, Winston Churchill sharply critiqued Haig's western front strategy and, in particular, described the Passchendaele campaign as "a forlorn expenditure of valour and life without equal in futility." He wrote in *The World Crisis*: "The disappointing captures of ground were relieved by tales of prodigious German slaughter. . . . The German losses were always on a far smaller scale. They had fewer troops in the cauldron."[36] Lloyd George regretted the extent to which his reputation was tainted by his association with Passchendaele. He later proclaimed with gusto:

> The reports passed on to the ministers were, as we all realised much later, grossly misleading. Victories were much overstated. Virtual defeats were represented as victories, however limited their scope. Our casualties were understated. Enemy losses became pyramidal. That was the way the military authorities presented the situation to Ministers—that was their active propaganda in the Press. All disconcerting and discouraging facts were suppressed in the reports received from the front by the War Cabinet—every bright feather of success was waved and flourished in our faces.[37]

Field Marshal Haig remained at GHQ for the battles of 1918; the politicians considered his relief in the middle of that year, but stayed their hand for want of an obvious successor and a faith that Foch had command matters in hand at a higher level. Nevertheless, Lloyd George's failure to dispense with Haig should be weighed against his enthusiasm for the formation of an Allied Supreme War Council and the eventual appointment of an Allied generalissimo: Both of those developments were of war-winning significance in the closing months of 1918.

# Notes

## PREFACE

1. P. Gibbs, *From Bapaume to Passchendaele* (London: Heinemann, 1918), 157.

2. G.C. Wynne, *If Germany Attacks* (London: Faber and Faber, 1940), 273.

3. R. Blake, ed., *The Private Papers of Douglas Haig, 1914–1919* (London: Eyre and Spottiswoode, 1952), 239–40.

4. C.E. Callwell, *Field-Marshal Sir Henry Wilson*, vol. 1 (London: Cassell, 1927), 354–55, 359.

5. W.S. Churchill, *The World Crisis, 1916–1918*, vol. 2 (London: Thornton Butterworth, 1927), 338–39.

## CHAPTER 1

1. J. Keegan, *The First World War* (London: Hutchinson, 1998), 34–35.

2. D.R. Woodward, *Lloyd George and the Generals* (London: Associated Universities, 1983), 28.

3. J.E. Edmonds, *Military Operations France and Belgium, 1915*, vol. 2 (London: Macmillan, 1936), 393.

4. War Office, *Statistics of the Military Effort of the British Empire during the Great War, 1914–1920* (London: His Majesty's Stationery Office, 1922), 359.

5. J.P. Harris, *Douglas Haig and the First World War* (Cambridge, UK: Cambridge University, 2008), 14.

6. G. Micholls, *A History of the 17th Lancers*, vol. 2 (London: Macmillan, 1931), 51; D. Reitz, *Commando* (London: Faber and Faber, 1929), 222–28; Marquess of Anglesey, *A History of the British Cavalry*, vol. 4 (London: Secker and Warburg, 1986), 230–31; W.K. Hancock, *Smuts: The Sanguine Years, 1870–1919* (Cambridge, UK: Cambridge University, 1962), 136.

7. D. Haig, *Cavalry Studies* (London: Hugh Rees, 1907); G.J. De Groot, "Educated Soldier or Cavalry Officer? Contradictions in the Pre-1914 Career of Douglas Haig," *War and Society*, September 1986, 58–63.

8. Haig, *Cavalry Studies*, 8, 18.

9. Dorothy, Countess Haig, *The Man I Knew* (Edinburgh: Moray, 1936), 32.

10. L. Wolff, *In Flanders Fields* (London: Longmans, 1959), xiv; Harris, *Douglas Haig*, 50; G.J. De Groot, *Douglas Haig, 1861–1928* (London: Unwin Hyman, 1988), 140.

11. Wolff, *In Flanders Fields*, xiv.

12. J. Beach, *Haig's Intelligence: G.H.Q. and the German Army, 1916–1918* (Cambridge, UK: Cambridge University, 2013), 50.

13. P. Gibbs, *Realities of War* (London: Heinemann, 1920), 26.

14. J.F.C. Fuller, *Memoirs of an Unconventional Soldier* (London: Ivor Nicholson and Watson, 1936), 142.

15. B. Bond, *The Victorian Army and the Staff College, 1854–1914* (London: Eyre Methuen, 1972), 274–75.

16. W. Robertson, *From Private to Field-Marshal* (London: Constable, 1921), 66.

17. R. Jenkins, *Asquith* (London: Collins, 1986), 383; W. Robertson, *Soldiers and Statesmen, 1914–1918*, vol. 1 (London: Cassell, 1926), 71.

18. Woodward, *Lloyd George*, 43.

19. Robertson, *From Private to Field-Marshal*, 98.

20. M. Hankey, *The Supreme Command, 1914–1918*, vol. 2 (London: Allen and Unwin, 1961), 446.

21. J.E. Edmonds, *Military Operations France and Belgium, 1916*, vol. 2 (London: Macmillan, 1938), xvi.

22. War Office, *Statistics of the Military Effort*, 360; R. Prior and T. Wilson, *The Somme* (Sydney: University of New South Wales, 2005), 301.

23. J. Sheldon, *The German Army at Cambrai* (Barnsley, UK: Pen and Sword, 2009), 1–2.

24. Woodward, *Lloyd George*, 274.

25. R. Blake, *The Unknown Prime Minister: The Life and Times of Andrew Bonar Law, 1858–1923* (London: Eyre and Spottiswoode, 1955), 340; Woodward, *Lloyd George*, 133.

26. Blake, *The Unknown Prime Minister*, 234.

27. R. Blake, ed., *The Private Papers of Douglas Haig, 1914–1919* (London: Eyre and Spottiswoode, 1952), 192.

28. Hankey, *The Supreme Command*, vol. 1, 361.

29. A.J. Marder, *From the Dreadnought to Scapa Flow*, vol. 5 (London: Oxford University, 1970), 111; A.A. Wiest, *Passchendaele and the Royal Navy* (London: Greenwood, 1995), 73.

30. E. Greenhalgh, *Victory through Coalition* (Cambridge, UK: Cambridge University, 2005), 140, 146.

31. R.A. Doughty, *Pyrrhic Victory: French Strategy and Operations in the Great War* (Cambridge, MA: Belknap Harvard, 2005), 354; C. Falls, *The Great War, 1914–1918* (New York: Putnam, 1959), 278; J.E. Edmonds, *A Short History of World War I* (London: Oxford University, 1951), 279.

32. C. Barnett, *The Swordbearers* (London: Hodder and Stoughton, 1963), 203; A. Bernede, "Third Ypres and the Restoration of Confidence in the Ranks of the French Army," in *Passchendaele in Perspective*, ed. P.H. Liddle (London: Leo Cooper, 1997), 88–89.

33. Barnett, *The Swordbearers*, 235–36.

34. Doughty, *Pyrrhic Victory*, 364; G.C. Oram, *Military Executions during World War I* (Basingstoke, UK: Palgrave Macmillan, 2003), 43, 111.

# CHAPTER 2

1. J.E. Edmonds, *Military Operations France and Belgium, 1917*, vol. 2 (London: Macmillan, 1948), 23.

2. E. Greenhalgh, *Victory through Coalition* (Cambridge, UK: Cambridge University, 2005), 150.

3. C. Barnett, *The Swordbearers* (London: Hodder and Stoughton, 1963), 206.

4. C.E. Callwell, *Field-Marshal Sir Henry Wilson*, vol. 1 (London: Cassell, 1927), 354–55, 359.

5. R. Blake, ed., *The Private Papers of Douglas Haig, 1914–1919* (London: Eyre and Spottiswoode, 1952), 234.

6. A.A. Wiest, *Passchendaele and the Royal Navy* (London: Greenwood, 1995), 96.

7. D. Stevenson, *Cataclysm: The First World War as Political Tragedy* (London: Allen Lane, 2004), 329.

8. S.J. Wilson, *The Seventh Manchesters* (London: Longmans, 1920), 47; M. Farndale, *History of the Royal Regiment of Artillery*, vol. 1 (London: Royal Artillery Institution, 1986), 213.

9. E. Wyrall, *The History of the 19th Division, 1914–1918* (London: Arnold, 1932), 83–84.

10. C.H. Dudley Ward, *Regimental Records of the Royal Welch Fusiliers (23rd Foot)*, vol. 3 (London: Forster Groom, 1928), 311.

11. A.T. Paterson, *The Thirty-Ninth: The History of the 39th Battalion, A.I.F.* (Uckfield, UK: Naval and Military, 2010), 103.

12. C. Harington, *Tim Harington Looks Back* (London: John Murray, 1940), 55.

13. C. Harington, *Plumer of Messines* (London: John Murray, 1940), 59; E.M. Spiers, *Haldane: An Army Reformer* (Edinburgh: Edinburgh University, 1980), 74.

14. Edmonds, *Military Operations France and Belgium, 1917*, vol. 2, 91–92; H. Hagenlücke, "The German High Command," in *Passchendaele in Perspective*, ed. P.H. Liddle (London: Leo Cooper, 1997), 49–50; C.E.W. Bean, *The A.I.F. in France*, vol. 4 (Sydney: Angus and Robertson, 1933), 598.

15. L. Wolff, *In Flanders Fields* (London: Longmans, 1959), 90–91; Edmonds, *Military Operations France and Belgium, 1917*, vol. 2, 31.

16. A. Eden, *Another World, 1897–1917* (London: Allen Lane, 1976), 137.

17. Harington, *Tim Harington Looks Back*, 56.

18. E.N. Gladden, *Ypres, 1917* (London: Kimber, 1967), 32, 45.

19. Bean, *The A.I.F. in France*, vol. 4, 582.

20. O.E. Burton, *The Auckland Regiment* (Auckland: Whitcombe and Tombs, 1922), 143.

21. J. Sheldon, *The German Army at Passchendaele* (Barnsley, UK: Pen and Sword, 2007), 4; T. Henshaw, *The Sky Their Battlefield* (London: Grub Street, 1995), 8.

22. Wolff, *In Flanders Fields*, 96.

23. Bean, *The A.I.F. in France*, vol. 4, 592.

24. T. Denman, *Ireland's Unknown Soldiers: The 16th (Irish) Division in the Great War* (Dublin: Irish Academic, 1992), 111.

25. Edmonds, *Military Operations France and Belgium, 1917*, vol. 2, 54.

26. Edmonds, *Military Operations France and Belgium, 1917*, vol. 2, 61.

27. Eden, *Another World*, 141.

28. Gladden, *Ypres, 1917*, 61.

29. Denman, *Ireland's Unknown Soldiers*, 111–12.

30. Harington, *Tim Harington Looks Back*, 60.

31. G.C. Wynne, *If Germany Attacks* (London: Faber and Faber, 1940), 275.

32. Burton, *The Auckland Regiment*, 146; D. Ferguson, *The History of the Canterbury Regiment, N.Z.E.F., 1914–1919* (Auckland: Whitcombe and Tombs, 1921), 163.

33. Wynne, *If Germany Attacks*, 276–77.

34. Sheldon, *The German Army at Passchendaele*, 29.

35. Sheldon, *The German Army at Passchendaele*, 10, 12.

36. Wolff, *In Flanders Fields*, 103.

37. Bean, *The A.I.F. in France*, vol. 4, 682.

38. Bean, *The A.I.F. in France*, vol. 4, 682; Edmonds, *Military Operations France and Belgium, 1917*, vol. 2, 87–88.

39. Eden, *Another World*, 124.

## CHAPTER 3

1. K. Grieves, "The 'Recruiting Margin' in Britain: Debates on Manpower during the Third Battles of Ypres," in *Passchendaele in Perspective*, ed. P.H. Liddle (London: Leo Cooper, 1997), 390.

2. D.R. Woodward, *Lloyd George and the Generals* (London: Associated University, 1983), 170–71.

3. W.K. Hancock, *Smuts: The Sanguine Years, 1870–1919* (Cambridge, UK: Cambridge University, 1962), 424, 435–36; L.S. Amery, *My Political Life*, vol. 2 (London: Hutchinson, 1953), 99.

4. A.A. Wiest, *Passchendaele and the Royal Navy* (London: Greenwood, 1995), 106.

5. R. Blake, ed., *The Private Papers of Douglas Haig, 1914–1919* (London: Eyre and Spottiswoode, 1952), 239–40.

6. Woodward, *Lloyd George*, 177.

7. Woodward, *Lloyd George*, 178.

8. Wiest, *Passchendaele*, 107; Woodward, *Lloyd George*, 178.

9. A.J. Marder, *From the Dreadnought to Scapa Flow*, vol. 4 (London: Oxford University, 1969), 204.

10. Wiest, *Passchendaele*, 109.

11. Marquess of Anglesey, *A History of the British Cavalry*, vol. 4 (London: Secker and Warburg, 1986), 264–65; A. Farrer-Hockley, *Goughie* (London: Hart-David, MacGibbon, 1975), 65–68.

12. Dorothy, Countess Haig, *The Man I Knew* (Edinburgh: Moray, 1936), 126; I.F.W. Beckett, *Johnnie Gough, V.C.* (London: Donovan, 1989), 2.

13. T. Travers, "A Particular Style of Command: Haig and G.H.Q., 1916–18," *Journal of Strategic Studies*, 1987, 370.

14. Farrer-Hockley, *Goughie*, 213–14.

15. J. Sheldon, *The German Army at Cambrai* (Barnsley, UK: Pen and Sword, 2009), 20.

16. H. Hagenlücke, "The German High Command," in *Passchendaele in Perspective*, ed. Liddle, 50; G.C. Wynne, *If Germany Attacks* (London: Faber and Faber, 1940), 83–84.

17. J. Sheldon, *The German Army at Passchendaele* (Barnsley, UK: Pen and Sword, 2007), 34.

18. Sheldon, *The German Army at Passchendaele*, 36.

19. T. Henshaw, *The Sky Their Battlefield* (London: Grub Street, 1995), 193; J.H. Morrow, *The Great War in the Air* (Washington: Smithsonian Institution, 1993), 217–18.

20. Wiest, *Passchendaele*, 139–40.

21. Sheldon, *The German Army at Passchendaele*, 36–37.

22. J.E. Edmonds, *Military Operations France and Belgium, 1917*, vol. 2 (London: Macmillan, 1948), 122.

23. E. Wyrall, *The Gloucestershire Regiment in the War, 1914–1918* (London: Methuen, 1931), 217; Wiest, *Passchendaele*, 130, 135–36; R. Bacon, *The Dover Patrol* (London: Hutchinson, 1920), 209.

24. S. Ewart, *Historical Records of the Queen's Own Cameron Highlanders*, vol. 4 (Edinburgh: Blackwood, 1931), 191–92.

25. W.G. Macpherson, *Medical Services General History*, vol. 3 (London: His Majesty's Stationery Office, 1924), 170, 180.

26. L.F. Haber, *The Poisonous Cloud: Chemical Warfare in the First World War* (Oxford: Clarendon, 1986), 233.

27. B.H. Liddell Hart, *The Tanks*, vol. 1 (London: Cassell, 1959), 7, 47.

28. A.G. Stern, *Tanks, 1914–1918: The Log-Book of a Pioneer* (London: Hodder and Stoughton, 1919), 98; J.P. Harris, *Men, Ideas and Tanks* (Manchester, UK: Manchester University, 1995), 67.

29. Harris, *Men, Ideas and Tanks*, 70.

30. Stern, *Tanks*, 107–8; D. Lloyd George, *War Memoirs*, vol. 1 (London: Odhams, 1938), 385.

31. Stern, *Tanks*, 116.

32. Harris, *Men, Ideas and Tanks*, 68.

33. Hart, *The Tanks*, vol. 1, 120.

34. T. Wilson, *The Myriad Faces of War* (Cambridge, UK: Polity, 1986), 487.

## CHAPTER 4

1. C.E.W. Bean, *The A.I.F. in France*, vol. 4 (Sydney: Angus and Robertson, 1933), 699; H. Hagenlücke, "The German High Command," in *Passchendaele in Perspective*, ed. P.H. Liddle (London: Leo Cooper, 1997), 51.

2. Crown Prince Rupprecht of Bavaria, "Further Experiences of the Arras Battle," 13/5/1917, Australian War Memorial 45/32/34.

3. D. Sutherland, *War Diary of the Fifth Seaforth Highlanders* (London: Bodley Head, 1920), 121.

4. D. Horner, *The Gunners: A History of Australian Artillery* (Sydney: Allen and Unwin, 1995), 161.

5. G. Werth, "Flanders 1917 and the German Soldier," in *Passchendaele in Perspective*, ed. Liddle, 325.

6. J.E. Edmonds, *Military Operations France and Belgium, 1917*, vol. 2 (London: Macmillan, 1948), 130.

7. C. Headlam, *The History of the Guards Division in the Great War, 1915–1918*, vol. 1 (London: John Murray, 1924), 227.

8. C.H. Dudley Ward, *The 56th Division* (London: John Murray, 1921), 151.

9. Edmonds, *Military Operations France and Belgium, 1917*, vol. 2, 137–38.

10. J. Terraine, ed., *General Jack's Diary, 1914–1918* (London: Eyre and Spottiswoode, 1964), 227.

11. F.E. Whitton, *The Prince of Wales's Leinster Regiment (Royal Canadians)*, vol. 2 (Aldershot, UK: Gale and Polden, 1924), 368.

12. Edmonds, *Military Operations France and Belgium, 1917*, vol. 2, 131.

13. War Office, *Statistics of the Military Effort of the British Empire during the Great War, 1914–1920* (London: His Majesty's Stationery Office, 1922), 65.

14. W.A. Watson, *King George's Own Central India Horse* (Edinburgh: Blackwood, 1930), 358.

15. M. Hankey, *The Supreme Command, 1914–1918*, vol. 2 (London: Allen and Unwin, 1961), 683.

16. Hankey, *The Supreme Command*, vol. 2, 684; D.R. Woodward, *Lloyd George and the Generals* (London: Associated University, 1983), 183.

17. Woodward, *Lloyd George*, 184; A.A. Wiest, *Passchendaele and the Royal Navy* (London: Greenwood, 1995), 116.

18. Edmonds, *Military Operations France and Belgium, 1917*, vol. 2, 104–6.

19. D.R. Woodward, ed., *The Military Correspondence of Field-Marshal Sir William Robertson* (London: Bodley Head, 1989), 208.

20. Edmonds, *Military Operations France and Belgium, 1917*, vol. 2, 108; D.T. Zabecki, *Steel Wind: Colonel Georg Bruchmueller and the Birth of Modern Artillery* (Westport, CT: Praeger, 1994), 16; I.M. Brown, *British Logistics on the Western Front, 1914–1919* (Westport, CT: Praeger, 1998), 235.

21. R. Prior and T. Wilson, *Passchendaele: The Untold Story* (London: Yale, 1996), 87–88.

22. Brigadier General J. Charteris, "Notes on the Situation, 29th July, 1917," Australian War Memorial 45/33/6.

23. J. Charteris, *At G.H.Q.* (London: Cassell, 1931), 236.

24. C.C. Repington, *The First World War, 1914–1918*, vol. 2 (London: Constable, 1920), 8; R. Blake, ed., *The Private Papers of Douglas Haig, 1914–1919* (London: Eyre and Spottiswoode, 1952), 249.

25. J. Sheldon, *The German Army at Passchendaele* (Barnsley, UK: Pen and Sword, 2007), 52; Hagenlücke, "The German High Command," 51.

26. C. Falls, *The Gordon Highlanders in the First World War, 1914–1919* (Uckfield, UK: Naval and Military, 2014), 156.

27. F.W. Bewsher, *The History of the 51st (Highland) Division, 1914–1918* (Edinburgh: Blackwood, 1921), 210; L. James, ed., *The History of King Edward's Horse* (London: Sifton, Praed, 1921), 220.

28. S. Snelling, *Victoria Crosses of the First World War: Passchendaele, 1917* (Stroud, UK: Sutton, 1998), 8–9.

29. J.H. Boraston and C.E.O. Bax, *The Eighth Division in War, 1914–1918* (London: Medici Society, 1926), 133–34, 139–40.

30. Blake, *The Private Papers of Douglas Haig*, 250–51.

31. Edmonds, *Military Operations France and Belgium, 1917*, vol. 2, 178.

32. Hagenlücke, "The German High Command," 51; Sheldon, *The German Army at Passchendaele*, 95, 97.

33. Sheldon, *The German Army at Passchendaele*, 91.

34. Headlam, *The Guards Division*, vol. 1, 257.

35. H. Gordon, *The Unreturning Army: A Field-Gunner in Flanders, 1917–1918* (London: Dent, 1967), 70–71.

36. A.M. McGilchrist, *The Liverpool Scottish, 1900–1919* (Liverpool: Henry Young, 1930), 128.

37. Blake, *The Private Papers of Douglas Haig*, 250.

38. J. Charteris, *Field-Marshal Earl Haig* (London: Cassell, 1929), 273; J. Hussey, "The Flanders Battleground and the Weather in 1917," in *Passchendaele in Perspective*, ed. Liddle, 149.

39. W.S. Churchill, *The World Crisis, 1916–1918*, vol. 2 (London: Thornton Butterworth, 1927), 337, 339.

40. L. Wolff, *In Flanders Fields* (London: Longmans, 1959), xvi.

41. Field Marshal D. Haig, "Report on the Battle of 31st July, and Its Results," 4/8/1917, Australian War Memorial 45/33/5.

42. Sheldon, *The German Army at Passchendaele*, 104; Crown Prince Rupprecht of Bavaria, "The War Diary of Crown Prince Rupprecht," *The Army Quarterly*, 1929, 298; Charteris, *At G.H.Q.*, 246.

43. C.D. Baker-Carr, *From Chauffeur to Brigadier* (London: Ernest Benn, 1930), 245–46.

44. Woodward, *The Military Correspondence of Field-Marshal Robertson*, 215–16.

# CHAPTER 5

1. F.E. Whitton, *The Prince of Wales's Leinster Regiment (Royal Canadians)*, vol. 2 (Aldershot, UK: Gale and Polden, 1924), 429.

2. T. Denman, *Ireland's Unknown Soldiers: The 16th (Irish) Division in the Great War* (Dublin: Irish Academic, 1992), 114, 119.

3. K. Grieves, "The 'Recruiting Margin' in Britain: Debates on Manpower during the Third Battle of Ypres," in *Passchendaele in Perspective*, ed. P.H. Liddle (London: Leo Cooper, 1997), 391, 394.

4. J. Sheldon, *The German Army at Passchendaele* (Barnsley, UK: Pen and Sword, 2007), 109.

5. Sheldon, *The German Army at Passchendaele*, 119–20.

6. H.A. Foley, ed., *Scrap Book of the 7th Battalion Somerset Light Infantry* (Aylesbury, UK: privately published, 1932), 79; E. Wyrall, *The History of the Somerset Light Infantry (Prince Albert's), 1914–1919* (London: Methuen, 1927), 200.

7. G.W.L. Nicholson, *Canadian Expeditionary Force, 1914–1919* (Ottawa: R. Duhamel, 1962), 297; J.E. Edmonds, *Military Operations France and Belgium, 1917*, vol. 2 (London: Macmillan, 1948), 222–26, 230.

8. S. Snelling, *Victoria Crosses of the First World War: Passchendaele, 1917* (Stroud, UK: Sutton, 1998), 87.

9. Snelling, *Victoria Crosses*, 93; S. Gillon, *The Story of the 29th Division* (London: Thomas Nelson, 1925), 130–31.

10. W. De B. Wood, *The History of the King's Shropshire Light Infantry in the Great War, 1914–1918* (London: Medici Society, 1925), 185; V.E. Inglefield, *The History of the Twentieth (Light) Division* (London: Nisbet, 1921), 159.

11. Denman, *Ireland's Unknown Soldiers*, 122; Edmonds, *Military Operations France and Belgium, 1917*, vol. 2, 196.

12. R. Prior and T. Wilson, *Passchendaele: The Untold Story* (London: Yale, 1996), 104.

13. Sheldon, *The German Army at Passchendaele*, 137–38.

14. Field Marshal D. Haig, "Report on the Operations in Flanders from 4th August to 20th August," 20/8/1917, Australian War Memorial 45/33/5.

15. C.D. Baker-Carr, *From Chauffeur to Brigadier* (London: Ernest Benn, 1930), 251.

16. Baker-Carr, *From Chauffeur to Brigadier*, 254; Prior and Wilson, *Passchendaele*, 106.

17. T. Travers, "A Particular Style of Command: Haig and G.H.Q., 1916–18," *Journal of Strategic Studies*, 1987, 365.

18. Baker-Carr, *From Chauffeur to Brigadier*, 255.

19. J. Stewart and J. Buchan, *The Fifteenth (Scottish) Division, 1914–1919* (Edinburgh: Blackwood, 1926), 178.

20. P. Scott, "Law and Orders: Discipline and Morale in the British Armies in France, 1917," in *Passchendaele in Perspective*, ed. Liddle, 359.

21. Scott, "Law and Orders," 359.

22. E.D. Vaughan, *Some Desperate Glory* (London: F. Warne, 1981), 228.

23. C.E. Carrington, *The War Record of the 1/5th Battalion The Royal Warwickshire Regiment* (Birmingham, UK: Cornish, 1922), 56.

24. War Office, *Statistics of the Military Effort of the British Empire during the Great War, 1914–1920* (London: His Majesty's Stationery Office, 1922), 364.

25. D.R. Woodward, *The Military Correspondence of Field-Marshal Sir William Robertson* (London: Praeger, 1989), 217; D.R. Woodward, *Lloyd George and the Generals* (London: Associated University, 1983), 233.

26. R. Blake, ed., *The Private Papers of Douglas Haig, 1914–1919* (London: Eyre and Spottiswoode, 1952), 252.

27. Blake, *The Private Papers of Douglas Haig*, 252; Edmonds, *Military Operations France and Belgium, 1917*, vol. 2, 209.

28. J.P. Harris, "Haig and the Tank," in *Haig: A Re-appraisal 70 Years On*, ed. N. Cave and B. Bond (London: Leo Cooper, 1999), 150; J.F.C. Fuller, *Memoirs of an Unconventional Soldier* (London: Ivor Nicholson and Watson, 1936), 176.

29. A. Conan Doyle, *The British Campaigns in Europe, 1914–1918* (London: G. Bles, 1928), 558.

30. Stewart and Buchan, *The Fifteenth (Scottish) Division*, 192.

31. J. Macartney-Filgate, *History of the 33rd Divisional Artillery in the War, 1914–18* (London: Vacher, 1921), 133–34; C. Headlam, *The History of the Guards Division in the Great War, 1915–1918*, vol. 1 (London: John Murray, 1924), 283.

32. A.F. Brooke, "The Evolution of Artillery in the Great War," *The Journal of the Royal Artillery*, LIII, 1926–27, 247.

33. T.J. Mitchell and G.M. Smith, *Medical Services: Casualties and Medical Statistics of the Great War* (London: His Majesty's Stationery Office, 1931), 43.

34. Brooke, "The Evolution of Artillery," 248.

35. I.V. Hogg and L.F. Thurston, *British Artillery Weapons and Ammunition, 1914–1918* (London: Allan, 1972), 80–81, 126–27.

36. D.T. Zabecki, *Steel Wind: Colonel Georg Bruchmueller and the Birth of Modern Artillery* (Westport, CT: Praeger, 1994), 160–61; H. Jager, *German Artillery of World War One* (Marlborough, UK: Crowood, 2001), 34, 117; D. Nash, *German Artillery, 1914–1918* (London: Almark, 1970), 13–14.

37. C. Barnett, *The Swordbearers* (London: Hodder and Stoughton, 1986), 256; R.A. Doughty, *Pyrrhic Victory: French Strategy and Operations in the Great War* (Cambridge, MA: Belknap Harvard, 2005), 380–81; J. Keegan, *The First World War* (London: Hutchinson, 1998), 357; E. Greenhalgh, *The French Army and the First World War* (Cambridge, UK: Cambridge University, 2014), 236–39.

38. M. Hankey, *The Supreme Command, 1914–1918*, vol. 2 (London: Allen and Unwin, 1961), 693; S. Roskill, *Hankey: Man of Secrets*, vol. 1 (London: Collins, 1970), 422.

39. Hankey, *The Supreme Command*, vol. 2, 693.

40. Woodward, *Lloyd George*, 197.

41. Hankey, *The Supreme Command*, vol. 2, 695.

# CHAPTER 6

1. C.E.W. Bean, *The A.I.F. in France*, vol. 4 (Sydney: Angus and Robertson, 1933), 758; H. Hagenlücke, "The German High Command," in *Passchendaele in Perspective*, ed. P.H. Liddle (London: Leo Cooper, 1997), 52.

2. A.A. Wiest, *Passchendaele and the Royal Navy* (London: Greenwood, 1995), 154–55.

3. Wiest, *Passchendaele*, 157.

4. S. Ewart, ed., *Historical Records of the Queen's Own Cameron Highlanders*, vol. 3 (Edinburgh: Blackwood, 1931), 230.

5. E. Wyrall, *The Gloucestershire Regiment in the War, 1914–1918* (London: Methuen, 1931), 218.

6. S. Roskill, *Hankey: Man of Secrets*, vol. 1 (London: Collins, 1970), 422.

7. M. Hankey, *The Supreme Command, 1914–1918*, vol. 2 (London: Allen and Unwin, 1961), 696.

8. W.R. Woodward, *Lloyd George and the Generals* (London: Associated University, 1983), 198.

9. R. Blake, ed., *The Private Papers of Douglas Haig, 1914–1919* (London: Eyre and Spottiswoode, 1952), 254.

10. Hankey, *The Supreme Command*, vol. 2, 697.

11. D.R. Woodward, *Field-Marshal Sir William Robertson* (Westport, CT: Praeger, 1998), 157–58.

12. M. Gilbert, *Winston S. Churchill*, vol. 4 (London: Heinemann, 1975), 45–46.

13. Blake, *The Private Papers of Douglas Haig*, 255.

14. Blake, *The Private Papers of Douglas Haig*, 255.

15. R. Blake, *The Unknown Prime Minister: The Life and Times of Andrew Bonar Law, 1858–1923* (London: Eyre and Spottiswoode, 1955), 362; E. Greenhalgh, *Victory through Coalition* (Cambridge, UK: Cambridge University, 2005), 153.

16. Woodward, *Field-Marshal Sir William Robertson*, 147.

17. D.R. Woodward, ed., *The Military Correspondence of Field-Marshal Sir William Robertson* (London: Bodley Head, 1989), 225–26.

18. L. Wolff, *In Flanders Fields* (London: Longmans, 1959), 173.

19. J.H. Morrow, *The Great War in the Air* (Washington: Smithsonian Institution, 1993), 236.

20. Blake, *The Private Papers of Douglas Haig*, 255; J.E. Edmonds, *Military Operations France and Belgium, 1917*, vol. 2 (London: Macmillan, 1948), 251.

21. J. Ewing, *The History of the 9th (Scottish) Division, 1914–1919* (London: John Murray, 1921), 227.

22. S. Snelling, *Victoria Crosses of the First World War: Passchendaele, 1917* (Stroud, UK: Sutton, 1998), 122; J. Buchan, *The History of the South African Forces in France* (London: Thomas Nelson, 1920), 136–37.

23. Bean, *The A.I.F. in France*, vol. 4, 761.

24. H.R. Sandilands, *The 23rd Division, 1914–1919* (Edinburgh: Blackwood, 1925), 194–95.

25. E. Wyrall, *The History of the 19th Division, 1914–1918* (London: Arnold, 1932), 114; T. Bridges, *Alarms and Excursions* (London: Longmans, 1938), 196.

26. J. Sheldon, *The German Army at Passchendaele* (Barnsley, UK: Pen and Sword, 2007), 156.

27. Edmonds, *Military Operations France and Belgium, 1917*, vol. 2, 279.

28. Edmonds, *Military Operations France and Belgium, 1917*, vol. 2, 278; J.H. Boraston, ed., *Sir Douglas Haig's Despatches* (London: Dent, 1979), 122.

## CHAPTER 7

1. J. Sheldon, *The German Army at Passchendaele* (Barnsley, UK: Pen and Sword, 2007), 166.

2. N. Wanliss, *The History of the Fourteenth Battalion, A.I.F.* (Melbourne: The Arrow Printery, 1929), 240.

3. A.D. Ellis, *The Story of the Fifth Australian Division* (London: Hodder and Stoughton, 1919), 233; C.E.W. Bean, *The A.I.F. in France*, vol. 4 (Sydney: Angus and Robertson, 1933), 809.

4. Ellis, *Fifth Australian Division*, 247.

5. Ellis, *Fifth Australian Division*, 251–52; Sheldon, *The German Army at Passchendaele*, 169–71.

6. J.E. Edmonds, *Military Operations France and Belgium, 1917*, vol. 2 (London: Macmillan, 1948), 293.

7. Edmonds, *Military Operations France and Belgium, 1917*, vol. 2, 292; Bean, *The A.I.F. in France*, vol. 4, 832.

8. D. Lloyd George, *War Memoirs*, vol. 2 (London: Odhams, 1938), 1315.

9. M. Hankey, *The Supreme Command, 1914–1918*, vol. 2 (London: Allen and Unwin, 1961), 700.

10. Lloyd George, *War Memoirs*, vol. 2, 1316.

11. B.H. Liddell Hart, *The Memoirs of Captain Liddell Hart*, vol. 1 (London: Cassell, 1965), 365.

12. D.R. Woodward, ed., *The Military Correspondence of Field-Marshal Sir William Robertson* (London: Bodley Head, 1989), 229.

13. M. Occleshaw, *Armour against Fate: British Intelligence in the First World War* (London: Columbus, 1989), 341; Bean, *The A.I.F. in France*, vol. 4, 878.

14. A.A. Wiest, *Passchendaele and the Royal Navy* (London: Greenwood, 1995), 161.

15. A. Duff Cooper, *Haig*, vol. 2 (London: Faber and Faber, 1937), 164–65.

16. A.F. Home, *The Diary of a World War I Cavalry Officer* (Tunbridge Wells, UK: Costello, 1985), 150.

17. R. Blake, ed., *The Private Papers of Douglas Haig, 1914–1919* (London: Eyre and Spottiswoode, 1952), 256.

18. Lieutenant General L.E. Kiggell, "Record of a Conference Held at Second Army Headquarters, Cassel, at 11 A.M., 2 October 1917," Australian War Memorial 45/33/5.

19. T. Macdougall, ed., *War Letters of General Monash* (Sydney: Duffy and Snellgrove, 2002), 148–50.

20. Blake, *The Private Papers of Douglas Haig*, 256; Lloyd George, *War Memoirs*, vol. 2, 1657; D. French, *The Strategy of the Lloyd George Coalition, 1916–1918* (Oxford: Clarendon, 1995), 154.

21. Blake, *The Private Papers of Douglas Haig*, 258.

22. H. Hagenlücke, "The German High Command," in *Passchendaele in Perspective*, ed. P.H. Liddle (London: Leo Cooper, 1997), 53.

23. Edmonds, *Military Operations France and Belgium, 1917*, vol. 2, 300.

24. Sheldon, *The German Army at Passchendaele*, 198–99.

25. C. Pugsley, "The New Zealand Division at Passchendaele," in *Passchendaele in Perspective*, ed. Liddle, 281; H. Stewart, *The New Zealand Division, 1916–1919* (Auckland: Whitcombe and Tombs, 1921), 271.

26. E. Wren, *Randwick to Hargicourt: History of the 3rd Battalion, A.I.F.* (Sydney: Ronald G. McDonald, 1935), 260.

27. Sheldon, *The German Army at Passchendaele*, 195.

28. Sheldon, *The German Army at Passchendaele*, 196.

29. E. Gorman, *"With the Twenty-Second": A History of the 22nd Battalion, A.I.F.* (Melbourne: H.H. Champion, 1919), 65.

30. Sheldon, *The German Army at Passchendaele*, 205.

31. Edmonds, *Military Operations France and Belgium, 1917*, vol. 2, 304–5, 309.

32. C.T. Atkinson, *The Seventh Division, 1914–1918* (London: John Murray, 1927), 415.

33. J.E.B. Fairclough, *The First Birmingham Battalion in the Great War* (Birmingham, UK: Cornish, 1933), 113.

34. Sheldon, *The German Army at Passchendaele*, 202.

35. Edmonds, *Military Operations France and Belgium, 1917*, vol. 2, 316.

36. J. Davidson, *Haig: Master of the Field* (London: Nevill, 1953), 55.

37. J. Beach, *Haig's Intelligence: G.H.Q. and the German Army, 1916–1918* (Cambridge, UK: Cambridge University, 2013), 257.

38. L. Wolff, *In Flanders Fields* (London: Longmans, 1959), 194–95.

# CHAPTER 8

1. L.R. Lumley, *History of the Eleventh Hussars (Prince Albert's Own), 1908–1934* (London: Royal United Services Institute, 1936), 274.

2. A.F. Home, *The Diary of a World War I Cavalry Officer* (Tunbridge Wells, UK: Costello, 1985), 151; C.H. Dudley Ward, *Regimental Records of the Royal Welch Fusiliers (23rd Foot)*, vol. 3 (London: Forster Groom, 1928), 319.

3. C.C. Repington, *The First World War, 1914–1918*, vol. 2 (London: Constable, 1920), 80, 84.

4. D. French, *The Strategy of the Lloyd George Coalition, 1916–1918* (Oxford: Clarendon, 1995), 157.

5. G.C. Wynne, *If Germany Attacks* (London: Faber and Faber, 1940), 309.

6. J.F.C. Fuller, *Memoirs of an Unconventional Soldier* (London: Ivor Nicholson and Watson, 1936), 161.

7. P.G. Bales, *The History of the 1/4th Battalion Duke of Wellington's (West Riding) Regiment, 1914–1919* (Halifax, UK: Edward Mortimer, 1920), 163.

8. J.E. Edmonds, *Military Operations France and Belgium, 1917*, vol. 2 (London: Macmillan, 1948), 334.

9. C.E.W. Bean, *The A.I.F. in France*, vol. 4 (Sydney: Angus and Robertson, 1933), 901.

10. Bean, *The A.I.F. in France*, vol. 4, 906.

11. D.R. Woodward, *Lloyd George and the Generals* (London: Associated University, 1983), 208.

12. M. Hankey, *The Supreme Command, 1914–1918*, vol. 2 (London: Allen and Unwin, 1961), 713.

13. K. Jeffrey, *Field-Marshal Sir Henry Wilson* (Oxford: Oxford University, 2006), 203.

14. A.A. Wiest, *Passchendaele and the Royal Navy* (London: Greenwood, 1995), 162.

15. L. Wolff, *In Flanders Fields* (London: Longmans, 1959), 237; Bean, *The A.I.F. in France*, vol. 4, 908.

16. Bean, *The A.I.F. in France*, vol. 4, 910; Edmonds, *Military Operations France and Belgium, 1917*, vol. 2, 340.

17. J. Ewing, *The History of the 9th (Scottish) Division, 1914–1919* (London: John Murray, 1921), 243.

18. H. Stewart, *The New Zealand Division, 1916–1919* (Auckland: Whitcombe and Tombs, 1921), 285.

19. Bean, *The A.I.F. in France*, vol. 4, 928; Edmonds, *Military Operations France and Belgium, 1917*, vol. 2, 345; J.H. Boraston, ed., *Sir Douglas Haig's Despatches* (London: Dent, 1979), 130.

20. Wolff, *In Flanders Fields*, 238.

21. G.S. Hutchison, *The Thirty-Third Division in France and Flanders, 1915–1919* (London: Waterlow, 1921), 76.

22. S.J. Wilson, *The Seventh Manchesters* (London: Longmans, 1920), 47.

23. J. Sheldon, *The German Army at Passchendaele* (Barnsley, UK: Pen and Sword, 2007), 233.

24. J. Hussey, "The Flanders Battleground and the Weather in 1917," in *Passchendaele in Perspective*, ed. P.H. Liddle (London: Leo Cooper, 1997), 151.

25. Hussey, "The Flanders Battleground," 148–51.

26. Home, *The Diary of a World War I Cavalry Officer*, 151.

27. N.G. McNicol, *The Thirty-Seventh: History of the Thirty-Seventh Battalion, A.I.F.* (Melbourne: Modern Printing, 1936), 153.

28. Fuller, *Memoirs of an Unconventional Soldier*, 160.

29. W.T. Willcox, *The 3rd (King's Own) Hussars in the Great War, 1914–1918* (London: John Murray, 1925), 192.

30. Wiest, *Passchendaele and the Royal Navy*, 164.

31. Wiest, *Passchendaele and the Royal Navy*, 165.

32. Repington, *The First World War*, vol. 2, 98–99.

33. Repington, *The First World War*, vol. 2, 98–99.

34. Repington, *The First World War*, vol. 2, 101–2.

35. Woodward, *Lloyd George*, 209.

36. C.E.W. Bean, *The A.I.F. in France*, vol. 5 (Sydney: Angus and Robertson, 1937), 50.

37. D. Fraser, *Alanbrooke* (London: Collins, 1982), 78.

38. G.W.L. Nicholson, *Canadian Expeditionary Force, 1914–1919* (Ottawa: R. Duhamel, 1962), 313.

39. A.M.J. Hyatt, *General Sir Arthur Currie: A Military Biography* (Toronto: University of Toronto, 1987), 79.

40. A. Bernede, "Third Ypres and the Restoration of Confidence in the Ranks of the French Army," in *Passchendaele in Perspective*, ed. Liddle, 100; R.A. Doughty, *Pyrrhic Victory: French Strategy and Operations in the Great War* (Cambridge, MA: Belknap Harvard, 2005), 389; C. Barnett, *The Swordbearers* (London: Hodder and Stoughton, 1963), 257; E. Greenhalgh, *The French Army and the First World War* (Cambridge, UK: Cambridge University, 2014), 241–42.

41. D.R. Woodward, ed., *The Military Correspondence of Field-Marshal Sir William Robertson* (London: Bodley Head, 1989), 241.

42. C. Harington, *Tim Harington Looks Back* (London: John Murray, 1940), 63.

43. S. Snelling, *Victoria Crosses of the First World War: Passchendaele, 1917* (Stroud, UK: Sutton, 1998), 235.

44. E. Ludendorff, *My War Memories, 1914–1918*, vol. 2 (London: Hutchinson, 1919), 492.

45. Lieutenant General J.F.N. Birch to Chief of the General Staff, General Headquarters, 5/11/1917, Australian War Memorial 45/31/26.

46. J. Hawkes, *Mortimer Wheeler: Adventurer in Archaeology* (London: Weidenfeld and Nicolson, 1982), 57.

47. G.C. Oram, *Military Executions during World War I* (Basingstoke, UK: Palgrave Macmillan, 2003), 113.

48. Edmonds, *Military Operations France and Belgium, 1917*, vol. 2, 359; C.T. Atkinson, *The History of the South Wales Borderers, 1914–1918* (London: Medici Society, 1931), 347–49; Hussey, "The Flanders Battleground," 151; S. McCance, *History of the Royal Munster Fusiliers*, vol. 2 (Uckfield, UK: Naval and Military, 2009), 144–48.

49. H.M. Urquhart, *The History of the 16th Battalion (the Canadian Scottish), 1914–1919* (Toronto: Macmillan, 1932), 236.

50. Nicholson, *Canadian Expeditionary Force*, 327; War Office, *Statistics of the Military Effort of the British Empire during the Great War, 1914–1920* (London: His Majesty's Stationery Office, 1922), 632.

51. Wolff, *In Flanders Fields*, 23–24.

52. Edmonds, *Military Operations France and Belgium, 1917*, vol. 2, 361.

53. War Office, *Statistics of the Military Effort*, 262–63.

54. Bernede, "Third Ypres," 99.

55. G. Werth, "Flanders 1917 and the German Soldier," in *Passchendaele in Perspective*, ed. Liddle, 327.

56. Boraston, *Sir Douglas Haig's Despatches*, 108, 133; War Office, *Statistics of the Military Effort*, 334.

## CHAPTER 9

1. M. Hankey, *The Supreme Command, 1914–1918*, vol. 1 (London: Allen and Unwin, 1961), 207; A.A. Wiest, *Passchendaele and the Royal Navy* (London: Greenwood, 1995), 4.

2. D. Lloyd George, *War Memoirs*, vol. 2 (London: Odhams, 1938), 1368.

3. D.R. Woodward, *Lloyd George and the Generals* (London: Associated University, 1983), 213.

4. K. Jeffrey, *Field-Marshal Sir Henry Wilson* (Oxford: Oxford University, 2006), 207.

5. P. Warner, *Passchendaele: The Story behind the Tragic Victory of 1917* (London: Sidgwick and Jackson, 1988), 234.

6. R. Prior and T. Wilson, *Passchendaele: The Untold Story* (London: Yale, 1996), 179.

7. W.S. Churchill, *The World Crisis, 1916–1918*, vol. 2 (London: Thornton Butterworth, 1927), 343.

8. C.D. Baker-Carr, *From Chauffeur to Brigadier* (London: Ernest Benn, 1930), 263; W. Miles, *Military Operations France and Belgium, 1917*, vol. 3 (London: Macmillan, 1948), 4–5.

9. J. Williams, *Byng of Vimy* (London: Secker and Warburg, 1983), 21.

10. B.H. Liddell Hart, *The Tanks*, vol. 1 (London: Cassell, 1959), 130.

11. J.F.C. Fuller, *Memoirs of an Unconventional Soldier* (London: Ivor Nicholson and Watson, 1936), 171.

12. Hart, *The Tanks*, vol. 1, 131.

13. Miles, *Military Operations France and Belgium, 1917*, vol. 3, 6.

14. Fuller, *Memoirs of an Unconventional Soldier*, 171.

15. W.H.L. Watson, *A Company of Tanks* (Edinburgh: Blackwood, 1920), 44–45; C.E.W. Bean, *The A.I.F. in France*, vol. 4 (Sydney: Angus and Robertson, 1933), 272–73.

16. Fuller, *Memoirs of an Unconventional Soldier*, 108–9; Watson, *A Company of Tanks*, 70.

17. Fuller, *Memoirs of an Unconventional Soldier*, 171; Williams, *Byng of Vimy*, 175; Miles, *Military Operations France and Belgium, 1917*, vol. 3, 6; Hart, *The Tanks*, vol. 1, 131.

18. Fuller, *Memoirs of an Unconventional Soldier*, 171.

19. Fuller, *Memoirs of an Unconventional Soldier*, 178; J. Davidson, *Haig: Master of the Field* (London: Nevill, 1953), 69.

20. Williams, *Byng of Vimy*, 177.

21. Williams, *Byng of Vimy*, 177; Miles, *Military Operations France and Belgium, 1917*, vol. 3, 8–9.

22. Fuller, *Memoirs of an Unconventional Soldier*, 179.

23. C. Falls, *The Gordon Highlanders in the First World War, 1914–1919* (Uckfield, UK: Naval and Military, 1958), 167.

24. Miles, *Military Operations France and Belgium, 1917*, vol. 3, 17.

25. J.P. Harris, *Douglas Haig and the First World War* (Cambridge, UK: Cambridge University, 2008), 394.

26. Miles, *Military Operations France and Belgium, 1917*, vol. 3, 306.

27. Miles, *Military Operations France and Belgium, 1917*, vol. 3, 308.

28. Miles, *Military Operations France and Belgium, 1917*, vol. 3, 309, 311.

29. E. Wyrall, *History of the King's Regiment (Liverpool), 1914–1919*, vol. 3 (London: Arnold, 1935), 541.

30. Miles, *Military Operations France and Belgium, 1917*, vol. 3, 27–28.

31. D.R. Woodward, *Field Marshal Sir William Robertson* (Westport, CT: Praeger, 1998), 175.

32. Baker-Carr, *From Chauffeur to Brigadier*, 260.

33. Fuller, *Memoirs of an Unconventional Soldier*, 199; Miles, *Military Operations France and Belgium, 1917*, vol. 3, 353.

34. Baker-Carr, *From Chauffeur to Brigadier*, 261; Watson, *A Company of Tanks*, 42.

35. F.W. Bewsher, *The History of the 51st (Highland) Division, 1914–1918* (Edinburgh: Blackwood, 1921), 235.

36. Hart, *The Tanks*, vol. 1, 128.

37. T. Travers, *How the War Was Won* (London: Routledge, 1992), 20–21.

38. Miles, *Military Operations France and Belgium, 1917*, vol. 3, 25.

39. Falls, *The Gordon Highlanders*, 165–66.

40. H.A. Jones, *The War in the Air*, vol. 4 (Oxford: Clarendon, 1934), 429; T. Henshaw, *The Sky Their Battlefield* (London: Grub Street, 1995), 251–52.

# CHAPTER 10

1. J. Sheldon, *The German Army at Cambrai* (Barnsley, UK: Pen and Sword, 2009), 17–18.

2. Sheldon, *The German Army at Cambrai*, 38.

3. Sheldon, *The German Army at Cambrai*, 6, 28–29; W. Miles, *Military Operations France and Belgium, 1917*, vol. 3 (London: Macmillan, 1948), 47–48.

4. Sheldon, *The German Army at Cambrai*, 36.

5. C. Falls, *The History of the 36th (Ulster) Division* (London: Constable, 1996), 142; Sheldon, *The German Army at Cambrai*, 31; Miles, *Military Operations France and Belgium, 1917*, vol. 3, 48–49.

6. W. Seymour, *The History of the Rifle Brigade in the War of 1914–1918*, vol. 2 (London: Rifle Brigade Club, 1936), 168; F.W. Bewsher, *The History of the 51st (Highland) Division, 1914–1918* (Edinburgh: Blackwood, 1921), 236; T.O. Marden, ed., *A Short History of the 6th Division, 1914–1919* (London: Hugh Rees, 1920), 36.

7. J. Williams, *Byng of Vimy* (London: Secker and Warburg, 1983), 184–85.

8. D.G. Browne, *The Tank in Action* (Edinburgh: Blackwood, 1920), 65.

9. B.H. Liddell Hart, *The Tanks*, vol. 1 (London: Cassell, 1959), 135.

10. Miles, *Military Operations France and Belgium, 1917*, vol. 3, 334.

11. E. Wyrall, *History of the King's Regiment (Liverpool), 1914–1919*, vol. 3 (London: Arnold, 1935), 545.

12. M. Farndale, *History of the Royal Regiment of Artillery*, vol. 1 (London: Royal Artillery Institution, 1986), 222.

13. Bewsher, *The History of the 51st (Highland) Division*, 239.

14. S. Foot, *Three Lives* (London: Heinemann, 1934), 194.

15. F. Loraine Petre, *The History of the Norfolk Regiment*, vol. 2 (Norwich, UK: Jarrold, 1924), 275.

16. Sheldon, *The German Army at Cambrai*, 68.

17. Sheldon, *The German Army at Cambrai*, 46–47.

18. Sheldon, *The German Army at Cambrai*, 49, 56.

19. Falls, *The History of the 36th (Ulster) Division*, 156.

20. Bewsher, *The History of the 51st (Highland) Division*, 241.

21. D. Sutherland, *War Diary of the Fifth Seaforth Highlanders* (London: Bodley Head, 1920), 137.

22. Sutherland, *War Diary*, 139; Miles, *Military Operations France and Belgium, 1917*, vol. 3, 57; Bewsher, *The History of the 51st (Highland) Division*, 242; C. Falls, *The Gordon Highlanders in the First World War, 1914–1919* (Uckfield, UK: Naval and Military, 1958), 168.

23. B. Hammond, *Cambrai 1917* (London: Weidenfeld and Nicolson, 2008), 141.

24. Miles, *Military Operations France and Belgium, 1917*, vol. 3, 56–58; Bewsher, *The History of the 51st (Highland) Division*, 245.

25. Miles, *Military Operations France and Belgium, 1917*, vol. 3, 90; Bewsher, *The History of the 51st (Highland) Division*, 260.

26. Sheldon, *The German Army at Cambrai*, 92.

27. J.A. Taylor, *Deborah and the War of the Tanks, 1917* (Barnsley, UK: Pen and Sword, 2016), 243.

# CHAPTER 11

1. W. Seymour, *The History of the Rifle Brigade in the War of 1914–1918*, vol. 2 (London: Rifle Brigade Club, 1936), 175.

2. S.G.P. Ward, *Faithful: The Story of the Durham Light Infantry* (London: Nelson, 1963), 393; E. Wyrall, *The West Yorkshire Regiment in the War, 1914–1918*, vol. 2 (London: John Lane, 1927), 154.

3. T.O. Marden, ed., *A Short History of the 6th Division, 1914–1919* (London: Hugh Rees, 1920), 39.

4. W. Miles, *Military Operations France and Belgium, 1917*, vol. 3 (London: Macmillan, 1948), 21; S. Gillon, *The Story of the 29th Division* (London: Thomas Nelson, 1925), 147.

5. Gillon, *The Story of the 29th Division*, 152–53.

6. Miles, *Military Operations France and Belgium, 1917*, vol. 3, 72.

7. F. Fox, *The Royal Inniskilling Fusiliers in the World War* (London: Constable, 1928), 112–13.

8. J. Sheldon, *The German Army at Cambrai* (Barnsley, UK: Pen and Sword, 2007), 91–92.

9. Sheldon, *The German Army at Cambrai*, 109–10.

10. B. Hammond, *Cambrai 1917* (London: Weidenfeld and Nicolson, 2008), 167.

11. Sheldon, *The German Army at Cambrai*, 114.

12. Sheldon, *The German Army at Cambrai*, 115.

13. S. Foot, *Three Lives* (London: Heinemann, 1934), 196.

14. Lord Carnock, *The History of the 15th The King's Hussars, 1914–1922* (Gloucester, UK: Crypt House, 1932), 145.

15. Marquess of Anglesey, *A History of the British Cavalry*, vol. 4 (London: Secker and Warburg, 1986), 121–22.

16. J.M. Brereton, *A History of the 4th/7th Royal Dragoon Guards* (Catterick, UK: The Regiment, 1982), 333–34.

17. Miles, *Military Operations France and Belgium, 1917*, vol. 3, 81.

18. H. Hudson, *History of the 19th King George's Own Lancers, 1858–1921* (Aldershot, UK: Gale and Polden, 1937), 176–77.

19. E. Tennant, *The Royal Deccan Horse in the Great War* (Uckfield, UK: Naval and Military, 2008), 59.

20. J.E.B. Seely, *Adventure* (London: Heinemann, 1930), 273.

21. Miles, *Military Operations France and Belgium, 1917*, vol. 3, 70–71.

22. Anglesey, *A History of the British Cavalry*, vol. 4, 132.

23. Anglesey, *A History of the British Cavalry*, vol. 4, 134.

24. Anglesey, *A History of the British Cavalry*, vol. 4, 134–35, 137.

25. Sheldon, *The German Army at Cambrai*, 116–17.

26. Miles, *Military Operations France and Belgium, 1917*, vol. 3, 94.

27. Miles, *Military Operations France and Belgium, 1917*, vol. 3, 98.

## CHAPTER 12

1. Lord Somers, *The War History of the Sixth Tank Battalion* (Uckfield, UK: Naval and Military, 2003), 51; S. Gillon, *The Story of the 29th Division* (London: Thomas Nelson, 1925), 146.

2. W. Miles, *Military Operations France and Belgium, 1917*, vol. 3 (London: Macmillan, 1948), 88; B. Cooper, *The Ironclads of Cambrai* (London: Souvenir, 1967), 135, 137.

3. Miles, *Military Operations France and Belgium, 1917*, vol. 3, 279–81.

4. J. Charteris, *Field-Marshal Earl Haig* (London: Cassell, 1929), 285.

5. C.R.M.F. Cruttwell, *A History of the Great War, 1914–1918* (Oxford: Clarendon, 1934), 473.

6. D. Sutherland, *War Diary of the Fifth Seaforth Highlanders* (London: Bodley Head, 1920), 142.

7. J.M. Brereton, *A History of the 4th/7th Royal Dragoon Guards* (Catterick, UK: The Regiment, 1982), 336.

8. T. Travers, *How the War Was Won* (London: Routledge, 1992), 24.

9. D.R. Woodward, *Field-Marshal Sir William Robertson* (Westport, CT: Praeger, 1998), 176; D.R. Woodward, *Lloyd George and the Generals* (London: Associated University, 1983), 228.

10. E. Wyrall, *History of the King's Regiment (Liverpool), 1914–1919*, vol. 3 (London: Arnold, 1935), 545.

11. J. Sheldon, *The German Army at Cambrai* (Barnsley, UK: Pen and Sword, 2007), 130.

12. Sheldon, *The German Army at Cambrai*, 137.

13. J. Beach, *Haig's Intelligence: G.H.Q. and the German Army, 1916–1918* (Cambridge, UK: Cambridge University, 2013), 263.

14. M.M. Haldane, *History of the Fourth Battalion, the Seaforth Highlanders* (London: Witherby, 1928), 243.

15. T. Henshaw, *The Sky Their Battlefield* (London: Grub Street, 1995), 254.

16. C.T. Atkinson, *The History of the South Wales Borderers, 1914–1918* (London: Medici Society, 1931), 355.

17. Miles, *Military Operations France and Belgium, 1917*, vol. 3, 107–8.

18. R. Blake, ed., *The Private Papers of Douglas Haig, 1914–1919* (London: Eyre and Spottiswoode, 1952), 268–69.

19. J.H. Boraston, ed., *Sir Douglas Haig's Despatches* (London: Dent, 1979), 159–60.

20. Travers, *How the War Was Won*, 26.

234 Notes

21. Blake, *The Private Papers of Douglas Haig*, 269.

22. Haldane, *History of the Fourth Battalion*, 245.

23. Miles, *Military Operations France and Belgium, 1917*, vol. 3, 123–25.

24. F.E. Whitton, *History of the 40th Division* (Aldershot, UK: Gale and Polden, 1926), 93–94, 99; W. Moore, *A Wood Called Bourlon* (London: Leo Cooper, 1988), 95–96.

25. W.H.L. Watson, *A Company of Tanks* (Edinburgh: Blackwood, 1920), 189–90.

26. Sheldon, *The German Army at Cambrai*, 165.

27. L.J.C. Southern, *The Bedfordshire Yeomanry in the Great War* (Bedford, UK: Rush and Warwick, 1935), 71.

28. Miles, *Military Operations France and Belgium, 1917*, vol. 3, 134.

29. C. Falls, *The Gordon Highlanders in the First World War, 1914–1919* (Uckfield, UK: Naval and Military, 2014), 171; Miles, *Military Operations France and Belgium, 1917*, vol. 3, 128.

30. F. Ponsonby, *The Grenadier Guards in the Great War of 1914–1918*, vol. 2 (London: Macmillan, 1920), 271.

31. Miles, *Military Operations France and Belgium, 1917*, vol. 3, 139.

32. Miles, *Military Operations France and Belgium, 1917*, vol. 3, 148.

33. Whitton, *History of the 40th Division*, 152.

34. Sheldon, *The German Army at Cambrai*, 179.

35. C. Headlam, *The History of the Guards Division in the Great War, 1915–1918*, vol. 1 (London: John Murray, 1924), 304–7.

36. Headlam, *The History of the Guards Division*, 308.

37. Travers, *How the War Was Won*, 27.

38. Sheldon, *The German Army at Cambrai*, 205.

39. E. Greenhalgh, *The French Army and the First World War* (Cambridge, UK: Cambridge University, 2014), 246.

40. J.P. Harris, *Douglas Haig and the First World War* (Cambridge, UK: Cambridge University, 2008), 403; Beach, *Haig's Intelligence*, 266.

41. T.O. Marden, ed., *A Short History of the 6th Division, 1914–1919* (London: Hugh Rees, 1920), 36.

## CHAPTER 13

1. J. Sheldon, *The German Army at Cambrai* (Barnsley, UK: Pen and Sword, 2007), 208, 305–6.

2. Sheldon, *The German Army at Cambrai*, 218.

3. D.T. Zabecki, *The German 1918 Offensives* (New York: Routledge, 2006), 69–70; T.T. Lupfer, *The Dynamics of Doctrine: The Changes in German Tactical Doctrine during the First World War* (Fort Leavenworth, KS: United States Army Command and General Staff College, 1981), 42.

4. A.M. McGilchrist, *The Liverpool Scottish, 1900–1919* (Liverpool: Henry Young, 1930), 144.

5. T. Travers, *How the War Was Won* (London: Routledge, 1992), 28; E. Wyrall, *History of the King's Regiment (Liverpool), 1914–1919*, vol. 3 (London: Arnold, 1935), 554.

6. W. Miles, *Military Operations France and Belgium, 1917*, vol. 2 (London: Macmillan, 1948), 169, 300.

7. J. Beach, *Haig's Intelligence: G.H.Q. and the German Army, 1916–1918* (Cambridge, UK: Cambridge University, 2013), 265.

8. H. Whalley-Kelly, *"Ich Dien": The Prince of Wales's Volunteers (South Lancashire), 1914–1934* (Aldershot, UK: Gale and Polden, 1935), 123–25; McGilchrist, *The Liverpool Scottish*, 156.

9. A. Conan Doyle, *The British Campaigns in Europe, 1914–1918* (London: G. Ples, 1928), 611.

10. Miles, *Military Operations France and Belgium, 1917*, vol. 3, 179–80.

11. S. Hare, *The Annals of the King's Royal Rifle Corps*, vol. 5 (London: John Murray, 1932), 255–56.

12. E. Wyrall, *The History of the Somerset Light Infantry (Prince Albert's), 1914–1919* (London: Methuen, 1927), 234.

13. Travers, *How the War Was Won*, 28.

14. A.H. Maude, *The 47th (London) Division, 1914–1919* (London: Amalgamated, 1922), 125.

15. F. Loraine Petre, *The Royal Berkshire Regiment (Princess Charlotte of Wales's)*, vol. 2 (Reading, UK: The Barracks, 1925), 38–41.

16. Maude, *The 47th (London) Division*, 127.

17. Miles, *Military Operations France and Belgium, 1917*, vol. 3, 228.

18. Marquess of Anglesey, *A History of the British Cavalry*, vol. 4 (London: Secker and Warburg, 1986), 147; Miles, *Military Operations France and Belgium, 1917*, vol. 3, 232; W.A. Watson, *King George's Own Central India Horse* (Edinburgh: Blackwood, 1930), 368.

19. Anglesey, *A History of the British Cavalry*, vol. 4, 147.

20. D.E. Whitworth, ed., *A History of the 2nd Lancers (Gardner's Horse), 1809–1922* (Uckfield, UK: Naval and Military, 2006), 106–7.

21. Whitworth, *A History of the 2nd Lancers*, 111–12.

22. Miles, *Military Operations France and Flanders, 1917*, vol. 3, 234.

23. Watson, *King George's Own Central India Horse*, 373.

24. B. Hammond, *Cambrai 1917* (London: Weidenfeld and Nicholson, 2008), 409.

25. Miles, *Military Operations France and Belgium, 1917*, vol. 3, 227, 248.

26. Sheldon, *The German Army at Cambrai*, 288–89.

27. Sheldon, *The German Army at Cambrai*, 309.

28. Lupfer, *The Dynamics of Doctrine*, 43; Zabecki, *The German 1918 Offensives*, 70.

29. Sheldon, *The German Army at Cambrai*, vii.

30. Sheldon, *The German Army at Cambrai*, 304.

31. Miles, *Military Operations France and Belgium, 1917*, vol. 3, 273.

32. J.F.C. Fuller, *Memoirs of an Unconventional Soldier* (London: Ivor Nicholson and Watson, 1936), 220.

33. C.D. Baker-Carr, *From Chauffeur to Brigadier* (London: Ernest Benn, 1930), 275.

34. W.S. Churchill, *The World Crisis, 1916–1918*, vol. 2 (London: Thornton Butterworth, 1927), 348.

35. Baker-Carr, *From Chauffeur to Brigadier*, 294.

36. Churchill, *The World Crisis*, vol. 2, 381.

37. Beach, *Haig's Intelligence*, 266.

38. B. Millman, *Pessimism and British War Policy, 1916–1918* (London: Frank Cass, 2001), 106.

39. J.P. Harris, *Douglas Haig and the First World War* (Cambridge, UK: Cambridge University, 2008), 408.

40. Harris, *Douglas Haig*, 414; D. Lloyd George, *War Memoirs*, vol. 2 (London: Odhams, 1938), 1339.

41. B.H. Liddell Hart, *The Tanks*, vol. 1 (London: Cassell, 1959), 155; Ministry of Munitions, *The Official History of the Ministry of Munitions*, vol. 12, part 3 (Uckfield, UK: Naval and Military, 2008), 93.

42. R. Blake, ed., *The Private Papers of Douglas Haig, 1914–1919* (London: Eyre and Spottiswoode, 1952), 273.

43. R. Prior and T. Wilson, *Passchendaele: The Untold Story* (London: Yale, 1996), 181; M. LoCicero, *A Moonlight Massacre: The Night Operation on the Passchendaele Ridge, 2 December 1917* (Solihull, UK: Helion, 2014).

44. P. Gibbs, *Realities of War* (London: Heinemann, 1920), 396.

45. E. Ludendorff, *My War Memories, 1914–1918*, vol. 2 (London: Hutchinson, 1919), 491.

46. Sheldon, *The German Army at Cambrai*, 312.

47. Sheldon, *The German Army at Cambrai*, 315–16.

48. J.H. Boraston, ed., *Sir Douglas Haig's Despatches* (London: Dent, 1979), 133.

49. B.H. Liddell Hart, *The Real War, 1914–1918* (Boston: Little, Brown, 1930), 343.

50. B. Bond, *The Victorian Army and the Staff College, 1854–1914* (London: Eyre Methuen, 1972), 288; T. Travers, *The Killing Ground* (London: Allen and Unwin, 1987), 108.

51. Bond, *The Victorian Army*, 297; Travers, *The Killing Ground*, 108, 120.

## CHAPTER 14

1. C. Barnett, *The Swordbearers* (London: Hodder and Stoughton, 1963), 265.

2. D.T. Zabecki, *The German 1918 Offensives* (New York: Routledge, 2006), 25; J.L. Wallach, *The Dogma of the Battle of Annihilation* (Westport, CT: Greenwood, 1986), 183–84.

3. Zabecki, *The German 1918 Offensives*, 99.

4. M. Geyer, "German Strategy in the Age of Machine Warfare, 1914–1945," in *Makers of Modern Strategy*, ed. P. Paret (Princeton, NJ: Princeton University, 1986), 551–52.

5. C.E.W. Bean, *The A.I.F. in France*, vol. 4 (Sydney: Angus and Robertson, 1933), 946; S. Roskill, *Hankey: Man of Secrets*, vol. 1 (London: Collins, 1970), 463.

6. G.J. De Groot, *Douglas Haig, 1861–1928* (London: Unwin Hyman, 1988), 354.

7. J. Charteris, *Field-Marshal Earl Haig* (London: Cassell, 1929), 389; T. Travers, "A Particular Style of Command: Haig and G.H.Q., 1916–18," *Journal of Strategic Studies*, London: Frank Cass, 1987, 367.

8. J.P. Harris, *Douglas Haig and the First World War* (Cambridge, UK: Cambridge University, 2008), 411, 416–17.

9. C.C. Repington, *The First World War, 1914–1918*, vol. 2 (London: Constable, 1920), 173.

10. R. Blake, ed., *The Private Papers of Douglas Haig, 1914–1919* (London: Eyre and Spottiswoode, 1952), 277–78.

11. Blake, *The Private Papers of Douglas Haig*, 278.

12. C.L. Mowat, *Britain between the Wars, 1918–1940* (London: Methuen, 1956), 512–13.

13. W.S. Churchill, *The World Crisis, 1916–1918*, vol. 2 (London: Thornton and Butterworth, 1927), 377.

14. Harris, *Douglas Haig*, 430; D.R. Woodward, *Field-Marshal Sir William Robertson* (Westport, CT: Praeger, 1998), 200–1; K. Jeffrey, *Field-Marshal Sir Henry Wilson* (Oxford: Oxford University, 2006), 218.

15. Blake, *The Private Papers of Douglas Haig*, 283; Charteris, *Field-Marshal Earl Haig*, 311.

16. J.E. Edmonds, *Military Operations France and Belgium, 1918*, vol. 1 (London: Macmillan, 1935), 2.

17. J. Keegan, *The First World War* (London: Hutchinson, 1998), 421.

18. T.T. Lupfer, *The Dynamics of Doctrine: The Changes in German Tactical Doctrine during the First World War* (Fort Leavenworth, KS: United States Army Command and General Staff College, 1981), 50; M. Middlebrook, *The Kaiser's Battle* (London: Allen Lane, 1978), 308–9.

19. Edmonds, *Military Operations France and Belgium, 1918*, vol. 1, 369.

20. E. Greenhalgh, "Myth and Memory: Sir Douglas Haig and the Imposition of Allied Unified Command in March 1918," *The Journal of Military History*, 2004, 800.

21. E. Greenhalgh, *Foch in Command* (Cambridge, UK: Cambridge University, 2011), 452.

22. J.E. Edmonds, *Military Operations France and Belgium, 1918*, vol. 5 (London: Macmillan, 1947), 584; R.F. Weigley, *History of the United States Army* (Bloomington: Indiana University, 1984), 377–78.

23. H.H. Herwig, *The First World War: Germany and Austria-Hungary, 1914–1919* (London: Arnold, 1997), 449.

24. Blake, *The Private Papers of Douglas Haig*, 239–40.

25. M. Hankey, *The Supreme Command, 1914–1918*, vol. 1 (London: Allen and Unwin, 1961), 207; A.A. Wiest, *Passchendaele and the Royal Navy* (London: Greenwood, 1995), 4.

26. L. Sondhaus, *German Submarine Warfare in World War I* (Boulder, CO: Rowman and Littlefield, 2017), 156.

27. Hankey, *The Supreme Command*, vol. 2, 702.

28. D. Lloyd George, *War Memoirs*, vol. 2 (London: Odhams, 1938), 1368.

29. J.E. Edmonds, *Military Operations France and Belgium, 1917* (London: Macmillan, 1948), vol. 2, 280.

30. J.H. Boraston, ed., *Sir Douglas Haig's Despatches* (London: Dent, 1979), 155.

31. J. Sheldon, *The German Army at Cambrai* (Barnsley, UK: Pen and Sword, 2009), 73; B. Cooper, *The Ironclads of Cambrai* (London: Souvenir, 1967), 120.

32. C.D. Baker-Carr, *From Chauffeur to Brigadier* (London: Ernest Benn, 1930), 270.

33. A. Green, *Writing the Great War: Sir James Edmonds and the Official Histories, 1915–1948* (London: Frank Cass, 2003), 49; B.H. Liddell Hart, "The Basic Truths of Passchendaele," *The Journal of the Royal United Services Institute*, London: Royal United Services Institute: 1959, 435–36.

34. T. Travers, *The Killing Ground* (London: Allen and Unwin, 1987), 101.

35. B.P. Hughes, ed., *History of the Royal Regiment of Artillery*, vol. 3 (London: Royal Artillery Institution, 1992), 160, 166–67; Repington, *The First World War*, vol. 2, 524; I.V. Hogg and L.F. Thurston, *British Artillery Weapons and Ammunition, 1914–1918* (London: Allan, 1972), 82–83.

36. Churchill, *The World Crisis, 1916–1918*, vol. 2, 338–39.

37. Lloyd George, *War Memoirs*, vol. 2, 1313.

# Bibliography

Amery, L.S. *My Political Life*. Vols. 1 and 2. London: Hutchinson, 1953.

Anglesey, Marquess of. *A History of the British Cavalry*. Vol. 4. London: Leo Cooper, 1986.

Atkinson, C.T. *The History of the South Wales Borderers, 1914–1918*. London: Medici Society, 1931.

———. *The Seventh Division, 1914–1918*. London: John Murray, 1927.

Bacon, R. *The Dover Patrol*. London: Hutchinson, 1920.

Baker-Carr, C.D. *From Chauffeur to Brigadier*. London: Ernest Benn, 1930.

Bales, P.G. *The History of the 1/4th Battalion Duke of Wellington's (West Riding) Regiment, 1914–1919*. Halifax, UK: Edward Mortimer, 1920.

Barnett, C. *The Swordbearers*. London: Hodder and Stoughton, 1963.

Beach, J. *Haig's Intelligence: G.H.Q. and the German Army, 1916–1918*. Cambridge, UK: Cambridge University, 2013.

Bean, C.E.W. *The A.I.F. in France*. Vol. 4. Sydney: Angus and Robertson, 1933.

———. *The A.I.F. in France*. Vol. 5. Sydney: Angus and Robertson, 1937.

Beckett, I.F.W. *Johnnie Gough, V.C.* London: Donovan, 1989.

Bernede, A. "Third Ypres and the Restoration of Confidence in the Ranks of the French Army." In *Passchendaele in Perspective*, edited by P.H. Liddle. London: Leo Cooper, 1997.

Bewsher, F.W. *The History of the 51st (Highland) Division, 1914–1918*. Edinburgh: Blackwood, 1921.

Birch, Lieutenant General J.F.N., to Chief of the General Staff, General Headquarters, 5/11/1917. Australian War Memorial 45/31/26.

Blake, R., ed. *The Private Papers of Douglas Haig, 1914–1919*. London: Eyre and Spottiswoode, 1952.

———. *The Unknown Prime Minister: The Life and Times of Andrew Bonar Law, 1858–1923*. London: Eyre and Spottiswoode, 1955.

Bond, B. *The Victorian Army and the Staff College, 1854–1914*. London: Eyre Methuen, 1972.

Boraston, J.H., ed. *Sir Douglas Haig's Despatches*. London: Dent, 1979.

Boraston, J.H. and C.E.O. Bax. *The Eighth Division in War, 1914–1918*. London: Medici Society, 1926.

Brereton, J.M. *A History of the 4th/7th Royal Dragoon Guards*. Catterick, UK: The Regiment, 1982.

Bridges, T. *Alarms and Excursions*. London: Longmans, 1938.

Brooke, A.F. "The Evolution of Artillery in the Great War." *The Journal of the Royal Artillery*, LIII, 1926–27.

Brown, I.M. *British Logistics on the Western Front, 1914–1919*. Westport, CT: Praeger, 1998.

Browne, D.G. *The Tank in Action*. Edinburgh: Blackwood, 1920.

Buchan, J. *The History of the South African Forces in France*. London: Thomas Nelson, 1920.

Burton, O.E. *The Auckland Regiment*. Auckland: Whitcombe and Tombs, 1922.

Callwell, C.E. *Field-Marshal Sir Henry Wilson*. 2 vols. London: Cassell, 1927.

Carnock, Lord. *The History of the 15th The King's Hussars, 1914–1922*. Gloucester, UK: Crypt House, 1932.

Carrington, C.E. *The War Record of the 1/5th Battalion The Royal Warwickshire Regiment*. Birmingham, UK: Cornish, 1922.

Charteris, J. *At G.H.Q.* London: Cassell, 1931.

———. *Field-Marshal Earl Haig*. London: Cassell, 1929.

———. "Notes on the Situation, 29th July, 1917." Australian War Memorial 45/33/6.

Churchill, W.S. *The World Crisis, 1916–1918*. 2 vols. London: Thornton Butterworth, 1927.

Cooper, A. Duff. *Haig*. 2 vols. London: Faber and Faber, 1936.

Cooper, B. *The Ironclads of Cambrai*. London: Souvenir, 1967.

Crozier, F.P. *A Brass Hat in No Man's Land*. London: Jonathan Cape, 1930.

Cruttwell, C.R.M.F. *A History of the Great War, 1914–1918*. Oxford: Clarendon, 1934.

Davidson, J. *Haig: Master of the Field*. London: Nevill, 1953.

De Groot, G.J. *Douglas Haig, 1861–1928*. London: Unwin Hyman, 1988.

———. "Educated Soldier or Cavalry Officer? Contradictions in the Pre-1914 Career of Douglas Haig." *War and Society*, September 1986.

Denman, T. *Ireland's Unknown Soldiers: The 16th (Irish) Division in the Great War*. Dublin: Irish Academic, 1992.

Doughty, R.A. *Pyrrhic Victory: French Strategy and Operations in the Great War*. Cambridge, MA: Belknap Harvard, 2005.

Doyle, A. Conan. *The British Campaigns in Europe, 1914–1918*. London: G. Bles, 1928.

Dudley Ward, C.H. *The 56th Division*. London: John Murray, 1921.

———. *History of the Welsh Guards*. London: London Stamp Exchange, 1988.

———. *Regimental Records of the Royal Welch Fusiliers (23rd Foot)*. Vol. 3. London: Forster Groom, 1928.

Eden, A. *Another World, 1897–1917*. London: Allen Lane, 1976.

Edmonds, J.E. *Military Operations France and Belgium, 1915*. Vol. 2. London: Macmillan, 1936.

———. *Military Operations France and Belgium, 1916*. Vol. 2. London: Macmillan, 1938.

———. *Military Operations France and Belgium, 1917*. Vol. 2. London: Macmillan, 1948.

———. *Military Operations France and Belgium, 1918*. Vols. 1 and 5. London: Macmillan, 1935.

———. *A Short History of World War I*. London: Oxford University, 1951.

Ellis, A.D. *The Story of the Fifth Australian Division*. London: Hodder and Stoughton, 1919.

Ewart, S., ed. *Historical Records of the Queen's Own Cameron Highlanders*. Vols. 3 and 4. Edinburgh: Blackwood, 1931.

Ewing, J. *The History of the 9th (Scottish) Division, 1914–1919*. London: John Murray, 1921.

Fairclough, J.E.B. *The First Birmingham Battalion in the Great War*. Birmingham, UK: Cornish, 1933.

Falls, C. *The Gordon Highlanders in the First World War, 1914–1919*. Uckfield, UK: Naval and Military, 2014.

———. *The Great War, 1914–1918*. New York: Putnam, 1959.

———. *The History of the 36th (Ulster) Division*. London: Constable, 1996.

———. *Military Operations France and Belgium, 1917*. Vol. 1. London: Macmillan, 1940.

Farndale, M. *History of the Royal Regiment of Artillery*. Vol. 1. London: Royal Artillery Institution, 1986.

Farrer-Hockley, A. *Goughie*. London: Hart-David, MacGibbon, 1975.

Ferguson, D. *The History of the Canterbury Regiment, N.Z.E.F., 1914–1919*. Auckland: Whitcombe and Tombs, 1921.

Foley, H.A., ed. *Scrap Book of the 7th Battalion Somerset Light Infantry*. Aylesbury, UK: published privately, 1932.

Foot, S. *Three Lives*. London: Heinemann, 1934.

Fox, F. *The Royal Inniskilling Fusiliers in the World War*. London: Constable, 1928.

Fraser, D. *Alanbrooke*. London: Collins, 1982.

French, D. *The Strategy of the Lloyd George Coalition, 1916–1918*. Oxford: Clarendon, 1995.

Fuller, J.F.C. *Memoirs of an Unconventional Soldier*. London: Ivor Nicholson and Watson, 1936.

———. "The Tactics of Penetration." *The Journal of the Royal Artillery*, 1926–27.

———. *Tanks in the Great War, 1914–1918*. London: John Murray, 1920.

Geyer, M. "German Strategy in the Age of Machine Warfare, 1914–1945." In *Makers of Modern of Strategy*, edited by P. Paret. Princeton, NJ: Princeton University, 1986.

Gibbs, P. *From Bapaume to Passchendaele*. London: Heinemann, 1918.

———. *Realities of War*. London: Heinemann, 1920.

Gilbert, M. *Winston S. Churchill*. Vol. 4. London: Heinemann, 1975.

Gillon, S. *The Story of the 29th Division*. London: Thomas Nelson, 1925.

Gladden, E.N. *Ypres, 1917*. London: Kimber, 1967.

Gordon, H. *The Unreturning Army: A Field-Gunner in Flanders, 1917–18*. London: Dent, 1967.

Gorman, E. *"With the Twenty-Second": A History of the 22nd Battalion, A.I.F.* Melbourne: H.H. Champion, 1919.

Green, A. *Writing the Great War: Sir James Edmonds and the Official Histories, 1915–1948*. London: Frank Cass, 2003.

Greenhalgh, E. *Foch in Command*. Cambridge, UK: Cambridge University, 2011.

———. *The French Army and the First World War*. Cambridge, UK: Cambridge University, 2014.

———. "Myth and Memory: Sir Douglas Haig and the Imposition of Allied Unified Command in March 1918." *The Journal of Military History*, 2004.

———. *Victory through Coalition*. Cambridge, UK: Cambridge University, 2005.

Grieves, K. "The 'Recruiting Margin' in Britain: Debates on Manpower during the Third Battle of Ypres." In *Passchendaele in Perspective*, edited by P.H. Liddle. London: Leo Cooper, 1997.

Haber, L.F. *The Poisonous Cloud: Chemical Warfare in the First World War.* Oxford: Clarendon, 1986.

Hagenlücke, H. "The German High Command." In *Passchendaele in Perspective*, edited by P.H. Liddle. London: Leo Cooper, 1997.

Haig, Countess Dorothy. *The Man I Knew.* Edinburgh: Moray, 1936.

Haig, D. *Cavalry Studies.* London: Hugh Rees, 1907.

Haig, Field Marshal D. "Report on the Battle of 31st July, and Its Results," 4/8/1917. Australian War Memorial 45/33/5.

Haig, Field Marshal D. "Report on the Operations in Flanders from 4th August to 20th August," 20/8/1917. Australian War Memorial 45/33/5.

Haldane, M.M. *History of the Fourth Battalion, the Seaforth Highlanders.* London: Witherby, 1928.

Hammond, B. *Cambrai 1917.* London: Weidenfeld and Nicolson, 2008.

Hancock, W.K. *Smuts: The Sanguine Years, 1870–1919.* Cambridge, UK: Cambridge University, 1962.

Hankey, M. *The Supreme Command, 1914–1918.* 2 vols. London: Allen and Unwin, 1961.

Hare, S. *The Annals of the King's Royal Rifle Corps.* Vol. 5. London: John Murray, 1932.

Harington, C. *Plumer of Messines.* London: John Murray, 1935.

———. *Tim Harington Looks Back.* London: John Murray, 1940.

Harris, J.P. *Douglas Haig and the First World War.* Cambridge, UK: Cambridge University, 2008.

———. "Haig and the Tank." In *Haig: A Re-appraisal 70 Years On*, edited by N. Cave and B. Bond. London: Leo Cooper, 1999.

———. *Men, Ideas and Tanks.* Manchester, UK: Manchester University, 1995.

Hawkes, J. *Mortimer Wheeler: Adventurer in Archaeology.* London: Weidenfeld and Nicolson, 1982.

Headlam, C. *The History of the Guards Division in the Great War, 1915–1918.* 2 vols. London: John Murray, 1924.

Henshaw, T. *The Sky Their Battlefield.* London: Grub Street, 1995.

Herwig, H.H. *The First World War: Germany and Austria-Hungary, 1914–1919.* London: Arnold, 1997.

Hogg, I.V. and L.F. Thurston. *British Artillery Weapons and Ammunition, 1914–1918.* London: Allan, 1972.

Home, A.F. *The Diary of a World War I Cavalry Officer.* Tunbridge Wells, UK: Costello, 1985.

Horner, D. *The Gunners: A History of Australian Artillery.* Sydney: Allen and Unwin, 1995.

Hudson, H. *History of the 19th King George's Own Lancers, 1858–1921.* Aldershot, UK: Gale and Polden, 1937.

Hughes, B.P., ed. *History of the Royal Regiment of Artillery.* Vol. 3. London: Royal Artillery Institute, 1992.

Hussey, J. "The Flanders Battleground and the Weather in 1917." In *Passchendaele in Perspective*, edited by P.H. Liddle. London: Leo Cooper, 1997.

Hutchison, G.S. *The Thirty-Third Division in France and Flanders, 1915–1919.* London: Waterlow, 1921.

Hyatt, A.M.J. *General Sir Arthur Currie: A Military Biography.* Toronto: University of Toronto, 1987.

Inglefield, V.E. *The History of the Twentieth (Light) Division.* London: Nisbet, 1921.

Jager, H. *German Artillery of World War One.* Marlborough, UK: Crowood, 2001.

James, L., ed. *The History of King Edward's Horse*. London: Sifton, Praed, 1921.

Jeffrey, K. *Field-Marshal Sir Henry Wilson*. Oxford: Oxford University, 2006.

Jenkins, R. *Asquith*. London: Collins, 1986.

Jones, H.A. *The War in the Air*. Vol. 4. Oxford: Clarendon, 1934.

Keegan, J. *The First World War*. London: Hutchinson, 1998.

Kiggell, Lieutenant General L.E. "Record of a Conference Held at Second Army Headquarters, Cassel, at 11 A.M., 2 October 1917." Australian War Memorial 45/33/5.

Kitchen, M. *The Silent Dictatorship*. New York: Holmes and Meier, 1976.

Liddell Hart, B.H. "The Basic Truths of Passchendaele." *The Journal of the Royal United Services Institute*, 1959.

———. *Foch: The Man of Orleans*. London: Eyre and Spottiswoode, 1931.

———. *The Memoirs of Captain Liddell Hart*. Vol. 1. London: Cassell, 1965.

———. *The Real War, 1914–1918*. Boston: Little, Brown, 1930.

———. *The Tanks*. Vol. 1. London: Cassell, 1959.

Lloyd, N. *Passchendaele*. London: Basic Books, 2017.

Lloyd George, D. *War Memoirs*. 2 vols. London: Odhams, 1938.

LoCicero, M. *A Moonlight Massacre: The Night Operation on the Passchendaele Ridge, 2 December 1917*. Solihull, UK: Helion, 2014.

Ludendorff, E. *My War Memories, 1914–1918*. 2 vols. London: Hutchinson, 1919.

Lumley, L.R. *History of the Eleventh Hussars (Prince Albert's Own), 1908–1934*. London: Royal United Services Institute, 1936.

Lupfer, T.T. *The Dynamics of Doctrine: The Changes in German Tactical Doctrine during the First World War*. Fort Leavenworth, KS: United States Command and General Staff College, 1981.

Macartney-Filgate, J.M. *History of the 33rd Divisional Artillery in the War, 1914–18*. London: Vacher, 1921.

Macdonald, A. *Passchendaele: The Anatomy of a Tragedy*. Auckland: Harper Collins, 2013.

Macdonald, L. *They Called It Passchendaele*. London: Joseph, 1978.

Macdougall, T., ed. *War Letters of General Monash*. Sydney: Duffy and Snellgrove, 2002.

Macpherson, W.G. *Medical Services General History*. Vol. 3. London: His Majesty's Stationery Office, 1924.

Marden, T.O., ed. *A Short History of the 6th Division, 1914–1919*. London: Hugh Rees, 1920.

Marder, A.J. *From the Dreadnought to Scapa Flow*. Vols. 2–5. London: Oxford University, 1965–1970.

Maude, A.H. *The 47th (London) Division, 1914–1919*. London: Amalgamated, 1922.

McCance, S. *History of the Royal Munster Fusiliers*. Vol. 2. Uckfield, UK: Naval and Military, 2009.

McGilchrist, A.M. *The Liverpool Scottish, 1900–1919*. Liverpool: Henry Young, 1930.

McNicol, N.G. *The Thirty-Seventh: History of the Thirty-Seventh Battalion, A.I.F.* Melbourne: Modern Printing, 1936.

Micholls, G. *A History of the 17th Lancers*. Vol. 2. London: Macmillan, 1931.

Middlebrook, M. *The Kaiser's Battle*. London: Allen Lane, 1978.

Miles, W. *Military Operations France and Belgium, 1917*. Vol. 3. London: Macmillan, 1948.

Millman, B. *Pessimism and British War Policy, 1916–1918*. London: Frank Cass, 2001.

Ministry of Munitions. *The Official History of the Ministry of Munitions*. 12 vols. Uckfield, UK: Naval and Military, 2008.

Mitchell, T.J. and G.M. Smith. *Medical Services: Casualties and Medical Statistics of the Great War*. London: His Majesty's Stationery Office, 1931.

Moore, W. *A Wood Called Bourlon*. London: Leo Cooper, 1988.

Morrow, J.H. *The Great War in the Air*. Washington: Smithsonian Institution, 1993.

Mowat, C.L. *Britain between the Wars, 1918–1940*. London: Methuen, 1956.

Nash, D. *German Artillery, 1914–1918*. London: Almark, 1970.

Neiberg, M.S. *Foch: Supreme Allied Commander in the Great War*. Lincoln: University of Nebraska, 2003.

Nichols, G.H.F. *The 18th Division in the Great War*. Edinburgh: Blackwood, 1922.

Nicholson, G.W.L. *Canadian Expeditionary Force, 1914–1919*. Ottawa: R. Duhamel, 1962.

Occleshaw, M. *Armour against Fate: British Intelligence in the First World War*. London: Colombus, 1989.

Oldham, P. *Pill Boxes on the Western Front*. London: Leo Cooper, 1995.

Oram, G.C. *Military Executions during World War I*. Basingstoke, UK: Palgrave Macmillan, 2003.

Passingham, I. *Pillars of Fire*. Stroud, UK: Sutton, 1998.

Paterson, A.T. *The Thirty-Ninth: The History of the 39th Battalion, A.I.F.* Uckfield, UK: Naval and Military, 2010.

Petre, F. Loraine. *The History of the Norfolk Regiment*. Vol. 2. Norwich, UK: Jarrold, 1924.

———. *The Royal Berkshire Regiment (Princess Charlotte of Wales's)*. Vol. 2. Reading, UK: The Barracks, 1925.

Ponsonby, F. *The Grenadier Guards in the Great War of 1914–1918*. Vol. 2. London: Macmillan, 1920.

Prior, R., and T. Wilson. *Passchendaele: The Untold Story*. London: Yale, 1996.

———. *The Somme*. Sydney: University of New South Wales, 2005.

Pugsley, C. "The New Zealand Division at Passchendaele." In *Passchendaele in Perspective*, edited by P.H. Liddle. London: Leo Cooper, 1997.

Reitz, D. *Commando*. London: Faber and Faber, 1929.

Repington, C.C. *The First World War, 1914–1918*. 2 vols. London: Constable, 1920.

Robertson, W. *From Private to Field-Marshal*. London: Constable, 1921.

———. *Soldiers and Statesmen, 1914–1918*. 2 vols. London: Cassell, 1926.

Roskill, S. *Hankey: Man of Secrets*. Vol. 1. London: Collins, 1970.

Rupprecht, Crown Prince of Bavaria. "Further Experiences of the Arras Battle," 13/5/1917. Australian War Memorial 45/32/34.

Rupprecht, Crown Prince of Bavaria. "The War Diary of Crown Prince Rupprecht." *The Army Quarterly*, 1929.

Sandilands, H.R. *The 23rd Division, 1914–1919*. Edinburgh: Blackwood, 1925.

Scott, P. "Law and Orders: Discipline and Morale in the British Armies in France, 1917." In *Passchendaele in Perspective*, edited by P.H. Liddle. London: Leo Cooper, 1997.

Seely, J.E.B. *Adventure*. London: Heinemann, 1930.

Seymour, W. *The History of the Rifle Brigade in the War of 1914–1918*. Vol. 2. London: Rifle Brigade Club, 1936.

Sheffield, G.S. *Forgotten Victory*. London: Headline, 2001.

Sheffield, G.S. and J.B. Bourne, eds. *Douglas Haig: War Diaries and Letters, 1914–1918*. London: Weidenfeld and Nicolson, 2005.

Sheldon, J. *The German Army at Cambrai*. Barnsley, UK: Pen and Sword, 2009.

———. *The German Army at Passchendaele*. Barnsley, UK: Pen and Sword, 2007.

Snelling, S. *Victoria Crosses of the First World War: Passchendaele, 1917.* Stroud, UK: Sutton, 1998.

Somers, Lord. *The War History of the Sixth Tank Battalion.* Uckfield, UK: Naval and Military, 2003.

Sondhaus, L. *German Submarine Warfare in World War I.* Boulder, CO: Rowman and Littlefield, 2017.

Southern, L.J.C. *The Bedfordshire Yeomanry in the Great War.* Bedford, UK: Rush and Warwick, 1935.

Spiers, E.M. *Haldane: An Army Reformer.* Edinburgh: Edinburgh University, 1980.

Stern, A.G. *Tanks, 1914–1918: The Log-Book of a Pioneer.* London: Hodder and Stoughton, 1919.

Stevenson, D. *Cataclysm: The First World War as Political Tragedy.* London: Allen Lane, 2004.

Stewart, H. *The New Zealand Division, 1916–1919.* Auckland: Whitcombe and Tombs, 1921.

Stewart, J. and J. Buchan. *The Fifteenth (Scottish) Division, 1914–1919.* Edinburgh: Blackwood, 1926.

Stubbs, K.D. *Race to the Front: The Material Foundations of Coalition Strategy in the Great War.* Westport, CT: Praeger, 2002.

Sutherland, D. *War Diary of the Fifth Seaforth Highlanders.* London: Bodley Head, 1920.

Taylor, J.A. *Deborah and the War of the Tanks, 1917.* Barnsley, UK: Pen and Sword, 2016.

Tennant, E. *The Royal Deccan Horse in the Great War.* Uckfield, UK: Naval and Military, 2008.

Terraine, J., ed. *General Jack's Diary, 1914–1918.* London: Eyre and Spottiswoode, 1964.

———. *The Road to Passchendaele.* London: Leo Cooper, 1977.

Travers, T. "Could the Tanks of 1918 Have Been War-Winners for the British Expeditionary Force?" *Journal of Contemporary History*, July 1992.

———. "The Evolution of British Strategy and Tactics on the Western Front in 1918: G.H.Q., Manpower, and Technology." *The Journal of Military History*, April 1990.

———. "The Hidden Army: Structural Problems in the British Officer Corps, 1900–1918." *Journal of Contemporary History*, 1982.

———. *How the War Was Won.* London: Routledge, 1992.

———. *The Killing Ground.* London: Allen and Unwin, 1987.

———. "A Particular Style of Command: Haig and G.H.Q., 1916–18." *Journal of Strategic Studies*, 1987.

Urquhart, H.M. *The History of the 16th Battalion (the Canadian Scottish), 1914–1919.* Toronto: Macmillan, 1932.

Vaughan, E.D. *Some Desperate Glory.* London: F. Warne, 1981.

Wallach, J.L. *The Dogma of the Battle of Annihilation.* Westport, CT: Greenwood, 1986.

Wanliss, N. *The History of the Fourteenth Battalion, A.I.F.* Melbourne: The Arrow Printery, 1929.

War Office. *Statistics of the Military Effort of the British Empire during the Great War, 1914–1920.* London: His Majesty's Stationery Office, 1922.

Ward, S.G.P. *Faithful: The Story of the Durham Light Infantry.* London: Nelson, 1963.

Warner, P. *Passchendaele: The Story behind the Tragic Victory of 1917.* London: Sidgwick and Jackson, 1988.

Watson, W.A. *King George's Own Central India Horse.* Edinburgh: Blackwood, 1930.

Watson, W.H.L. *A Company of Tanks.* Edinburgh: Blackwood, 1920.

Weigley, R.F. *History of the United States Army.* Bloomington: Indiana University, 1984.

Werth, G. "Flanders 1917 and the German Soldier." In *Passchendaele in Perspective*, edited by P.H. Liddle. London: Leo Cooper, 1997.

Whalley-Kelly, H. *"Ich Dien": The Prince of Wales's Volunteers (South Lancashire), 1914–1934*. Aldershot, UK: Gale and Polden, 1935.

Whitton, F.E. *History of the 40th Division*. Aldershot, UK: Gale and Polden, 1926.

———. *The Prince of Wales's Leinster Regiment (Royal Canadians)*. Vol. 2. Aldershot, UK: Gale and Polden, 1924.

Whitworth, D.E., ed. *A History of the 2nd Lancers (Gardner's Horse), 1809–1922*. Uckfield, UK: Naval and Military, 2006.

Wiest, A.A. *Passchendaele and the Royal Navy*. London: Greenwood, 1995.

Willcox, W.T. *The 3rd (King's Own) Hussars in the Great War, 1914–1919*. London: John Murray, 1925.

Williams, J. *Byng of Vimy*. London: Secker and Warburg, 1983.

Wilson, S.J. *The Seventh Manchesters*. London: Longmans, 1920.

Wilson, T. *The Myriad Faces of War*. Cambridge, UK: Polity, 1986.

Wolff, L. *In Flanders Fields*. London: Longmans, 1959.

Wood, W. De B. *The History of the King's Shropshire Light Infantry in the Great War, 1914–1918*. London: Medici Society, 1925.

Woodward, D.R. *Field-Marshal Sir William Robertson*. Westport, CT: Praeger, 1998.

———. *Lloyd George and the Generals*. London: Associated University, 1983.

———, ed. *The Military Correspondence of Field-Marshal Sir William Robertson*. London: Bodley Head, 1989.

———. *Trial by Friendship: Anglo-American Relations, 1917–1918*. Lexington: University of Kentucky, 1993.

Woollcombe, R. *The First Tank Battle: Cambrai, 1917*. London: Barker, 1967.

Wren, E. *Randwick to Hargicourt: History of the 3rd Battalion, A.I.F.* Sydney: Ronald G. McDonald, 1935.

Wylly, H.C. *The Poona Horse*. Vol. 2. London: Royal United Services Institution, 1933.

Wynne, G.C. *If Germany Attacks*. London: Faber and Faber, 1940.

Wyrall, E. *The Gloucestershire Regiment in the War, 1914–1918*. London: Methuen, 1931.

———. *The History of the 19th Division, 1914–1918*. London: Arnold, 1932.

———. *The History of the 62nd (West Riding) Division, 1914–1919*. Vol. 1. London: John Lane, 1925.

———. *The History of the Fiftieth Division, 1914–1919*. London: Percy Lund, Humphries, 1939.

———. *History of the King's Regiment (Liverpool), 1914–1919*. Vol. 3. London: Arnold, 1935.

———. *The History of the Somerset Light Infantry (Prince Albert's), 1914–1919*. London: Methuen, 1927.

———. *The West Yorkshire Regiment in the War, 1914–1918*. Vol. 2. London: John Lane, 1927.

Zabecki, D.T. *The German 1918 Offensives*. New York: Routledge, 2006.

———. *Steel Wind: Colonel Georg Bruchmueller and the Birth of Modern Artillery*. Westport, CT: Praeger, 1994.

# Index

CPSIA information can be obtained
at www.ICGtesting.com
Printed in the USA
BVHW042344151220
595408BV00002B/2